# THE HEIR APPARENT PRESIDENCY

# THE HEIR APPARENT PRESIDENCY

DONALD A. ZINMAN

UNIVERSITY PRESS OF KANSAS

Published by the University Press of Kansas (Lawrence, Kansas 66045), which was
organized by the Kansas Board of Regents and is operated and funded by Emporia
State University, Fort Hays State University, Kansas State University, Pittsburg State
University, the University of Kansas, and Wichita State University

Library of Congress Cataloging-in-Publication Data

Names: Zinman, Donald A., author.
Title: The heir apparent presidency / Donald A. Zinman.
Description: Lawrence, Kansas : University Press of Kansas, 2016. | Includes
bibliographical references and index.
Identifiers: LCCN 2015043969 | ISBN 9780700622078 (hardback) |
ISBN 9780700635238 (paperback) | ISBN 9780700622085 (ebook)
Subjects: LCSH: Presidents—United States—History—Case studies. | Political
leadership—United States—Case studies. | Madison, James, 1751–1836. |
Van Buren, Martin, 1782–1862. | Grant, Ulysses S. (Ulysses Simpson),
1822–1885. | Truman, Harry S., 1884–1972. | Bush, George, 1924– | BISAC:
POLITICAL SCIENCE / Political Process / Leadership. | POLITICAL SCIENCE /
Government / Executive Branch. | POLITICAL SCIENCE / History & Theory.
Classification: LCC E176.1 .Z56 2016 | DDC 973.09/9—dc23 LC record available at
http://lccn.loc.gov/2015043969.

British Library Cataloguing-in-Publication Data is available.

Printed in the United States of America

10 9 8 7 6 5 4 3 2 1

The paper used in this publication is acid free and meets the minimum requirements of
the American National Standard for Permanence of Paper for Printed Library Materials
Z39.48-1992.

*To Mom and Dad*

# CONTENTS

# PREFACE TO THE PAPERBACK EDITION

"This is not the outcome we wanted or we worked so hard for," Hillary Clinton told her supporters, as she formally conceded the 2016 presidential election to Donald Trump. Democrats were stunned. How could their candidate, with her sparkling resume of achievements and mainstream policy proposals, lose to such a flawed opponent? Clinton persistently held a small lead in pre-election polls, and Barack Obama, the outgoing Democratic incumbent, maintained respectable job approval ratings. The economy was strong overall, but not without some shortcomings. Yet in 2016, the coalition Obama built across two national elections never fully came together for his former secretary of state.

Hillary Clinton joined Al Gore, Hubert Humphrey, and many other candidates who failed to succeed a predecessor of their own party. Following two terms of controlling the executive branch, a party's task of holding the presidency grows significantly more difficult. George H. W. Bush, who overcame these challenges to win in 1988, faced numerous headwinds in office, notwithstanding his several accomplishments. Had Secretary Clinton prevailed, she would have found herself in the same sort of restrictive position as similarly situated presidents including James Madison and Martin Van Buren. Becoming an heir apparent president is no less demanding than the job of following a predecessor who lifted the hopes of the American people and achieved major policy goals.

Four years after Clinton's concession speech, Trump was defeated by Obama's vice president, Joe Biden. As a man who has spent a career in public office and is well within the mainstream of his party's ideological spectrum, Biden's more traditional political style differs from Obama's charisma and idealism. The undercurrent of the 2020 campaign was tense amid a backdrop of a global pandemic and a summer of protests and violence in America's streets. In the highest turnout election in over one hundred years, Biden won by positioning himself as a familiar, steady hand rather than a revolutionary. Across a range of policy issues, the new president proudly defended the record of the Obama administration and pledged to continue the unfinished business of the last Democratic White House.

Still, Biden does not neatly fit into the heir apparent role, given that he did not directly succeed Obama. The forty-sixth president entered office upon the departure of a very disruptive and unorthodox Republican predecessor. In addition to this, Trump's long-term impact upon American politics may very well prove to be more enduring than Obama's, thereby complicating Biden's task as a loyal disciple to the president he loyally served under for eight years. As much as Biden aims to continue the incomplete work of the Obama years, he faces a competing challenge against the rising force of right-wing nationalism in domestic politics. Arguably more than past presidents in the heir apparent station, Biden will need to establish a clear and distinct legacy of his own.

As this book demonstrates, no heir apparent presidential scenarios are identical. Ulysses S. Grant, a Republican in the ideological tradition of Abraham Lincoln, also assumed the office following an embattled and disruptive president of the opposition party. Nearly four years after Lincoln's assassination, Grant inherited a nation that remained torn by sectional division and the aftermath of a civil war. Lincoln had a transformative political impact upon the nation's future and thus enabled Grant to act as his first Republican heir apparent. Seldom can a chief executive leave enough of an imprint to be able to define a whole new generation of the American presidency.

This paperback edition of *The Heir Apparent Presidency* primarily focuses on five men who held the office as the first successor of a historically significant president from their own party. Their backgrounds and circumstances are different across time, but their political situations reveal many similarities. An heir apparent operates in a very constrained environment within a political landscape that remains very much defined by their predecessor. While heirs apparent have the ability to rack up accomplishments of their own, they struggle to get the credit, even as they surely have to contend with the policy consequences of their predecessors' mistakes. The ways and means they use to respond to these challenges, as well as new crises that occur, are likely to diminish their political standing in the long run.

Just as Obama and Biden have different backgrounds and political styles, so did Ronald Reagan and George H. W. Bush as well as other pairings of predecessors and heirs apparent. Every president has a different toolbox of political skills; sometimes they are effective, and sometimes they fall short. Any person in the heir apparent role, however, will find it difficult to avoid comparisons to their highly respected predecessor, especially when things go wrong. There is a narrow pathway to success for the heir apparent, but it lies in finding the perfect balance among stability, adjustment, change, and innovative techniques of communications.

Donald A. Zinman
Grand Valley State University
January 2023

# ACKNOWLEDGMENTS

My first passing interest in heir apparent presidents came during my last year in graduate school at the University of Texas. Upon my arrival at Grand Valley State University in 2006, I began to more systematically study the trials and travails of presidents who came into office on the shoulders of larger-than-life predecessors.

This research has been rewarding and fascinating, but *The Heir Apparent Presidency* would not have been possible without the support of so many people and institutions over the years. I will always owe a debt of gratitude to my mentors. Over the course of 12 years, first at Brandeis University, and then at UT, I was proud to be the student of Sidney Milkis, Walter Dean Burnham, and Bruce Buchanan.

Here at GVSU, I have had supportive colleagues since the day I arrived. The university granted me a sabbatical during the winter 2013 semester, for which I am very appreciative. I am also very thankful for the university's modernized library services and helpful staff. My political science colleagues at GVSU have made it a pleasure for me to come to the office every day. For this book, I want to particularly thank Paul Cornish and Erika King for reading early drafts of some of my chapters. Their feedback was most helpful.

I also appreciate the helpful critiques of colleagues outside of my university. Julia Azari and David Crockett read early drafts of my chapters and helped to steer me in the right direction. Two anonymous reviewers provided extremely useful feedback that helped me make this an all-around better book. I also extend my appreciation to Robert Demke for his thorough copyediting and to Mary Brooks for indexing the manuscript.

I extend my deepest appreciation to all the staff at the University Press of Kansas for their professionalism and accessibility. Chuck Myers, the director of UPK, was always available to answer my questions, and I appreciate the interest he has taken in my research over the years.

I am blessed to have special friends like Raquel Guzman, Rene Guzman, Damaris Nolasco, Heather Tafel, and Erika King. Finally, I am grateful for the love and support of my parents, Gary Zinman and Elda Zinman. My father, who passed away in February 2015, stimulated my interest in politics at a young age, and I'll never forget the long talks we used to have late into the night. My parents made it possible for me to be where I am today. I'm proud to be their heir apparent.

# THE HEIR APPARENT PRESIDENCY

# 1

# INTRODUCTION

## SUCCEEDING A GIANT

It is never easy to assume the mantle of leadership in the shadow of a larger-than-life predecessor. When the time comes for a person to lead, he or she will inevitably be judged according to the gold standard of the greats who came beforehand. That leader will face inevitable comparisons to his or her most immediate predecessor, especially if the predecessor was regarded as exemplary. Indeed, if there is an expectation that the successor lead along a similar trajectory as the predecessor, comparisons will be impossible to avoid. After winning three National Football League championships in the 1980s, San Francisco 49ers head coach Bill Walsh was succeeded by his defensive coordinator George Seifert.[1] The new coach had very big shoes to fill and very high standards to meet. Robert Eaton, the successor to Chrysler CEO Lee Iacocca, was compared to a prominent executive with a reputation for rebuilding a stagnant automaker.[2]

Seifert and Eaton followed different paths to their leadership positions, but they both followed larger-than-life predecessors with significant track records of success and records of innovation. The successors to Walsh and Iacocca had a mandate to maintain the winning models of their predecessors, although few observers expected these new leaders to compile similar records of success. Walsh and

Iacocca established bold and original approaches and their most immediate successors were expected to be faithful custodians rather than revolutionaries. In contrast, a coach who follows a predecessor who is fired after several losing seasons will have a mandate to repudiate previous strategies and tactics and develop new models for victory. Similarly, a CEO who replaces a failed predecessor will be expected to depart from discredited formulas of management and leadership.

Within any organization or institution, leadership demands some degree of apprenticeship, preparation, and knowledge of the successes and failures experienced by the leaders who came earlier. Men and women work their way through a complicated and sometimes unpredictable pathway of career advancement. Sometimes circumstances intervene, such as a death or an abrupt resignation. A new person is unexpectedly thrust into a leadership role, even if he or she may not be ready to assume the task. Varying pathways to leadership can be found in sports teams, corporations, nonprofit organizations, interest groups, political parties, and governments. American presidential history certainly reveals that there is no consistent preparation track for this office.

No matter how they get there, all leaders inherit problems, expectations, and adversaries. No matter what hand a new leader is dealt, he or she will be expected to leave the organization in a stronger position upon his or her departure. A new coach may have to contend with rivalries and personality conflicts that have been brewing for some time. A new corporate CEO may have to deal with emerging changes in his or her industry. Leaders of nations inherit social, political, economic, and foreign policy problems. Fairly or not, regardless of the organization or institution, all leaders will invite comparisons to the records of their predecessors.

After completing his or her tenure, even a transformative and trailblazing leader will not have solved all the problems facing the organization, institution, or team (and he or she may well have created new problems too). If the departing leader leaves behind a proud record of accomplishment and commands great respect, a successor may be positioned as an heir apparent. In this capacity, the successor is cast in the same philosophical and policy orientation as the predecessor. An heir apparent will pledge to continue building upon the achievements of the predecessor by following the same leadership trajectory. A commitment to continuity can earn the support of the predecessor's followers, but it also imposes constraints and deep expectations that may be very hard to meet. As the successor is committed to continuing along the predecessor's path, the new leader also inherits the problems and consequences resulting from the previous leader's choices. The predecessor's rivals may continue to jockey for position and the successor will surely generate new critics who draw unfavorable assessments against the previous leader's gold standard.

Indeed, circumstances always change between the predecessor's departure and the successor's tenure, thereby demanding alterations to the established pattern of leadership. If any aspect of the successor's leadership marks a clear departure from the record of the predecessor, old loyalists can quickly turn into critics. Leaders of institutions and organizations are chosen because of a commitment to a particular pattern of action. When that trajectory is disrupted, a leader may compromise the trust and support he or she depends upon from established allies.

If the predecessor is regarded as dominant and exemplary, adversaries and critics of the heir apparent may find a more vulnerable target, given the new power arrangements. Opponents may build real momentum to challenge the new leader, as well as the predecessor's achievements that the successor has pledged to protect. The predecessor's fierce loyalists will then expect the heir apparent to respond to opponents in accordance with principles and tactics of the predecessor. If this does not happen, the heir apparent leader will find him- or herself with a new crowd of critics.

These former supporters turned critics may loudly lament that the new leader fails to compare with the great predecessor. The incumbent will be accused of some combination of poor management, feckless negotiating, ineffective communication skills, and having a weak commitment to preserving the predecessor's record. Assertions will be made that the predecessor's hard-won achievements are being frittered away by a successor who has "betrayed" his or her supporters.

Regardless of their personal or professional relationship with each other, no two people can be expected to have identical styles of leadership and managerial skills. Obviously, the differences are greater when the successor has pledged publicly to reverse the approach of the predecessor. Even when the predecessor and the successor have pledged to follow a similar trajectory, however, differences in style and even substance will be revealing. Every change of leadership will bring differences of temperament, negotiating tactics, social skills, and how agendas are prioritized. One leader may be very charismatic, an excellent speaker, and very effective in dealing with the media. Then that leader's successor, who has pledged to the same means and ends, could be an uninspiring and dull public speaker who is prone to making public gaffes. Two leaders can have similar goals and ideologies, but one may be excellent at bargaining with other power brokers, while the other leader may lack this talent.

As a leader begins his or her stewardship, he or she will have an agenda, short-term goals, and long-term goals. Unexpected crises and developments will also surely intervene to disrupt those plans. Regardless of a leader's context and standing vis-à-vis the leaders who came before, the incumbent will want to compile achievements that are exclusive to his or her tenure. Indeed, the new leader may want to be bold by attempting to eclipse the achievements of previous leaders or to complete the unfinished work of his or her predecessor. Unfortunately, moving out of the shadow of a larger-than-life predecessor makes these tasks even more difficult, especially when an heir apparent takes over immediately or very soon after the titan's departure.

The challenges facing these heir apparent leaders are numerous, as I will discuss in greater detail. Still, they are challenges that can be met in the absence of catastrophic external events. In addition, strong organizational and communication skills can pay great dividends for a leader. Finally, there must be an appropriate balance between deference to established approaches of the predecessor and taking some risks by altering and refining the methods, the priorities, and even the goals of the previous leader.

Heir apparent leadership presents challenges across institutions and organizations, inside and outside of government, but my emphasis going forward will be on the American presidency. In the presidency, the problems, strengths, and flaws of the individual holding the office will manifest themselves early and transparently to all observers. Especially in the twenty-first century, and for many years in the previous century as well, presidents have been the most visible actors to casual and keen observers of American politics. The political and constitutional power that they yield on a domestic and international stage usually dwarfs the power of leaders outside of government. I will submit here that heir apparent leaders of any institution can observe a pattern of common problems, challenges, and opportunities by scrutinizing some of our past presidents who had to govern in this role. Some of these experiences may serve as valuable lessons to leaders who find themselves in the heir apparent position, even outside of government.

To be sure, there are different rules and practices in business, sports, and nonprofit organizations. Leadership within any organization or institution demands skills and talents that are very likely to be required in some degree in the American presidency. Inside and outside of government, skills in communication, bargaining, strategizing, and diplomacy are vital for a successful leader. Presidents and leaders outside of government must know how to set agendas, prioritize objectives, and choose when to fight and when to retreat in a conflict with adversaries.

## SUCCESSION AND THE PRESIDENCY

The presidency was designed by the Constitution's Framers, in Article II, to be a robust and independent office while still not occupying the center of American political and governmental life. In *Federalist Papers* Nos. 67–77, Alexander Hamilton carefully explicates the necessity for specific presidential powers under the Constitution, while assuring citizens that the chief executive's powers will be limited by other actors.[3] Yet from the eighteenth century to the present, through a long succession of strong and weak executives, the overarching trajectory of presidential power and influence was one of steady growth. Explanations and consequences for the growth of the presidency have been extensively covered by other scholars.[4]

"To reverse and undo what has been done by a predecessor," Hamilton said, "is very often considered by a successor as the best proof he can give of his own capacity and desert."[5] The very act of presidential succession contributes to the growth of presidential power over the long run. Presidential failure can breed the very conditions that enable stronger presidents to remake the American political and governmental landscape: James Buchanan was succeeded by Abraham Lincoln and Herbert Hoover was succeeded by Franklin D. Roosevelt. Strong and successful presidents can then bequeath significant accomplishments to their successors. A like-minded successor wants to preserve, protect, and extend the achievements of the predecessor, which was the role of Roosevelt's successor, Harry Truman. However, even a successor from a different political persuasion will seek to at least maintain the power and influence of the office to take the nation in a different direction. Dwight Eisenhower, the first Republican president in twenty years, inherited an office in 1953 that grew exponentially as a consequence of the New Deal, World War II, and the Cold War. As president, Eisenhower charted a somewhat different course than his New Deal Democratic predecessors, but he did not seek (nor would circumstances permit) a diminution of presidential power.

Many presidential biographies and scholarly studies reveal the impulse in every president to surpass the accomplishments of the men who came before him. Lyndon Johnson came of age politically as a young congressman who firmly attached himself to Franklin Roosevelt's New Deal. As president himself, Johnson sought to surpass Roosevelt's achievements.[6] James Polk was a Democrat in the Jacksonian tradition, and was mentored by the General himself. As president, Polk used the office to aggressively achieve Jacksonian goals in the domestic and international arenas.[7] Theodore Roosevelt sought to use the presidential office on a much more personal level than any of his predecessors, while also reinvigorating the reformist spirit of Abraham Lincoln's Republican Party.[8] Barack Obama's documented fascination with the presidency of his ideological opposite, Ronald Reagan, suggests that Obama sought to emulate Reagan's communicative talents. Obama envisioned using the office as a vehicle for twenty-first-century progressivism, just as Reagan once used the office to advance conservatism.[9]

Still, the aforementioned cases are not examples of an heir apparent assuming the office from a like-minded predecessor who is regarded as a powerful and significant president. Years elapsed as developments established some distance between one president and another. In the intervening years, the other party won the presidency and attempted to take the nation in a different direction, new foreign and domestic crises occurred, the demographics of the nation changed, and public policies evolved in unanticipated directions. The new president began with more of a clean slate and smaller shadows of great predecessors lurking in the background.

The heir apparent president's dilemma is different. Presidents who are successful with policy accomplishments are very likely to enlarge the influence of their office, either as a consequence of their achievements or as a means of executing their goals. For a like-minded heir apparent, preserving those achievements, as well as the power and influence of the office, serves as a test of the depth and durability of the predecessor's footprint. Presidents that are recognized as "great" or well above average will be inextricably tied to their most immediate like-minded successors. The heir apparent's struggles to establish an identity of his or her own may clash with the imperatives of preserving, protecting, and defending the predecessor's achievements. How a successor in this role navigates the challenges of being in such a large shadow will tell us more about how presidents set agendas, respond to crises, manage coalitions, and establish identities of their own.

# 2

# SECOND IN LINE IN POLITICAL TIME

## THE PRESIDENT AS A REGIME MANAGER

Some American presidents will establish a legacy through a record of policy achievements and personal political stature that will cast an enduring footprint upon many decades of American political development. Other presidents will fail more often than they succeed and leave office with a sparse and forgettable record. Another possibility is that they may leave with a record of destructive policy choices that set the nation on a regressive course. Still other presidents will fall somewhere between these two extreme categories, racking up a record of positive policy achievements and innovations, tempered by unforeseen policy consequences and moments of poor political calculus. Lyndon Johnson, for example, achieved numerous accomplishments in the arenas of civil rights and social welfare policy, only to see his presidency eroded by the Vietnam War.[1] Indeed, even highly ranked presidents will be prone to poor decisions and policy failures, such as Franklin Roosevelt's decision to intern Japanese Americans in the Second World War and Thomas Jefferson's Embargo Act in 1807.

The president has the ability to shape the political and governmental landscape, but his actions will also be influenced by the circumstances of the existing political and governmental environment.[2] Some presidents will more often find themselves as the captive of their political environment, while other presidents will more often find themselves as a builder of a new political environment. Regardless of one's talents as a politician, opportunity is not created equally for presidents. One president may inherit a nation on the brink of civil war from a discredited predecessor of the opposition party, affording significant opportunities to "think anew and act anew."[3] Another president may assume office with grand designs to overhaul the nation's health care system, only to find that the American people have little appetite for a major expansion of the social welfare state.[4]

Stephen Skowronek depicts many American presidents as the leading figure in a governing regime.[5] In this role, the president leads a dominant governing coalition in the pursuit of long-term policy objectives.[6] In Skowronek's categorization, the regime coalition is backed by a dominant political party, interest groups, and activists who hold power over a controlling share of the institutions and processes in American government. The center of gravity within the American political system is set at a point determined by this governing regime. The regime establishes the boundaries of mainstream political debate and action, guided by fundamental ideologies concerning the role of government, economic policies, social arrangements, and constitutional norms.[7]

Historically, presidents have arbitrated disputes between fellow party members, carefully used patronage to satisfy restive party factions, brokered deals with stakeholders in and out of government, and advocated publicly for policy agendas.[8] The emphasis of these tasks has shifted over many years, but the leadership position of the president remains vital within a governing regime. Unfortunately for presidents, their ability to positively influence American government and politics will be limited by what Skowronek calls "political time," which is like the biological clock of a governing regime.[9]

At an early point in political time, a regime is ascendant. A president who constructs a new regime has broad authority to tear down the remnants of the old order and plant the foundations of a new equilibrium in politics and government. Skowronek calls such presidents *reconstructive*, for they assume office in opposition to an old, discredited, divided, and unpopular regime. Thomas Jefferson, Andrew Jackson, Abraham Lincoln, Franklin Roosevelt, and Ronald Reagan fall into this esteemed category, for they were the builders of new regimes.[10] These presidents are the supporting actors in the chapters that follow, as they blaze the trail for the heirs apparent who are the leading actors of this book.

Related to the heirs apparent under examination here are the presidents that Skowronek categorizes as regime *articulators*. Such presidents are numerous across history, assuming office as adherents of the established governing regime. In office they struggle to maintain the support of all regime factions, while still charting an innovative course of their own.[11] As political time moves along, matters become even more difficult for the presidents Skowronek calls *disjunctive*. These presidents, such as Herbert Hoover and Jimmy Carter, govern in affiliation with a collapsing regime.[12] Finally, presidents who govern in opposition to the governing regime function as *preemptive* presidents, who must navigate a political universe dominated by a hostile political establishment.[13]

## UNDERSTANDING HOW POLITICAL TIME MOVES

Heir apparent presidents to the reconstructive regime builders identified above would seem to neatly fit into the articulator category. Martin Van Buren assumed office as the protégé of Andrew Jackson and a disciple of his political philosophy. James Polk was not Jackson's most immediate successor, but he too was a Democrat in the Jacksonian tradition. Both men would fall under the category of articulators to the Jacksonian Democratic regime. Similarly, Harry Truman and Lyndon Johnson would be classified as articulators of the New Deal Democratic regime of Franklin Roosevelt.

Because this articulator category is very large, however, it is fair to ask if the problems and characteristics of these presidents are generalizable across such a sweeping classification. Van Buren and Truman directly succeeded the builders of their respective governing regimes, while Polk and Johnson entered office several years after each respective regime was already well established. A president who is an heir apparent to a regime-building predecessor assumes office amid a political climate where memories of his predecessor are still very fresh. The predecessor's policy legacy is only beginning to manifest itself. Unforeseen policy consequences begin to take shape. Because of the attachment to his predecessor, the heir apparent will have the task of cleaning up a mess that will only multiply his political baggage. Martin Van Buren, for example, had to contend with a resurgent Whig opposition on his watch, as his presidency was consumed by the consequences of Jacksonian economic policies. The problems of heir apparent presidents warrant their own thorough examination, as they are tightly bound in time and political ideology to their very Herculean predecessors. The challenges of being heir apparent to a larger-than-life predecessor are different from the plight of governing with a greater political and personal separation from other presidents.

The challenges of the heir apparent role are unique from those of presidents who enjoy a greater degree of political and personal separation from regime builders. In comparison to presidents in the heir apparent position, these midlife regime articulators may enjoy greater latitude to experiment, innovate, and test the boundaries of their governing philosophy. Compared to Harry Truman, John F. Kennedy and Lyndon Johnson enjoyed a greater distance in time from Roosevelt, the builder of the New Deal regime. Truman assumed office upon Roosevelt's death and was tasked with ending a major war and protecting the New Deal from a renewed assault by adversaries. Truman's efforts to innovate in the arenas of civil rights and social welfare policy faced many more limitations than Johnson's initiatives on these same fronts several years later.

The clock of political time starts over once again upon the replacement of an old regime with a new one. Skowronek warns us, however, that the cycle of political time is less transparent today, as compared to the political landscape of the nineteenth and early twentieth centuries. He attributes this phenomenon to progressively stronger institutions of opposition that complicate the kind of regime-changing politics that Jefferson, Jackson, Lincoln, and

Roosevelt catalyzed.[14] In spite of long-term phenomena concerning political time, the presidency of George H. W. Bush reveals that being heir apparent to a powerful and transformative predecessor remains a significant challenge.

In seeking to answer questions about the dilemma of the heir apparent president, it is necessary to more closely examine similar heir apparent presidencies across history. How does an heir apparent handle the policy consequences of his predecessor? To what degree is the heir apparent constricted by his predecessor's record and policy achievements? Is the heir apparent bound to protect his predecessor's policy achievements at all costs, or is there room to compromise and modify? What kind of opposition does an heir apparent face, not only from obvious adversaries, but also from allies? We begin by identifying how one becomes an heir apparent president, followed by a discussion of the challenges, opportunities, conflicts, and obligations that are common to the presidents in this category. Subsequent chapters will provide specific analyses of the presidents who best exemplify the heir apparent role as successor to a regime-building predecessor.

As explicated in table 2.1, regime builders are defined identically with the presidents Skowronek categorizes as reconstructive. The heir apparent presidents under consideration in this study were the first presidents of the same party to succeed their respective regime builders. In all cases save for one, the heir apparent is the immediate successor of a regime builder. Ulysses S. Grant most directly succeeded Andrew Johnson as president, who did not formally belong to the Republican Party (and was repudiated by Republicans to the point of impeachment), making Grant the better example of a Republican heir apparent to Lincoln.

The experience of the heir apparent is likely to see a gradual activation of the problems and conflicts that will only intensify on the watch of subsequent regime-affiliated presidents. A full accounting of the plight of the heir apparent president will help us to better understand the rhythms of political time.[15] More generally, the story of the heir apparent presidency may teach us some important lessons about democratic leadership when it is passed on to a designated successor from a successful and transformative predecessor.

**Table 2.1**
**Regime Builders and Heirs Apparent**

| Regime | Dominant Party | Regime Builder | Heir Apparent |
|---|---|---|---|
| Jeffersonian | Democratic-Republican | Thomas Jefferson | James Madison |
| Jacksonian | Democratic | Andrew Jackson | Martin Van Buren |
| Civil War Republican | Republican | Abraham Lincoln | Ulysses S. Grant |
| New Deal | Democratic | Franklin D. Roosevelt | Harry Truman |
| Reagan Republican | Republican | Ronald Reagan | George H. W. Bush |

## BECOMING AN HEIR APPARENT PRESIDENT

Just as there is no singular track to the presidency, there is no singular pathway to being anyone's heir apparent. Over two hundred years of presidential history reveals a diverse pattern of routes to the Constitution's highest office. Martin Van Buren, for example, was a keen political tactician and party builder. He aggressively promoted Andrew Jackson's presidency while also working his way into Jackson's inner circle, where he would be well positioned to be the anointed Jacksonian Democrat in the presidential election of 1836.[16] Harry Truman, however, had little interest in the presidency as a career goal and only found himself as Roosevelt's vice president as the product of a compromise brokered at his party's convention in the interest of maintaining unity.[17] George H. W. Bush had a long career in politics, government, and business, and made one unsuccessful run for his party's presidential nomination before serving as Ronald Reagan's vice president for eight years. James Madison's pre-presidential pathway included service as secretary of state, which was a very common stepping-stone in the years of the early republic. Ulysses S. Grant, on the other hand, was not actively involved in partisan political affairs during his prepresidential career.[18]

One who aspires to be an heir apparent will use his predecessor's base of political support, as well as the institutions and processes that define the existing American political regime. To work one's way up through the apparatus of the party, a prospective heir apparent will need to work through the political landscape established by the regime-building predecessor. A president in the heir apparent role will also face challenges associated with inheriting a base of political support from a powerful predecessor. Each heir apparent identified above sought to rally the political base of his respective predecessor when running for election and reelection. As Truman's victory in 1948 revealed, it is likely that the heir apparent will be unable to command the same level of electoral dominance as his predecessor. Emerging intraparty divisions start to worsen and the opposition party starts to find exploitable weaknesses in the governing regime party.[19]

The electoral track record for heirs apparent is less impressive when compared to their regime-building predecessors. All of the regime builders won reelection by very convincing margins, while the record for their respective successors is rather mixed. Van Buren and Bush were defeated for reelection outright, while Madison faced an opponent who proved to be far more competitive than Jefferson faced in his reelection contest. Truman, facing the voters for the first time in 1948, prevailed in spite of his divided party, but with a margin that fell short of Roosevelt's electoral victories. Grant is alone among heirs apparent, for he did achieve a very convincing margin of reelection in 1872, which nonetheless revealed weaknesses in the national Republican Party coalition.[20]

Table 2.2 compares the electoral records of heirs apparent and their predecessors. As table 2.3 reveals, regime-building predecessors cumulatively won election and reelection by more impressive margins than heirs apparent. Every predecessor was not only reelected to a second term by a large margin but also increased his support in the Electoral College and the popular vote, save for Andrew Jackson's slight dip in the popular vote in 1832. Roosevelt, who broke George Washington's two-term tradition in 1940, did see reduced support in his 1940 and 1944 reelections. Even so, Roosevelt's third- and fourth-term reelections still outpaced Truman's Electoral College and popular vote totals in 1948. Among heirs apparent who did win a second term, they had to contend with significant divisions within their own party and a resurgent opposition

**Table 2.2**
**Electoral Records of Heirs Apparent and Predecessors**

| President | Second Term? | First-Term Election | Second-Term Election |
|---|---|---|---|
| Jefferson | ✔ | Electoral Votes: 52.90% | Electoral Votes: 92.05% |
| *Madison* | ✔ | Electoral Votes: 69.32% | Electoral Votes: 58.72% |
| Jackson | ✔ | Electoral Votes: 68.20% | Electoral Votes: 76.00% |
| | | Popular Vote: 55.93% | Popular Vote: 54.74% |
| *Van Buren* | | Electoral Votes: 57.82% | Electoral Votes: 20.41% |
| | | Popular Vote: 50.79% | Popular Vote: 46.82% |
| Lincoln | ✔ | Electoral Votes: 59.41% | Electoral Votes: 90.99% |
| | | Popular Vote: 39.65% | Popular Vote: 55.03% |
| *Grant* | ✔ | Electoral Votes: 72.79% | Electoral Votes: 81.25% |
| | | Popular Vote: 52.66% | Popular Vote: 55.58% |
| Roosevelt* | ✔ | Electoral Votes: 88.89% | Electoral Votes: 98.49% |
| | | Popular Vote: 57.41% | Popular Vote: 60.80% |
| *Truman* | ✔ | NA | Electoral Votes: 57.06% |
| | | | Popular Vote: 49.55% |
| Reagan | ✔ | Electoral Votes: 90.89% | Electoral Votes: 97.58% |
| | | Popular Vote: 50.75% | Popular Vote: 58.77% |
| *Bush* | | Electoral Votes: 79.18% | Electoral Votes: 31.23% |
| | | Popular Vote: 53.37% | Popular Vote: 37.45% |

*Roosevelt's third-term reelection resulted in the incumbent winning 84.56% of the electoral vote and 54.72% of the popular vote. In his fourth-term reelection, Roosevelt won 81.36% of the electoral vote and 53.39% of the popular vote.

Heir apparent presidents are identified in italics.

Source: Electoral data comes from Dave Leip's presidential election website "Atlas of US Presidential Elections," www.uselectionatlas.org/. The popular vote is applicable beginning in 1828, as popular selection of presidential electors did not become widespread until 1824. See also Donald A. Zinman, "Passing the Torch through Political Time: Heir Apparent Presidents and the Governing Party," *White House Studies* 9, no. 1 (2009): 55. Truman was elected to serve a second term in 1948 after serving nearly the entire length of Roosevelt's fourth term.

**Table 2.3**
**Means of Electoral Records of Heirs Apparent and Predecessors**

| President | Electoral Votes | Popular Vote |
|---|---|---|
| Predecessor | 81.78% | 54.12% |
| Heir Apparent | 58.64% (Winners Only: 68.02%) | 49.46% (Winners Only: 52.39%) |

Source: Electoral data comes from Dave Leip's presidential election website "Atlas of US Presidential Elections," www.uselectionatlas.org/. The popular vote is applicable beginning in 1828, as popular selection of presidential electors did not become widespread until 1824. See also Donald A. Zinman, "Passing the Torch through Political Time: Heir Apparent Presidents and the Governing Party," *White House Studies* 9, no. 1 (2009): 55.

party, two phenomena that will be discussed in greater detail below and in subsequent chapters.

## FIRST FOLLOWER-IN-CHIEF

The heir apparent role results in different approaches to handling the policies, ideologies, and legacy of the predecessor. Even when independent actions are taken, these decisions are likely to be framed in the context of the predecessor's principles and long-term goals. In the heir apparent capacity, the president will utilize three approaches: maintaining continuity, expanding the commitments of the governing regime, and correcting administrative deficiencies and unforeseen consequences from the predecessor's policies. In addition, some policy remedies will blend all three approaches. In their unique situation, they are expected to act as strong leaders while loyally following a governing philosophy that has been implemented by a predecessor and popularly legitimized. As a politician jockeying for position, as a bargainer seeking policy achievement, and as an administrative manager, a successful heir apparent president must master these approaches to leadership, even when they clash.

### Continuity: Protector-in-Chief

An heir apparent's mandate will differ from that of his predecessor. The predecessor is the builder and the heir apparent is the first custodian. A predecessor catalyzes a revolution in politics and government with enduring consequences: Jeffersonian democracy, Jacksonian democracy, sectional civil war and the abolition of slavery, the New Deal, and the Reagan Revolution. An heir apparent will be elected upon a promise to preserve, protect, and defend his predecessor's achievements and fundamental governing philosophy. The predecessors identified above, on the other hand, revolutionized fundamental assumptions and workings of government that had been in place for a generation or more.

Under a continuity approach, existing policies are maintained with little or no changes. The mission and scope of the predecessor's programs continue along virtually the same trajectory. Commitments are also made to defend the status quo from attacks by critics. George Bush promised very loudly in the 1988 campaign to protect Ronald Reagan's tax cuts from Democrats in Congress, and Harry Truman made a robust defense of the New Deal in the 1948 campaign.[21] In the face of demands for corrections and reversals to his predecessor's policies, an heir apparent may hunker down and insist on continuity.

### Expanding Commitments

Presidents bring goals with them when they assume office, but the slow machinery of government and politics competes with the limitations of time within a president's tenure. Even the most powerful presidents will fall short of accomplishing all of their goals, given the diffused nature of American constitutional government, abrupt changes in political momentum, and the intervention of domestic and international crises. Legislation that is achieved may fall short of the president's intended level of ambition and scope. The task of finishing these matters of unfinished business will have to fall to like-minded successors, who may or may not be able to bring these long-term policy goals to fruition.

Finishing unfulfilled commitments takes a president beyond mere continuity of existing policies. An heir apparent who assumes office with a mandate to continue the policy course of his predecessor can be expected to carry the baton forward by attempting to complete his predecessor's unfinished business. Here the heir apparent practices the expansion approach. Shifting political circumstances and the quality of the new president's political acumen do not guarantee success, but this course of action permits the heir apparent to follow the same trajectory as the predecessor, which may minimize risks from within the governing coalition. For example, Grant advocated passage of a constitutional amendment to guarantee black men the right to vote, codifying and expanding upon a principle Lincoln embraced on a narrow level near the end of his life.[22] Under Lincoln, this policy failed to see the light of day due to the limitations of time and practical political constraints. Grant could directly link himself to Lincoln's revolutionary politics by embracing this unfulfilled commitment.

Like any president affiliated with the governing regime, heirs apparent must reconcile their own agendas with the sacred policies and principles of their predecessors, as well as the practical realities of governing.[23] For the heir apparent, however, the task is all the more difficult, given his proximity in time to the regime builder. Heirs apparent are more tightly bound to the revolutionary politics of their party predecessor, as compared to a subsequent president who also claims allegiance to the reigning governing philosophy. We can also expect that any president will want to use the office on their own terms as individuals, with distinct goals, agendas, and techniques of leadership.[24] The heir apparent, just like subsequent regime affiliates, will attempt to chart a new course on certain issues and policies. Under the expansion approach, the predecessor's policies may be enlarged and extended. The expansion approach may also involve the heir apparent embarking upon new policy arenas by building off of the principles and overarching ideologies of the regime builder. The heir apparent, however, will find greater political constraints if he should choose to chart a new course that differs from his party predecessor's trajectory. Indeed, any president who is a disciple of an established regime may find himself with little political room to maneuver, if and when circumstances call for compromises in the reigning governing philosophy. For an heir apparent, this problem can be especially acute.

### *Correction: Repairer-in-Chief*

All policies are likely to generate unanticipated consequences. Popular policy ideas can be vulnerable to being rushed through the lawmaking process, with little concern for constitutional norms or operational effectiveness. Even policies that are in the overall best interest of the nation are very unlikely to function exactly as their advocates promised. Actors affected by the new policies may respond in unexpected ways to new rules, procedures, and governmental arrangements. Loopholes may be found in new laws as the intent of lawmakers and presidents is circumvented. Unanticipated complications, perhaps not considered during the lawmaking and implementation processes, can build up over several years and fall into the lap of the subsequent president.

A president of the opposition party who inherits such problems has an easier task, since he can wash his hands of the "failed" policies of the past. He will likely have been elected upon a promise to at least partially roll back his predecessor's policy choices. A president in opposition to a predecessor will begin in office with some flexibility from political allies to reverse his predecessor's trajectory, with an expectation of positive results in a reasonable amount of time. Roosevelt received very significant Democratic support in Congress for his New Deal initiatives in his first two years.[25] Inheriting a major recession from his Republican predecessor, Barack Obama achieved quick passage of a very large economic stimulus bill in February 2009 with almost unanimous Democratic support in Congress.[26] For a president who fits the heir apparent category as we have defined it here, the conundrum is more challenging.

In the heir apparent capacity, a president will inherit not only the challenges and unforeseen consequences of his predecessor's policies, but the associated political baggage as well. The heir apparent is likely to have been a leading political tactician or subordinate in his predecessor's administration. Two of the heirs apparent identified here served their predecessors in the cabinet, and three served as vice president. Fairly or not, service as a subordinate—or even just the party label—is enough to link any president to the recent predecessors of his party. Realistically, divorce or separation is not feasible.

Since the execution of public policies can evolve in unpredictable ways and unforeseen consequences begin to build up as the years transpire, the heir apparent will have to accept political and administrative responsibility. He will have to take measures to rectify shortcomings in his predecessor's policies, thereby jeopardizing support from a political base still wedded to the previous president's approaches. The heir apparent will have trouble getting much political credit for making mechanical repairs to his predecessor's course, as supporters feel betrayed and opponents feel emboldened by the president's tacit acknowledgment of deficiencies in the regime's governing philosophy. In contrast to his predecessor, the task of being a mop-up man will not be as glamorous as forging revolutionary new policies, but the heir apparent will stake his claim to the long-term project of his governing regime by acting as a responsible custodian. Part of a custodian's job is to clean up messes.

Facing policy consequences from an ideological predecessor's administration presents a variety of options for the heir apparent. Choices will have to be made within the context of the current political and public policy environment, not the political environment as it existed years before. The president can revert back to continuity, as noted above. Here he will resist demands for change, even in the face of failing policies, and pursue the same course as his party's predecessor, governing along the same ideological and programmatic lines. In contrast to his predecessor, who used an innovative policy agenda to play offense against a crumbling, older political order, the heir apparent is left to play defense with the same policy orthodoxy. This approach may satisfy some loyalists within the party coalition, but it will also generate criticism that the president is being inflexible and dogmatic in the face of pressing circumstances. In addition, this approach will allow the heir apparent no political distance from his predecessor's most controversial policies.

Conversely, an heir apparent can adopt a corrective approach. This course of action may call for the president to fix, modify, or tweak his predecessor's most controversial or failing initiatives, while still maintaining the core of the overarching policies. Administrative actions can be taken to repair the machinery of flagging policies and dysfunctional agencies. If necessary, people who are flouting the law can be held accountable. Pursuant to this approach, the president and his allies may call for legislation from Congress. This approach may do little to mollify hardened ideological critics, but it can satisfy party pragmatists and give the heir apparent some political space to govern in his own right.

A more drastic form of the corrective approach may call for the president to reverse parts of his predecessor's policies, tacitly admitting to the flaws of his party's governing philosophy. This course of action may be forced upon the president by failing policies and a stronger opposition party demanding change. Reversing policies will also do little to appease critics in the opposition party, for they will see such moves as a sign of weakness and political opportunity in the future. Inevitably, reversal will bring about accusations from members of the president's party that hard-won policy achievements are being frittered away and supporters are being stabbed in the back. In adopting the corrective approach, the president may claim to be acting in concert with the authentic spirit of his regime's governing philosophy. Whether they succeed or fail at repairing or reversing their predecessors' policies, even going down this pathway is likely to generate political costs for heirs apparent.

All presidents in the heir apparent category will likely oscillate between the continuity approach, the expansion approach, and the corrective approach, depending upon the issue and the political circumstances. A president may commence his tenure with a rigid posture and a robust defense of his predecessor's policies, followed by efforts to tweak and modify those policies, followed by outright reversals of the most troublesome policies. The heir apparent will also want to build off of the record and the established principles of his governing regime by creating new policies to address new and different issues. In addition, there will be efforts to finish some of the predecessor's unfulfilled agendas. An heir apparent president with this kind of inconsistent relationship with his predecessor's policies will be vulnerable to critics who say that the administration lacks ideological coherence.

## INTENSIFYING RESISTANCE

Presidents who fall into the heir apparent category will face similar patterns of political circumstances, even though the issues will differ across time. The approaches identified above suggest that these presidents will spend considerable time dealing with the policy consequences of their like-minded party predecessors. This imperative will clash with the heir apparent's mandate to protect his predecessor's policy achievements and the legitimacy of their party's governing orthodoxy. Within this context, these presidents will struggle with an adversarial political environment that can stall or reverse the long-term ambitions of the governing regime.

Opposition will crystallize on two central fronts. Heir apparent presidents will confront a resurgent opposition party and growing internal divisions within their own party coalition. The sources of division and opposition will start to build up during the predecessor's tenure, sometimes creating setbacks and diminished expectations for the administration. For example, after a substantial record of policy achievement, Roosevelt saw the emergence of a "conservative coalition" in Congress during his second term.[27] His initiatives faced opposition from Southern conservative Democrats and Republicans. The Conservative Coalition would trouble Truman and subsequent Democratic presidents for decades. Upon the predecessor's departure, critics inside and outside of the presidential party will have the time and space to build a countermovement and attack the deficiencies of the regime's governing record. These developments will be a real risk for heir apparent presidents.

Under Madison, a two-party system had yet to fully crystallize, but even within that era of Democratic-Republican dominance, the Federalist Party opposition managed to mount a short-lived comeback. Under Van Buren, the Whig opposition party united at a national level and embraced modern methods of campaign organizing to make Jackson's heir apparent a one-term president. Under Grant, the Democratic opposition strengthened as federal Reconstruction policies eased and the party's Southern base began to reassert itself at a national level once again. Under Truman, Republicans won control of both houses of Congress for the first time in eighteen years. Finally, Bush faced strong Democratic majorities in both chambers of Congress for his entire presidency, and like Van Buren, he was the one-term victim of an opposition party that was able to successfully revitalize itself.

All presidents must grapple with the likelihood of party losses in congressional midterm elections. Such setbacks are not limited to the weak and unpopular presidents. As table 2.4 reveals, the heir apparent presidents identified in this account maintained a worse overall record of party success in midterm elections, as compared to the overall party record of presidents identified as regime-building predecessors. Because predecessors operate in an environment where their party philosophy is ascendant, midterm losses are likely to be small and fleeting, or in rare cases like Roosevelt's Democrats

**Table 2.4**
**Midterm Congressional Party Seat Gains and Losses of Heirs Apparent and Predecessors by Percentage**

| Election Year | President | House | Senate |
|---|---|---|---|
| 1802 | Jefferson | 8.4 | 23.5 |
| 1806 | Jefferson | 1.4 | 2.9 |
| 1810 | *Madison* | 10.0 | 3.9 |
| 1814 | *Madison* | 2.4 | −9.4 |
| 1830 | Jackson | −4.7 | −2.1 |
| 1834 | Jackson | −0.5 | 8.3 |
| 1838 | *Van Buren* | −1.2 | −9.6 |
| 1862 | Lincoln | −12.8 | 1.5 |
| 1870 | *Grant* | −14.4 | −8.1 |
| 1874 | *Grant* | −33.0 | −3.0 |
| 1934 | Roosevelt | 1.8 | 10.4 |
| 1938 | Roosevelt | −16.6 | −7.3 |
| 1942 | Roosevelt | −10.3 | −9.4 |
| 1946 | *Truman* | −12.9 | −12.5 |
| 1950 | *Truman* | −6.4 | −5.2 |
| 1982 | Reagan | −6.2 | 2.0 |
| 1986 | Reagan | −0.9 | −8.0 |
| 1990 | *Bush* | −1.4 | −1.0 |
| Predecessor Mean | | −4.0 | 2.2 |
| Heir Apparent Mean | | −7.1 | −5.6 |

Heir apparent presidents are identified in italics. Numbers come from the total seat gains and losses based on the author's calculation from the official House and Senate lists of party membership at the start of each new Congress. These totals are based on Election Day results. Jackson's Democratic Party is listed as "Jacksonian" in the official lists until 1837. Senators were chosen by state legislatures prior to the twentieth century, but Senate election results are still indicative of political balances of power within states.

Source: Donald A. Zinman, "Passing the Torch through Political Time: Heir Apparent Presidents and the Governing Party," *White House Studies* 9, no. 1 (2009): 51–65, at 57.

in 1934, there are small party gains. After the period of ascendancy ends, heirs apparent function in a more stagnant political environment for their party, often producing more severe party losses.

Indeed, this phenomenon continues in presidential elections as well. As table 2.5 reveals, heirs apparent enjoy smaller coattail effects, as compared to regime-building predecessors. While presidents commonly sweep fellow party members into Congress upon their elections and reelections, a regime builder's electoral success is likely to penetrate deeper down the ballot. The starkest example here is Jefferson and Madison. Jefferson, the predecessor, brought about robust gains for his ascendant party in 1800 and 1804, while the heir apparent, Madison, was elected and reelected alongside Democratic-Republican party losses in Congress.

## INTERNAL DIVISIONS

Vulnerabilities are also generated from internal divisions within the heir apparent president's governing party. Indeed, any president must contend with internal party strife based upon conflicts over policy, strategy, tactics, or personality. As party leaders, modern presidents, and even some premodern presidents, have acted as arbiters and conciliators between feuding factions. Regime builders are no different in this respect, for even they faced within their parties critics who deplored their policy choices, competence, tactics, and even their character.[28] These presidents, however, were able to mollify, marginalize, or defeat disgruntled factions and proceed with an intact party coalition. Other presidents have not been so successful.

Heir apparent presidents may not only inherit the critics of their predecessors, but invite new criticisms as well. Lacking their predecessors' dominance over the political landscape, heir apparent presidents will confront more acute divisions and more aggressive critics within their parties. Here is where we will see cracks emerging in the national coalition crafted by the predecessor. The internal strife will reach such a level as to disrupt the party's national electoral coalition. When Madison, Grant, and Truman sought second terms,

Table 2.5
**Congressional Party Seat Gains and Losses in Successful Presidential
Elections for Heirs Apparent and Predecessors by Percentage**

| Election Year | President | House | Senate |
|---|---|---|---|
| 1800 | Jefferson | 20.8 | 18.8 |
| 1804 | Jefferson | 7.7 | 5.9 |
| 1808 | *Madison* | −16.9 | −2.9 |
| 1812 | *Madison* | −12.2 | −5.6 |
| 1828 | Jackson | 10.8 | −4.2 |
| 1832 | Jackson | 0.4 | −8.3 |
| 1836 | *Van Buren* | −6.2 | 17.3 |
| 1860 | Lincoln | 10.3 | 22.6 |
| 1864 | Lincoln | 24.3 | 8.8 |
| 1868 | *Grant* | −6.2 | 0.0 |
| 1872 | *Grant* | 12.2 | −12.2 |
| 1932 | Roosevelt | 22.3 | 12.5 |
| 1936 | Roosevelt | 3.0 | 7.3 |
| 1940 | Roosevelt | 1.1 | −3.1 |
| 1944 | Roosevelt | 5.1 | 0.0 |
| 1948 | *Truman* | 17.2 | 9.4 |
| 1980 | Reagan | 8.3 | 12.0 |
| 1984 | Reagan | 3.4 | −2.0 |
| 1988 | *Bush* | −0.7 | 0.0 |
| Predecessor Mean | | 9.8 | 5.9 |
| Heir Apparent Mean | | −1.8 | 0.9 |

Heir apparent presidents are identified in italics. Numbers come from the total seat gains and losses based on the author's calculation from the official House and Senate lists of party membership at the start of each new Congress. These totals are based on Election Day results. Jackson's Democratic Party is listed as "Jacksonian" in the official lists until 1837. Membership totals for the congressional session that began at the start of Lincoln's presidency (following the election of 1860) were affected by the exodus of Southern Democrats due to secession. The sectional crisis meant that Lincoln would enjoy a more strongly Republican Congress.

Source: Donald A. Zinman, "Passing the Torch through Political Time: Heir Apparent Presidents and the Governing Party," *White House Studies* 9, no. 1 (2009): 51–65, at 58.

they endured election-year defections from their parties. In 1992, George Bush had to beat back a primary challenger and lost some Republican votes in November to an independent candidate.[29]

Coalitional tensions during the tenure of the heir apparent will reveal more serious internal divisions in years to come. Truman, for example, prevailed in 1948 in spite of divisions within the New Deal Coalition, but tensions emerged over civil rights and foreign policy issues, which would only intensify in years to come.

Madison presided over a very large party coalition, but large party coalitions are likely to contain multiple rival factions. The Jeffersonian coalition broke up in the mid-1820s, but tensions between limited-government Jeffersonian purists and more nationalistic Democratic-Republicans began intensifying on Madison's watch.

On the heir apparent's watch, problems associated with managing a governing regime begin to escalate. As they practice a mixture of ideological purism, careful innovation, and compromise, charges of betrayal of party orthodoxy, accusations of ineffective political skills, and incompetence will weaken their presidencies. Some of these criticisms, which had been contained on the watch of the predecessor, will erupt with a greater intensity. Because heirs apparent have a close distance in time to the builders of their governing regimes, the strength of their predecessors' political legacy will cast an especially large shadow over all presidential actions. Heirs apparent will not enjoy the flexibility that the passage of time affords to subsequent presidents.

Sometimes heirs apparent will face a convergence of these sources of opposition in the form of a temporary alliance between the opposition party and dissident elements of the presidential party. Madison and Grant each faced reelection challenges from a coalition of their opposition party and disgruntled factions of their own party. Truman had to contend with opposition from the Republican and Southern Democratic Conservative Coalition in Congress.[30] Combined attacks from the opposition party and disgruntled factions of the governing regime will blend allegations of ideological betrayal and administrative inefficiency and mismanagement. Madison's vulnerability was a controversial war gone awry. Grant's vulnerability was a growing exasperation with Reconstruction measures.

## OTHER INCARNATIONS OF THE
## HEIR APPARENT PHENOMENON

A president who succeeds a recent predecessor of his own party will face constraints, risks, and opportunities. Here much will depend upon the heir apparent's political relationship with the predecessor and the predecessor's success in office. Other variables include the circumstances of the predecessor's departure, the context of the successor's election, and a president's place within the cycle of political time. The cases covered in subsequent chapters serve as the starkest examples of heirs apparent assuming office from a regime-building predecessor of their own party. Still, it should be acknowledged that common phenomena of the heir apparent presidency can be found to some degree if the successor has a political kinship with a predecessor who is considered above average.

While many of the phenomena that define an heir apparent presidency can be found in the presidencies of Adams and Taft, neither succeeded a regime builder. Both had large shoes to fill, but neither president ascended to the office with the expectation of protecting a relatively new governing regime. Adams was heir apparent to the constitutional presidency in an era that lacked a strong political party structure. Taft was the designated heir apparent to Republican Progressivism, which served as an innovation and alteration of a governing Republican regime going back several decades.[31]

## John Adams

"I am heir apparent you know and a succession is soon to take place," John Adams told his wife Abigail.[32] Simply by virtue of being the second person to occupy the constitutional office of the presidency, Adams played the heir apparent role. As the occupant of an office whose very design (and even its existence) provoked controversy at the Constitutional Convention,[33] Adams had to demonstrate that the presidency could be faithfully discharged by a man of less stature than George Washington. While some similarities can be found when comparing the heir apparent presidencies of Adams and the five cases that will be explicated here, his tenure comes under a set of circumstances that warrant different considerations and examinations.

The presidency was created as a somewhat antidemocratic bulwark against the proclivity of other elected officials to yield to unreasonable or hysterical popular demands. Defending the robust presidency in Article II of the Constitution, Hamilton wrote in *Federalist Paper* No. 71, "When occasions present themselves, in which the interests of the people are at variance with their inclinations, it is the duty of the persons whom they have appointed to be the guardians of those interests, to withstand the temporary delusion, in order to give them time and opportunity for more cool and sedate reflection."[34] The president was to be a statesman, a gentleman, a guardian of the national interest, and a man with significant experience in the service of his country. The president, it was hoped, would not be a clever politician skilled in the art of seducing the public. Nor would he be a mere servant to the fluctuations of public opinion. Washington "was the obvious choice" to serve as the first president, given his lifelong pattern of being a responsible and disinterested leader.[35]

Adams was the heir apparent to the constitutional presidency as it was most optimistically envisioned by the Framers. In Washington's absence, a man with a less heroic reputation would now have to assume the office and demonstrate that the presidency could be safely discharged. The challenge for Washington's successor would be a test for the presidency's constitutional design and limitations. Certainly Adams was a man of great stature himself, holding strong credentials as an American "Founding Father." He defeated Jefferson to win the first truly contested presidential election in history.[36] Political tensions had stimulated the beginnings of a two-party system in spite of the Founders' hostility to the creation of parties.[37]

While Washington governed in practice as a moderate Federalist, he maintained a nonpartisan administration and shunned party labels. Adams was a nominal Federalist, but like his predecessor, he sought to avoid overt partisanship as president.[38] Like subsequent heirs apparent, Adams found himself at odds with purists in his own party and a strengthening opposition party. Still, the party system of the late eighteenth century was only in its early development, as politicians were only beginning to line up (sometimes rather crudely) on different sides of the partisan aisle.[39] Under Adams, we can observe more of an heir apparent constitutional presidency, but less of an heir apparent partisan presidency, which is the focus of this study. While party politics was emerging in the 1790s, the presidency was not yet fully immersed in an institutionalized two-party system. Under Madison, the first major case we will turn to here, partisan fault lines were more sharply defined. Even under Madison, however, there was not the same level of rigidity as in the party systems presided over by Van Buren, Grant, Truman, and Bush.

Adams was confronted with dilemmas that forced him to consider new exercises of presidential authority, such as his decision to remove insubordinate members of his cabinet.[40] This was an action that was implied but not explicitly authorized by the Constitution. Indeed, many presidents faced the prospect of using their authority in ways that were neither explicitly authorized by the Constitution nor anticipated by the Framers. Even Washington was challenged for taking presidential actions that tested constitutional boundaries.[41] Adams, however, was the first president who did not command Washington's level of respect and deference to test the constitutional limitations of the office. His decision to dismiss pro-Hamilton cabinet officers marked an important early assertion of presidential supremacy over other executive branch leaders.

### William Howard Taft

Characteristics of an heir apparent presidency can be seen under William Howard Taft: a divided governing party, a stronger opposition party, and mounting policy consequences. Still, Taft's tenure did not follow a fully reconstructive presidency and a newly built governing regime. Fair arguments can be made that the achievements of Theodore Roosevelt rivaled the reconstructive brand of politics and policies brought about by Jefferson, Jackson, and Lincoln. Elements of a reconstructive shift in American politics are visible in the election results of 1896 and in the three presidential terms of William McKinley and Theodore Roosevelt that followed.[42] At the same time, their claims to the politics of reconstruction are limited, since these presidents did not act in repudiation of a regime controlled by a discredited opposition party. Rather, their innovations refined and strengthened an existing Republican majority and Republican model of governance. The most transformative projects in American political reconstruction engaged in a forceful rejection of the opposition party's ideologies and policy approaches.

Innovations in presidential action and style were also trademarks of Theodore Roosevelt's tenure. He was an energetic champion of progressive reform who used the powers of his office in ways that were deemed unacceptable for previous presidents.[43] Theodore Roosevelt's innovations in public policy and presidential style would seem to place Taft into the heir apparent role. Taft also held a political kinship with his predecessor, as he was a former Roosevelt administration cabinet secretary and a fellow progressive Republican. Although Taft did not share the same enthusiasm for the more aggressive and visible presidency of his predecessor, he was the recipient of constant advice from Roosevelt during the 1908 campaign.[44] Running as the unabashed progressive disciple of his predecessor, Taft won an overwhelming victory. Ideologically he was an heir apparent to the Progressive Republican cause, but stylistically Taft refused to follow his predecessor's lead by using the office in dynamic ways to achieve progressive policy goals.

His policy record was not neglectful of progressive objectives. As president, Taft in his policies on conservation continued progressive commitments.[45] A corporate income tax was implemented,[46] and his one-term administration brought more antitrust suits than Roosevelt's nearly two-term administration.[47] He signed the Mann-Elkins Act, which enhanced the Interstate Commerce Commission's powers over telecommunications and railroad rates; civil service reforms were extended into the Department of the Navy and the postal service.[48] He was a confident internationalist, as was his predecessor, using a so-called dollar diplomacy to advance American trading and economic interests in Latin America and the eastern hemisphere.[49]

In addition, Taft's vision of the chief executive's role in government most certainly did not emulate his predecessor's view, and that threatened numerous progressive policy achievements. Taft held the temperament of a judge dedicated to effective execution of the law, rather than that of an energetic activist politician. He instead promoted efficiency, working to improve government procedures and services with fiscal restraint.[50] His view of the presidency brushed aside Roosevelt's modernizations of the office; when policy innovation was warranted, Taft remained deferential and respectful to Congress, shunning the kind of overt public campaigning and assertiveness his predecessor so skillfully mastered.[51] As a consequence, conservative elements in Congress diminished major reforms dear to the hearts of Progressive activists, such as the Payne-Aldrich tariff.[52] Consistent with other heir apparent presidencies, the governing party suffered from a very severe party rupture in the early 1910s. Theodore Roosevelt repudiated his party successor more sharply than any president in history by challenging him for the Republican nomination in 1912 and then running against him as a third-party candidate.

## PROTECTING THE REVOLUTION: FIVE HEIRS APPARENT, FIVE REGIMES

James Madison, Martin Van Buren, Ulysses S. Grant, Harry Truman, and George H. W. Bush all played the heir apparent role as inheritors of regimes built by a recent party predecessor. All but Grant immediately assumed office upon a regime builder's departure from office. Subsequent chapters will examine the common challenges, risks, and opportunities that come with an heir apparent presidency in the large shadow of an especially revolutionary predecessor. Madison was the first custodian of Jefferson's "Revolution of 1800"; Van Buren, the brilliant party builder and tactician, was the first caretaker of Jacksonian democracy; Grant had to finish the task of the orderly and moderate Reconstruction envisioned by Lincoln; Truman was the feisty and plain-spoken defender of the New Deal; George Bush was the defender of the Reagan Revolution. Each heir apparent here was more than just the successor to a popular or above-average president. Rather, these heirs apparent are unique because they were uniquely charged with protecting the achievements of a revolutionary brand of politics and a newly installed political order.

As discussed above, the particular challenges facing presidents in this category will be examined in one chapter for each of these five heir apparent presidents. Each governing regime had vulnerabilities that put these presidencies at risk. These vulnerabilities were sometimes kept under control during the tenure of presidents with effective political skills. On other occasions, these presidents misjudged their political adversaries and exposed their governing coalition to significant setbacks. Either way, political time moves along in ways that are likely to cause increasingly greater complications for the heir apparent.

# 3

# JAMES MADISON:
# THE JEFFERSONIAN TORCH BEARER

## THE OPPOSITION PARTY ASSUMES POWER

Tracing their roots to the Anti-Federalist critics of the Constitution, Democratic-Republicans functioned as opponents of an expanded central state for more than a decade. As an opposition party, Democratic-Republicans were protective of states' rights, agrarianism, limited government, legislative supremacy over the executive, humility in foreign affairs, and opening up democratic processes. Asserting principles in an opposition stance, however, does not come with the obligations of governing. However, Jefferson and Madison could appreciate that Democratic-Republicans could not always realistically translate these principles into public policy as a governing party. This is a dilemma that will behoove any newly emergent opposition party assuming the reins of power.

Jefferson compared the Democratic-Republican victory of 1800 to the significance of the American Revolution.[1] The electoral outcome marked the first transition of American political power from a governing party to an opposition party. The election results were close but decisive in the long run. The outcome did not immediately appear to foreshadow the Federalist Party's slow demise, especially given the diffused nature of the American electoral and constitutional systems. Federalists lost a close presidential election and overwhelmingly lost control of the House of Representatives.

Their party began the Jefferson Administration with a strong minority base in the Senate, a firm base in the judiciary, and virtual parity with Democratic-Republicans in state governorships. By the end of Jefferson's tenure, however, Federalist Party strength had collapsed nationwide. When Madison succeeded Jefferson, there was little doubt that Democratic-Republicans now enjoyed an identity as the new American governing regime.

## MADISON'S JEFFERSONIAN REPUBLIC

As Democratic-Republicans consolidated their political gains from the Jefferson years, Madison inherited a republic facing domestic and international problems brought about by economic growth and modernization, as well as westward expansion. The United States was not yet close to being a major actor on the international stage, in spite of the demands from some Democratic-Republicans for an aggressive American stance. The indispensability of a sound central banking policy and the economic necessity of a national internal-improvement policy also continued to challenge traditional Jeffersonian principles. Jefferson was not a rigid ideologue as president, as he frequently departed from his regime's orthodoxy for the sake of political pragmatism. Whether or not his policy choices were consistent with Democratic-Republican principles, the actions of the Jefferson Administration bore the stamp of the governing party, including the consequences. As the Jefferson Administration's chief lieutenant and heir apparent, Madison could not escape political responsibility for his predecessor's policy consequences, even though Madison also had his predecessor's instincts for pragmatism and compromise. Overall, Madison maintained a Jeffersonian policy trajectory, as he advocated, defended, and extended Democratic-Republican principles into politics and government. At the same time, Madison's record as president lacks the revolutionary fervor of his predecessor, for he had to address Jefferson's policy shortcomings and the impracticality of Jeffersonian ideology in the real world. Indeed, some of Madison's choices exacerbated problems with Jeffersonian ideology, rather than rectifying unworkable policy situations.

As Jefferson was leaving office, Federalist opposition had weakened to nuisance levels, but divisions within the now very large Democratic-Republican coalition began to crystallize and infect the Madison cabinet. As is typical with any majority party that grows too large and too diverse, Democratic-Republicans were becoming too dominant for their own good. Tensions mounted between various party factions, each defined by a separate cast of leaders and a separate policy program that reflected their competing visions. In an era when state-level party organization was more important than national party cohesiveness, the strength of Democratic-Republican factions varied from state to state.

Maritime tensions with the British and French produced growing headaches for Madison, as Jefferson Administration cuts to the navy exposed American vulnerabilities at sea. Jefferson's sweeping Embargo Act, principally aimed at Britain and France, was enacted as a retaliatory measure, but it backfired. The policy was economically devastating and in spite of heavy-handed enforcement powers created by the law, defiant American shippers disobeyed the law with ease.[2] A new and slightly less restrictive embargo imposed during Madison's first year in office did little to rectify American grievances and proved similarly unenforceable.[3] Foreign policy tensions merged with tensions within the Democratic-Republican coalition, increasingly moving Madison into what was known as the War Hawk faction.

Territorial expansion continued slowly but certainly, testing Jeffersonian principles of limited national government and authority. The geographic size of the United States had recently doubled with the Louisiana Purchase, an act of the Jefferson Administration that tested the president's strict constitutional scruples. While the Jeffersonian creed stressed strict constitutional interpretation, it also celebrated the cultural and economic virtues of agrarianism. Western territorial expansion would extend the lifeline of America's predominantly agrarian character. On the one hand, territorial expansion opened up new opportunities for enterprising settlers and farmers, for they were the ideal Jeffersonian citizens, following their own economic destiny by living off the land. On the other hand, western expansion imposed new demands upon the federal government to integrate new communities into the national economy, establish territorial and local governments, and contend with escalations in tensions with Native American peoples. The Louisiana Purchase also brought with it an unresolved controversy for Madison concerning the status of Florida. With little political difficulty, Indiana was admitted to the union and funds were appropriated to extend the national Cumberland Road farther west.[4] Far more vexing for the Madison Administration were the new pressures upon the president to renege on past promises of respect for Native American territorial rights.[5] Like many early American presidents, Madison handled relations with Native Americans through a policy combination of compromise, confrontation, Western assimilation, and promises that were not always kept.[6]

## FROM FEDERALIST ARCHITECT TO JEFFERSONIAN HEIR APPARENT

Madison's path to an heir apparent presidency began with his political break from Treasury Secretary Alexander Hamilton and the Federalists. Madison never wavered in his view that a robust federal government was necessary, but this belief existed alongside a commitment to the judicious and cautious use of federal powers. Hamilton's economic plans for the nation's economy were particularly offensive to Madison. The treasury secretary's vision of a large expansion of federal responsibilities into national banking and assumption of state-level Revolutionary War debts provoked Madison's opposition upon policy and constitutional grounds.[7] The two men also clashed over President Washington's unilateral declaration of neutrality when Britain and France went to war in 1793.[8] Madison was a leading designer of the Constitution at the Philadelphia Convention of 1787 and a meticulous defender of the document in the *Federalist Papers*. He was qualified to be a prominent spokesperson for the Federalist causes of strong national government and limited democracy. Soon after the Constitution's implementation, however, Madison evolved into one of the leading voices of opposition to the administration's federal consolidation of power, which he believed came at the expense of the states and the people.[9] From his perch in the House of Representatives, he was frequently consulted in the early years of the Washington Administration on policy matters and constitutional procedures, but this tapered off as Madison assumed a leading opposition role.[10]

As a private citizen during John Adams's presidency, Madison partook in a collaborative project with Vice President Jefferson, as both men were alarmed over the Alien and Sedition Acts. Amid heightened tensions with France, this package of laws tightened citizenship requirements for immigrants and vaguely criminalized speech and printed words deemed to be "seditious." Jefferson authored a resolution, adopted by the Kentucky legislature in 1798, calling upon states to declare these laws unconstitutional. Madison penned a similar resolution on behalf of Virginia. Stopping just short of advocating outright nullification by the states, Madison argued that states had a duty to resist unconstitutional legislation from Washington, DC.[11]

The position of secretary of state was a common stepping-stone to the presidency in the early republic, and Madison was correctly assumed to be President Jefferson's top choice for the post when the new administration assumed office in 1801. In this role, Madison served as Jefferson's top advisor and counselor.[12] Here, at Jefferson's right hand, Madison played a leading role in most important episodes of the administration, including many issues and problems that would persist into his own presidency. Madison was also the central player in Jefferson's efforts to block some of Adams's last-minute judicial appointments, culminating in the Supreme Court's *Marbury v. Madison* (1803) ruling. The personal and professional relationship between these two men was the strongest of all of the predecessor/heir apparent couplings being covered in this account. Hence, there was no room for Madison to escape the intraparty animosity Jefferson had earned by his second term.

In an era of amorphous party organizations and not entirely well-defined party labels, Madison represented an early example of a party-switching politician. Like that of other men of his generation, Madison's embrace of the party system was done with reluctance and out of political necessity. Like a future heir apparent president, Martin Van Buren, Madison was a party builder at the legislative level, articulating arguments and strategic themes. Both men also established and strengthened close relationships with their future presidential predecessors. The party system of Madison's era did not match the sophistication of Van Buren's era, but both men earned credibility as faithful advocates for their respective parties in the context of offensive and defensive legislative advocacy. Subsequently, they served in the administrations of their presidential predecessors as loyal lieutenants.

### *The Election of 1808: Reassembling the Jeffersonian Coalition*

Jefferson governed in an environment of growing Democratic-Republican political momentum, which peaked in his landslide reelection in 1804. As Madison prepared for his own elevation to the presidency, Democratic-Republican strength vis-à-vis the Federalist opposition was very strong. However, as Jefferson abided by Washington's practice of stepping down after two terms, the presidential election of 1808 exposed simmering tensions within the Democratic-Republican coalition. There was even a minor Federalist Party resurgence. Both of these threats failed to derail Madison's election, but they did lay the groundwork for a more challenging landscape of opposition during his presidency.

The Federalist Party renominated their 1804 presidential nominee Charles Cotesworth Pinckney, a lawyer and Revolutionary War officer. Badly weakened, the Federalists had experienced a steady decline in Congress and state governorships during the Jefferson years.[13] The unpopularity of the embargo and intraparty squabbling among Democratic-Republicans gave Federalists an opportunity, even if the odds were still long. An ascendant governing party facing a diminished opposition party must still contend with its accumulating policy record. A governing party with major policy vulnerabilities and internal divisions can temporarily lose power, even as the opposition party fails to fundamentally redirect the nation's ideological and policy trajectory.[14] Federalists now had an opening to hitch Madison to the deficiencies of the Jefferson Administration.

First, however, Madison had to quell a rebellion against his candidacy from the multiplying factions of his own party. As Jefferson's tenure was ending, Democratic-Republican camps included mainline Jeffersonians, Old Republicans (or Quids), the Clinton faction, and the "Invisibles." The Old Republicans, led by Representative John Randolph of Roanoke, had become disillusioned by Jefferson's increasingly flexible interpretation of the Constitution, and accused him of abandoning the principles of limited government and states' rights. They favored James Monroe as Jefferson's successor.[15] Opposition also came from the Clintonian faction, which was based in New York, and centered on Vice President George Clinton's political adherents. They disliked the embargo, challenged Virginia's domination of the Democratic-Republican Party, and demanded their share of patronage, given New York's important place in the national party coalition.[16] The Invisibles' base of power was in the Senate, where they were led by Senators William Giles of Virginia and Samuel Smith of Maryland.[17] Their opposition to Madison was an extension of their growing opposition to Jefferson in his second term. Lacking a unifying ideology, and internally divided in their own right, the Invisibles frequently teamed up with other factions and Federalists in opposition to Jefferson and Madison.[18] Personal dislike and distrust of Jefferson, and any disciple associated with him, were central motivations for the Invisibles.[19] Fortunately for Madison, no single faction was able to unite around an alternative and develop a successful strategy to overtake Jefferson's top lieutenant.

The mechanism used to nominate presidential and vice presidential candidates of this era was the congressional nominating caucus, giving party members in Congress the ultimate authority over the selection of candidates. This elite-based approach was already becoming controversial by the time Madison was a candidate. At the behest of Madison's supporters, the caucus was scheduled early to blunt the momentum of rival candidates, which included Monroe and Vice President Clinton.[20] On January 23, 1808, the caucus was boycotted by numerous anti-Madison members of Congress, who believed the process was "a gross assumption of power not delegated by the people," unconstitutional, and stacked in favor of the secretary of state.[21] Madison prevailed with 83 votes out of the 89 caucus voters (out of 149 members who were invited), while Monroe and Clinton received only three votes each.[22]

Intraparty headaches did not end for Madison with his victory in the caucus. Some Clinton and Monroe supporters continued to advocate for their respective candidates. Monroe retained a strong base of support in Virginia, while Clinton commanded strong support in New York and Pennsylvania. Some Democratic-Republican newspapers denounced the caucus and only reluctantly endorsed Madison, while the *American Citizen* newspaper in New York continued to advocate for Clinton.[23] These efforts were not successful, but they revealed intraparty personal rivalries, procedural controversies, and ideological differences that would only multiply during Madison's presidency and beyond. Similar episodes of lukewarm enthusiasm or outright opposition from intraparty factions can be found in the first presidential campaigns of Van Buren, Truman, and Bush. All heir apparent presidents in this account faced challenges for their party nomination, save for Grant, but other factions failed to unify around an alternative and overcome the institutional support of the designated successor. These presidents sought office at times when their respective party establishments were vulnerable to internal challenges from political rivals. At the same time, their parties were resilient enough to maintain control over the policies, ideologies, and nominations of presidential candidates.

In the general election, Federalist newspapers and pamphlets excoriated Madison and Jefferson over the deleterious effects of the embargo (which they denounced as the "Dambargo") and lamented "French influence" in foreign policy.[24] Democratic-Republican publications countered Federalist charges that Madison was weak of character and lacked independence, given his close ties to Jefferson.

To vindicate his record and stress his qualifications for promotion to the presidency, pro-Madison papers published the secretary of state's official correspondence pertaining to the Monroe-Pinkney Treaty. The treaty from 1806 sought to end British impressments of American seamen, but it was repudiated by Jefferson as ineffective and falling short of the administration's goals.[25] Indeed, Madison's correspondence revealed him to be a staunch defender of American interests who acted with objectivity and resolve in his dealings with other nations.[26] Jefferson cleared the way for more of Madison's official correspondence to be released to Congress and the public during the thick of the 1808 presidential campaign.[27]

When the presidential electors submitted their votes, the Democratic-Republican electoral coalition was solidly reassembled behind Madison, though a little less robustly than four years before. Federalists carried Delaware again and reclaimed most of their New England stronghold (where the embargo was very unpopular), which had been lost in 1804. Pinckney also won scattered electoral votes in Maryland and North Carolina. The Clinton movement in New York produced only six electoral votes for their candidate, while the Monroe movement in Virginia fizzled. Madison dominated the South, the West, and Pennsylvania and carried 13 of New York's 19 electoral votes. In the 10 states that permitted popular selection of presidential electors, Madison electors scored nearly two-thirds of the popular vote,[28] but Democratic-Republican slippage was evident in 1808 congressional elections: Federalists gained one Senate seat and 24 seats in the House. These results still left them entrenched in the congressional minority, but gave Federalists a spark of momentum with which to challenge the new president, perhaps in combination with anti-Madison Democratic-Republican factions.

Jefferson and Madison governed in an era when party labels existed, but a fully mature and sophisticated party system had yet to materialize. Both parties lacked a strong base of grassroots support in the electorate and both parties had only very limited organization at the national level. And the very idea of two-party competition was not seen as a favorable attribute: Democratic-Republicans and Federalists regarded each other as illegitimate opponents who were somehow perverting the true spirit of disinterested constitutional government.[29] As early as his first election to the presidency, Madison experienced phenomena that are common to heir apparent presidents, even under the first party system, which was limited.

## PROTECTING THE JEFFERSONIAN REPUBLIC ON JEFFERSONIAN TERMS

Strict adherence to orthodox Democratic-Republican principles was often not feasible or desirable for Madison. He encountered a more dangerous international stage than his predecessor, which also served to complicate the nation's economic landscape. Unlike subsequent heirs apparent, Madison had the advantage of a limited opposition party and disorganized opposition factions within his own party. These phenomena made it possible for Madison to gingerly maneuver away from strict Jeffersonian orthodoxy when necessary, just as his predecessor himself had done. Much like Jefferson, Madison often acted with pragmatism to moderate or even abandon Democratic-Republican policy commitments in the interest of protecting long-term goals, economic stability, and national security. Lacking robust Federalist opposition, Madison could depart from Jeffersonian orthodoxy on Jeffersonian terms. Blending the three approaches of maintaining continuity, expanding his regime's policy commitments, and correcting administrative deficiencies, Madison followed his predecessor's ideological and policy trajectory. Even where Jefferson's policies themselves departed from Jeffersonian philosophy, Madison forged ahead, gradually steering his party and the nation away from the most purist interpretations of Democratic-Republican ideology. Still, Madison's pliant handling of Democratic-Republican commitments did not preclude him from taking actions in defense of orthodox principles.

### Saying No

The veto is one of the strongest defensive weapons a president possesses, as it can be a tool to maintain continuity. It can be used to protect the principles and commitments of the president's party and administration from challenges by opponents. An heir apparent president can use the veto to reassert the orthodox principles of his governing regime and burnish his credentials as a protector of his predecessor's hard-earned achievements. Jefferson vetoed no legislation as president, but Madison used his pen to veto five pieces of legislation he found constitutionally objectionable and offensive to orthodox Jeffersonian principles. The veto was used by Madison to maintain continuity and resist policy changes that departed from Jeffersonian orthodoxy.

The matter of separation of church and state provided two opportunities for Madison to maintain strict adherence to Jeffersonian principles. In February 1811, Madison vetoed a bill that called for incorporating the Episcopal Church in Washington, DC. He rejected this measure as "a precedent for giving to religious societies as such a legal agency in carrying into effect a public and civil duty."[30] A week later, another veto was issued upon a bill that set aside land for use by the Baptist Church in the Mississippi Territory. Again, Madison's veto was based upon his reading of the First Amendment's Establishment Clause.[31]

Madison was also concerned about the ongoing use of Supreme Court justices on the judicial circuit. In his annual message in 1816, Madison recommended that Congress reform this practice and reorganize lower-level courts.[32] Four years before, he vetoed a bill that would have expanded the circuit-riding role of Supreme Court justices. His veto message called the measure impractical and "a precedent for modifications and extensions of judicial services encroaching on the constitutional tenure of judicial offices."[33] The veto was consistent with the Jeffersonian principle of a constitutionally limited role for the justices of the highest court. Madison was not about to expand a practice he regarded as outdated, unfeasible, and potentially disruptive to the judiciary's proper constitutional place.

Where Madison acted in defense of strict constitutional construction, he did not always act consistently. Jeffersonian orthodoxy scorned federal support for internal improvements like roads, bridges, and canals. Yet Jefferson himself signed the law that authorized construction of the national Cumberland Road.[34] Madison signed off on the construction contract during his presidency,[35] and in 1815 the president approved an additional $100,000 to expand the road westward.[36] Much to the shock of internal-improvement boosters like House Speaker Henry Clay and Representative John C. Calhoun, Madison vetoed a measure known as the Bonus Bill on the last full day of his presidency. This legislation would have funded road and canal construction with surplus revenue from the Second National Bank.[37] In his veto message, Madison acknowledged the merits of internal improvements on policy grounds, but reverted to a strict constitutional construction that may have gone beyond Jefferson himself:

> Seeing that such a power is not expressly given by the Constitution, and believing that it can not be deduced from any part of it without an inadmissible latitude of construction and a reliance on insufficient precedents; believing also that the permanent success of the Constitution depends on a definite partition of powers between the General and the State Governments, and that no adequate landmarks would be left by the constructive extension of the powers of Congress as proposed in the bill, I have no option but to withhold my signature from it.[38]

Through his handling of the internal-improvement issue, Madison adhered to continuity by resisting projects he regarded as unconstitutional, but he also committed to finishing and expanding the Cumberland Road project. In his annual message in 1815, he spoke favorably of internal improvements, though Madison also supported a constitutional amendment to authorize this policy.[39] On the one hand, Madison observed the Jeffersonian principle of a limited federal role in economic development and followed his regime's constitutional principles on this policy. On the other hand, this annual message implied that doctrinaire adherence to Jeffersonian orthodoxy might not be compatible with economic growth, given Madison's advocacy of internal improvements, national banking, military strength, and higher tariffs.[40]

### Mr. Madison's Bank

Elsewhere, Madison continued on Jefferson's policy trajectory, even when it skewed away from the preferences of Democratic-Republican purists. On national banking, Madison's approaches waxed and waned, but gradually moved toward a probanking position. On this issue Madison could assert orthodox Jeffersonian principles and stoutly oppose a national bank, or he could follow the actual record of his predecessor and tolerate the Bank's existence. Yet Madison was confronted with a more demanding challenge on this issue. The National Bank's twenty-year charter was due to expire on Madison's watch in March 1811. By this time, the president had reached the conclusion that the Bank was a vital instrument in preserving the nation's credit and economic stability. Madison's old constitutional objections were laid aside in view of the Bank's long record of steady and effective performance.[41] Much like Jefferson, who was resigned to tolerating the Bank's financial entrenchment in the nation's economy,[42] Madison gave way in his philosophical principles to presidential responsibilities over a stable economy. This was an especially acute issue given that Jefferson left office with an economy wracked by the Embargo Act. For any governing coalition, economic turmoil will have the gradual effect of wearing down that regime's legitimacy to govern over time.

Unfortunately for Madison, opposition to the Bank was still very strong from Democratic-Republicans of various factions, and the president downplayed his support for renewing the charter.[43] Nineteenth-century practices frowned upon presidents interjecting themselves into the rough-and-tumble of the legislative process, but Treasury Secretary Albert Gallatin actively lobbied Congress for recharter on behalf of the administration. In the Senate, the Bank recharter bill lost by one vote, due to Vice President Clinton's tie-breaking "no" vote.[44] The Bank's looming expiration, disappearance, and second rechartering debate ultimately forced Madison to take a sharper affirmative or negative position on the institution, in contrast to his predecessor.

Financing the war with Britain was cumbersome in the Bank's absence. Madison now held the position that the institution, shortcomings and all, was economically indispensable.[45] Congress began working on a new national bank bill in 1814, but the lengthy legislative debate drifted away from the objectives envisioned by Madison and Treasury Secretary Alexander Dallas. The final bill was the product of much maneuvering by anti-Madison and anti-Bank Democratic-Republicans, as well as mischievous Federalists.[46] Madison vetoed the final legislation on January 30, 1815, on the grounds that the bill was poorly conceived:

> Waiving the question of the constitutional authority of the Legislature to establish an incorporated bank as being precluded in my judgment by repeated recognitions under varied circumstances of the validity of such an institution in acts of the legislative, executive, and judicial branches of the Government, accompanied by indications, in different modes, of a concurrence of the general will of the nation, the proposed bank does not appear to be calculated to answer the purposes of reviving the public credit, of providing a national medium of circulation, and of aiding the Treasury by facilitating the indispensable anticipations of the revenue and by affording to the public more durable loans.[47]

This time Madison confined his objections to the effectiveness and accountability of the new proposed bank, rather than its constitutionality. Indeed, the veto message revealed a pragmatic willingness to support a second national bank, but Madison was convinced by Dallas and Monroe to veto this measure.[48] The bank bill pushed by Dallas, and brushed aside by Congress, essentially reinstated the Hamiltonian banking system of the first National Bank.[49] The president recommended a national bank in his annual message to Congress in December 1815.[50] A new bank bill, along the broad outlines of the first banking system, was smoothly enacted and signed by the president the following April.

On the banking issue, Madison's flexibility revealed that he evolved from an approach based upon continuity to an approach based upon correction of a flawed policy formula. At the start of his presidency, Madison maintained Jefferson's policy of toleration and cordial dislike toward the Bank. The problem with simply tolerating the institution, rather than forcefully and affirmatively advocating for it, is that opponents were well positioned to mobilize and capitalize upon the Bank's political vulnerabilities. In subsequent years, Madison did become an increasingly forceful advocate for the Bank's rechartering and its economic value to the nation. After experiencing the wartime consequences of the Bank's absence, Madison went beyond Jefferson's passive toleration of the institution toward an affirmative defense of a new charter. By the end of his tenure, Madison boosted the Bank as a corrective departure from Jefferson's handling of this policy.

## Making the Tariff Protective

Madison endorsed a moderate corrective course from the Jeffersonian principle of free trade and low tariffs. A rising industrial base required a reexamination of Jeffersonian assumptions of economic policy. As he moved toward a greater federal role in banking and internal improvements, Madison also requested and won enactment of a modest protective tariff.[51] The annual message in 1815 acknowledged the benefits of this policy to the nation's nascent manufacturing base and overall prosperity. And it was not inconsistent with Democratic-Republican practices to rely heavily upon tariffs for raising revenue. Indeed, Jefferson signed tariff increases in March 1804 to pay for the Barbary War.[52] Jefferson's administration gradually repealed domestic and excise taxes, meaning that the federal treasury would be almost exclusively filled by tariffs.[53] Madison not only legitimized his party's use of tariffs for raising revenue, but also opened the door to using the tariff as a protective economic device and a means to challenge rival nations. Advocated by Secretary Dallas, the tariff was a carefully targeted and temporary measure to challenge British economic power and boost the nation's industrial base in the event of another war. In the context of military preparedness vis-à-vis the British, and long disconnected from the days of Hamilton's advocacy of tariffs, Southern Democratic-Republican members of Congress strongly supported the measure.[54] The bill passed with a large bipartisan vote, rolling over the objections of Old Republican leader John Randolph in the House.[55]

## Watering Down the "Dambargo"

Jefferson's embargo policy required Madison to correct disastrous consequences. As the Embargo Act failed to deliver on its promises, a revision was enacted in the closing months of Jefferson's presidency. The new policy for Madison to enforce was the Non-Intercourse Act of 1809, which continued to restrict trade with Britain and France, but loosened shipping elsewhere. Under the law the president could lift trade restrictions with Britain and France if these countries halted their interference with American shippers.[56] Early indications and diplomacy suggested that the law might change British behavior. Madison initially lifted trade restrictions on Britain, but then used constitutionally creative contortions to reinstate them when it became apparent that British policies would not change.[57] Misunderstandings, misleading statements, and a British diplomat who disobeyed his instructions all combined to dash any hopes for a normalization of Anglo-American trade relations. Like the Jefferson embargo, the Non-Intercourse Act was also impossible to realistically enforce.[58]

The next step in this stumbling trade war was called Macon's Bill #2. Rep. Nathaniel Macon's first attempt to revise the Non-Intercourse Act failed in Congress (Macon's Bill #1). The second revision did not actually have Macon's support, but it became law in May 1810. This law sought to play off of the economic rivalry between Britain and France by cutting trade off from one country if and when the other country respected American trading neutrality. Instead, France's Napoleon I deceived Madison into believing that France would lift trade restrictions upon the United States. Because of the French deception, the Macon law then called for the reimposition of trade restrictions on Britain in early 1811. Nothing was gained economically or politically and war with Britain was now more likely.[59]

In his heir apparent role as repairer-in-chief, Madison's actions here were a total failure. Faced with a nonintercourse policy that was a major economic, diplomatic, and political failure, Madison sought to adjust, rather than substantially reverse, course. The Embargo Act and its two successor policies still restricted American trade with Britain and France very broadly. Madison's approaches here pleased no one, and failed to rectify fundamental grievances with these two nations. Instead, the futility of using trade restrictions as a means to challenge these major world powers was only further confirmed and supplemented by bad diplomatic maneuvers. Federal powers had to be enhanced to enforce restrictions on commerce with major trading partners, which was anathema to a political party dedicated to free trade and limited government. By only tweaking his predecessor's record in this disastrous policy, Madison drove his party and administration further away from Jeffersonian orthodoxy. As economic and diplomatic consequences continued to mount during Madison's first term, practical distinctions between the Embargo Act, the Non-Intercourse Act, and the Macon law could be very hard to distinguish. Abandoning nonintercourse altogether would have likely generated criticism from within the Democratic-Republican coalition anyway. British and French offenses on the seas would have likely continued. On the other hand, ironically, Madison could have made a more politically fresh start by repudiating his own predecessor's departure from Jeffersonian principles of free trade, limited government, and the humble conduct of foreign affairs.

## The Pursuit of Florida

The acquisition of Spanish-controlled West Florida presented an opportunity for Madison to act upon his predecessor's unfulfilled ambitions. Here the heir apparent worked to expand the commitments of his governing regime. Acting in full accordance with Jefferson's long-term territorial policy goals, Madison pursued a gradual annexation of West Florida.[60] Jefferson believed that his administration's purchase of the Louisiana Territory included West Florida, although Spain begged to differ. With his hands full of other sensitive foreign policy situations, Jefferson let the matter languish for his successor. The United States did not make a move upon the poorly defended territory until political and military unrest made it possible. In the summer of 1810, Madison sent a representative to West Florida to promote a revolution. Like so many revolutions, it spiraled out of control, with a clash in Baton Rouge and rebels asserting an independent Republic of West Florida. Unwilling to negotiate with the unrecognized republic, Madison ordered the annexation of West Florida in a secret proclamation on October 27, 1810. American military forces moved in accordingly. Madison attempted to use similar tactics to acquire East Florida by way of a covert operation, but the plan fizzled.[61]

Just as Jefferson used admittedly supple means of constitutional interpretation to acquire the Louisiana Territory, Madison stretched constitutional scruples still further in the quest for territorial gain. Indeed, American claims to West Florida were debatable. Pursuant to the previous administration's policy that West Florida was always part of the Louisiana acquisition, Madison acted to secure territory he believed was covered by the Senate-ratified treaty of 1803. The president was not authorized by Congress to simply take West Florida, and with military forces to boot. The president's secret proclamation, made while Congress was adjourned, conveniently shielded him from being held accountable by the legislative branch. Once the proclamation was made public, Federalists denounced Madison for acting without congressional approval. However, the administration did seek and receive congressional authorization for its unsuccessful mission to acquire East Florida.[62]

## *Flying with the War Hawks*

Major grievances with the British continued as Madison assumed office from Jefferson. Disputes continued over impressment, trade policy, and allegations of British support for Native American attacks on white American settlements in the West. Madison was not a War Hawk by nature, as he frowned upon militarism and judged the nation to be poorly prepared for war with the still powerful

British Empire.[63] Nonetheless, the Jefferson Administration's failure to rectify fundamental grievances with Great Britain produced increasingly serious consequences. Madison was forced into a corrective policy stance, which itself produced still more failure and hardship.

The administration continued to seek a peaceful solution, but as diplomacy floundered, Madison's actions and rhetoric moved ever closer to the prowar camp. Similar to John Adams during the Quasi-War with France, Madison embraced his presidential responsibilities to adequately prepare the nation for a possible war. In the months leading up to war, Madison called upon Congress to improve and streamline the training of militia officers, create a science-based military academy to supplement West Point, and enlarge military personnel and munitions.[64] Plans were made to increase the army to over 35,000 men, but discussion of new policies became bogged down in political bickering.[65] Naval policies continued the Jefferson Administration's approach of relying upon gunboats.[66] Politically and militarily, Madison's preparatory efforts were mostly unsuccessful and too late. Lack of military readiness and modernization produced a series of humiliating setbacks, culminating in the burning of the national capital in August 1814. General Andrew Jackson's overwhelming victory in New Orleans the following January, however, generated an outpouring of patriotic fervor.[67] That moment of victory on the battlefield coincided with the unrelated Treaty of Ghent, which formally ended the war.

Unlike so many future American presidents, Madison would not lead a unified party into war. The war was especially unpopular in New England, divisive within the Democratic-Republican Party, and universally opposed by Federalists, as reflected in the congressional vote in June 1812 to declare war.[68] Detailing American grievances against the British on June 1, 1812, Madison did not explicitly ask for a declaration of war in his written message. The president was careful to show due deference to congressional powers in this arena.[69] On top of the numerous Democratic-Republican groups Madison faced at the time of his election, he also found himself pressured by the War Hawk faction, particularly in the House. Younger and predominantly from the South and the West, War Hawks confidently called for military solutions to American grievances with the British.[70] Their leaders included Calhoun and Speaker Clay, who was consolidating power in the House. Meanwhile, Democratic-Republican opposition came from the Clintonian faction and the weakening Quid faction.[71] Senate Invisibles preferred a more limited war, but voted for the final resolution calling for unlimited war.[72]

Democratic-Republican orthodoxy frowned upon a professionalized and permanent army as dangerous to liberty and state sovereignty; state militias were to be preferred. Democratic-Republicans worried that the army was a stronghold of Federalist political influence. Even Jefferson appreciated the value of a standing army to national security, and was not convinced that the state militias were an effective alternative. Brushing aside the concerns of some in his party, Jefferson chose not to wholly dismantle the army built by the Adams Administration. Instead, he gradually facilitated the appointment of a Democratic-Republican officer corps while easing Federalists out of the military hierarchy.[73] Early in his presidency, Madison followed the same course, but as the nation moved toward a war footing, he began appointing Federalists to officer commissions. This caused grumbling from other Democratic-Republicans, but by offering commissions to Federalists, Madison used the patronage process (however ineffectively) to build bipartisan support for the war.[74]

Renewed emphasis upon military preparedness revealed Madison's corrective policy stance concerning his regime's traditional approaches to national defense. Postwar demobilization included a downsized but still credible military. Haphazard planning and ill-conceived cutbacks leading up to the War of 1812 required Madison to give due attention to the imperatives of professionalization and the continuity of a robust peacetime military. Tensions with Britain, Spain, and the Barbary States had hardly subsided. The president encouraged Congress to consider additional military schools, investment in the navy, and reforms to the militia system.[75] In April 1816, Madison signed off on legislation to preserve a robust standing military that could protect American points of vulnerability.[76] While the officer corps was shrunk dramatically from wartime levels, the active duty army still consisted of over 10,000 men in 1816 and over 8,400 men in 1817. These troop numbers far surpassed the decade of prewar troop levels.[77] Funds were also appropriated to build up the navy and construct new ships (not all of which were built).[78]

### *The Election of 1812: The Federalist Bear Market Rally*

In spite of a still immature American political party system, and in spite of their own disdain for grassroots party building, Federalists capitalized upon the policy problems and intraparty difficulties of Madison and the Democratic-Republicans. After a decade of steady (and sometimes precipitous) decline, Federalists reasserted themselves as a credible opposition party in Northeastern states. Federalist Party strength in both chambers of Congress steadily declined throughout the Jefferson Administration. Federalists held 35.8% of House seats in 1801, and only 18.3% of seats in 1807. In the Senate, Federalists held 44.1% of seats in 1801, and only 17.6% of seats in 1807. Federalists held seven state governorships in 1801 and only two by 1808.[79]

The pattern of an opposition party resurgence under an heir apparent president is evident under Madison's tenure. Signs of a Federalist resurgence can be traced back to Madison's election in 1808, as noted above, but signs of opposition momentum also manifested during the war. After again losing seats in the 1810 congressional elections, Federalists posted modest gains in both chambers in 1812. In 1814, Federalists had mixed results: small losses in the House (four seats) and moderate gains in the Senate (four seats).[80] Federalist state governorships momentarily surged to five in 1809, slipped back to two in 1810, but grew to seven in 1814 and 1815.[81]

Unfortunately for Federalists, their comeback was temporary and regionally limited to the Northeast, particularly New England. A party seeking to revitalize itself after years in the wilderness requires some degree of renewed national appeal and reaching out to new political constituencies. Federalists instead merely rallied their old New England stronghold and met with only limited success elsewhere. Democratic-Republican hegemony in the South and the West proceeded though the Madison years, though with concomitant intraparty squabbling in some states. After belatedly adopting more sophisticated grassroots organizing tactics, Federalists improved their national standing to a small degree.[82] During the Madison presidency, Federalists still remained well entrenched in the minority within Congress, never achieving more than 37.4% of membership in either chamber.[83]

Vulnerabilities were everywhere for the incumbent president. There had never been an American presidential election in wartime, much less during a controversial war. Democratic-Republican divisions that had opened up during the Jefferson presidency continued to sharpen and mutate, with the political stakes and tensions intensifying due to the war. In their efforts to exploit intraparty Democratic-Republican feuding, Federalists teamed up with the Clintonian faction to oppose Madison's reelection in 1812. A fusion ticket of Federalists and New York–based anti-Madison Democratic-Republicans nominated New York Lieutenant Governor DeWitt Clinton for president. For his own part, the president was renominated unanimously in his own party's congressional nominating caucus. Attendance at the caucus included about two-thirds of Democratic-Republicans in Congress. As anti-Madison members failed to coalesce around an alternative, they boycotted the caucus.[84]

Clinton was a war opponent, but his campaign clumsily appealed to supporters and opponents. The Democratic-Republican campaign resorted to a common tactic for the incumbent party in wartime: patriotic appeals and insinuations that the opposition was unpatriotic and not a reliable alternative to protect national security.[85] The outcome revealed a genuinely competitive race, as Madison won only 128 electoral votes to Clinton's 89. Clinton won all of New England, save for Vermont, and won the old Federalist stronghold of Delaware. Clinton delivered his home state of New York, New Jersey, and nearly half of Maryland's electoral votes. Madison swept the South and the West, as well as Pennsylvania. In the states that permitted popular selection of electors, Madison electors won 53% of the vote, a large drop from 1808.[86]

The Federalist comeback can best be described as what Wall Street calls a "bear market rally": a modest and temporary rally amid a long-term period of decline.[87] In a case of bad timing and poor public relations, Federalists were embarrassed when news of their Hartford Convention became public. This meeting of New England Federalists in December 1814 and January 1815 produced a variety of constitutional reform proposals. Secession from the union was also allegedly discussed. Madison saw to it that the convention's report was well known to the public.[88] Coinciding with the Ghent peace treaty and Jackson's victory at New Orleans, the Hartford Convention stalled the Federalist Party's resurgence. Federalist disintegration resumed: their losses in Congress escalated, Monroe was elected president in 1816 with no credible Federalist opposition, and he was reelected with no opposition at all in 1820. The party diminished into irrelevancy in the 1820s. Subsequent opposition parties who faced an heir apparent president would perform far better at building a broader national base for the future.

## HEIR APPARENT TO AN IMPERFECT JEFFERSONIANISM

The record of Madison's presidency revealed that he never completely repudiated Federalist policies. He pragmatically embraced enhanced federal responsibilities in the arenas of national banking, internal improvements, and protective tariffs. After learning some hard lessons on the battlefield, this president also embraced greater military professionalization and preparedness. Madison continued the process of gradual abdication of purist Jeffersonian commitments that was already well underway during Jefferson's second term. Sometimes Madison acted irregularly on his principles, as revealed by the Bonus Bill veto. Sometimes he acted with notable political clumsiness and refused to concede mistakes, as revealed by the fiascos over the Non-Intercourse Act and the Macon law. At the same time, this president could lay claim to acting in concert with his predecessor's policy trajectory, even if Madison actually departed from the most doctrinaire interpretations of the Jeffersonian creed.

Parties provide an organizational base for opposition interests to organize and advance agendas, a political fact of life that was still in its developing stages during Madison's tenure. An opposition party also forces the governing party to adhere to a core set of principles and commitments, but Democratic-Republicans did not embrace the virtues of two-party competition. Rather, they sought to conquer and absorb their Federalist adversaries, sometimes by way of refining and moderating Hamiltonian policies. As a consequence, the governing party looked increasingly unwieldy and incoherent. Federalists were also too tardy and reluctant in their attempts to build a popularly based political party at a national level. Hence, Madison had far more vexing difficulties with his own governing party. Dissident Democratic-Republicans spoke through their leaders in Congress, state governments, and the newspapers they controlled. They often succeeded at modifying, delaying, and defeating Madison's initiatives, but they also squabbled among themselves and failed to coalesce behind common leaders and a common critique of their president.

Amid a still fluid and unsophisticated political party system, Madison could take advantage of the limited clout of his intraparty and opposition party critics. In his capacity as Jefferson's heir apparent, Madison used all three of the approaches explicated in the previous chapter: protecting continuity, expanding the commitments of his governing regime, and repairing flaws in his predecessor's policies. Madison did not always accomplish these tasks with the greatest of success. Sometimes the administration only succeeded in worsening existing policy problems and sharpening existing political tensions. In spite of some bad and unpopular choices, Madison could forge ahead, refining the Jeffersonian republic through his own uniquely Madisonian approach to the Jeffersonian model.

# 4

# MARTIN VAN BUREN:
# THE UNFORTUNATE MOP-UP MAN

## THE JACKSONIAN DEMOCRACY VAN BUREN INHERITED

Frequently referred to as "The Democracy," the Democratic Party was born out of the remains of the bloated Democratic-Republican Party. In the mid-1820s, the old Jeffersonian party was a collection of different camps, each defined by a separate cast of leaders, signature issues, and regional bases of strength. Supporters of Andrew Jackson defined themselves as the "democratic" wing of the old Jeffersonian party. Similar to the Jeffersonians of a generation before, they viewed themselves as being in opposition to an elitist cadre of mercantilists, financiers, and entrenched bureaucrats taking advantage of government privileges at the expense of the common people. Using different tactics of political organization, Jacksonian Democrats aspired to return the nation to the purest manifestations of Jeffersonian values.

To a sharper degree than the Jeffersonians, Jacksonian Democrats promoted populist democracy through vehicles such as slogans, mass rallies, parades, grassroots organizing, and speeches by political candidates (though rarely presidential candidates). Partisan newspapers, which were part of the previous party system, continued to proliferate. Property qualifications were lifted for adult white males in state after state, thereby expanding the electorate to include many more economically downscale voters—the political base for Jacksonian Democrats. Jacksonians unabashedly promoted political parties as the natural extension of the popular will, to the point of even welcoming an organized opposition party. Jacksonians believed that political parties should be hierarchical and meritocratic organizations that democratically represented their constituencies. Conventions would make procedures more transparent, diffuse power away from Washington, DC, toward the states, and prevent a small elite from controlling party affairs. Patronage would reward party loyalists with jobs and other favors while preventing the federal government from falling under the permanent control of unaccountable and entrenched bureaucrats.

Westward expansion would maintain the agrarian character of the nation envisioned by early Jeffersonians, while making land ownership available to most Americans. Jacksonians honored states' rights, just as their Jeffersonian predecessors did, for state governments were closer and more accountable to the people. At the same time, Jacksonian Democrats stoutly opposed states' rights extremists who spoke of nullification or secession. Similarly, antislavery abolitionists were treated as misguided agitators who would tear the nation apart. Jacksonian Democrats held that slavery was a constitutional right of property ownership. Otherwise, the most democratic way to handle the slavery issue was to allow the states to establish their own policies in concert with their own values. The federal government would respect whatever choice each state made, while vigorously enforcing fugitive slave laws. Small government was deemed the natural complement of personal freedom, while debt would make government beholden to powerful creditors. They feared that wealthy and politically well-connected people and institutions would take advantage of an overly large and powerful federal government. Somewhat ironically, Jackson acted as if the best way to protect ordinary citizens, defend limited government, and promote democratization was through stronger presidential powers.[1]

Jackson was both a democratic revolutionary and a bulwark against Whig reformers. Democrats championed reforms to make politics and government the business of common citizens, and resisted Henry Clay's American System of internal improvements, a

National Bank, and protective tariffs. Jacksonian democracy also held no place for African Americans (free or slave), while regarding Native Americans as troublesome impediments to territorial growth and national harmony. These issues brought about polarizing policy debates through the medium of a more democratized party system. Jackson was a towering political figure, but these controversies and a fully mobilized Whig opposition revealed real vulnerabilities in the Jacksonian Democratic regime by the time Van Buren assumed the presidency.

Jackson's second term was consumed by his successful efforts to put the National Bank out of business. In July 1832, the president vetoed a bill to recharter the Bank for another 20 years. Reelected to another term that fall, Jackson was not content to let the Bank's existing charter simply expire after four years. Jackson engaged in a grueling fight to remove the federal government's deposits from the Bank. Funds were moved to state-chartered banks, which were usually controlled by Jacksonian Democrats. A censure enacted by the Senate in March 1834 did not faze the president. Meanwhile, financial markets trembled, investors lost confidence, and bankers called in loans.[2]

In spite of the Bank War, the economy was experiencing a speculative boom in the mid-1830s. As cotton prices spiked and the money supply expanded significantly, government land sales surged. So much revenue was pouring into the federal treasury that Jacksonian Democrats briefly achieved their dream of paying off the national debt. The Bank War may have killed off the Jacksonians' biggest public enemy, but it failed to stop rampant speculative behavior and the proliferation of paper money at the state level.[3] To slow down the speculative frenzy over government-owned lands, Jackson issued a Specie Circular order on July 11, 1836. The new policy required payment of only gold or silver for government-owned lands.[4] Previously that year, Jackson reluctantly signed another law disbursing surplus revenues to the states, although this seemed to only fuel more speculation.[5]

Economic modernization will always challenge any governing regime in unanticipated ways. As modes of production, distribution, and consumption shift, changes emerge in old ways of life and cultural norms. Populations move, new political constituencies surface, and demographics change. The Jacksonian Democratic regime was no different. As land-hungry settlers fueled a speculative bubble, Jacksonians turned more of their attention to Native Americans, in search of a "humane" way to remove them to the West. Mechanization, industrialization, and the growth of corporations brought about a "market revolution" in the economy and significant cultural anxiety.[6] All sectors of the national economy became increasingly linked. Demand for federal support of internal improvements increased accordingly, as farmers and industrialists required quality infrastructure to move their goods to market. Demand for protective tariffs of new American industries also challenged national Jacksonian leaders, who worried that such policies put the government in the business of playing economic favorites. The Second Bank of the United States was now a well-entrenched institution with a close linkage to corporations, financiers, and powerful politicians. Just like their Jeffersonian predecessors, Jacksonian Democrats were ambivalent at best, if not outright opposed to federal involvement in these policies. However, economic changes moved in different directions and at different paces in the various states. As dictated by their state and local interests, elements of the national Jacksonian Democratic coalition were far from unified on each of these policies.

At the nucleus of many major policy debates was the North-South sectional rivalry, which was really a proxy fight over the issue of slavery. Few mainstream politicians desired a substantive and direct debate over the status of slavery, given the ability of that issue to tear both political parties apart from within. The House actually enacted a "gag rule" in 1836 to stifle any debate that would consider slavery's restriction.[7] In addition, as antislavery literature was beginning to circulate in the South during Jackson's second term, Vice President Van Buren also supported the administration's policy of confiscating such material from the mails.[8] Other issues, including territorial expansion, tariffs, and even internal improvements, all raised questions about the sectional balance of power, and slavery by extension. Democratic and Whig politicians could endeavor to craft national policies to maintain the North-South equilibrium, as well as the fragile national coalition of each party.

## THE "LITTLE MAGICIAN" ASCENDS

Similar to Madison, Van Buren was a leading builder of his party, both within his own state and at a national level. In this role, Van Buren built an alliance with his presidential predecessor, ultimately creating the Democratic Party around the popular Jackson. Van Buren joined the Jackson Administration following a long political career in New York. In his state, Van Buren became known as the "Little Magician" for his impressive political skills within the Democratic-Republican Party. As a young politician, he was part of DeWitt Clinton's faction; however, Van Buren split with the Clintonians in 1813. Van Buren's "Bucktail" faction purported to represent purist Jeffersonian values and sought to moderate the more commercial-minded Clintonian faction. In the legislature, Bucktails valued party discipline and professionalized techniques of party organization. Bucktails formed the Albany Regency, an early version of a political machine, upon which Van Buren shaped his state's party and his own political career.[9] As a United States senator, Van Buren supported Treasury Secretary William Crawford in the disputed presidential election of 1824, but then worked to build a unified coalition around Jackson for the 1828 election.[10]

Working his own way up the New York political ladder, Van Buren's Albany Regency machine helped deliver him the gubernatorial election of 1828. He did not stay long, however, as he soon returned to Washington, DC, as secretary of state in the Jackson Administration. Jackson then planned to send Van Buren to Great Britain to serve as the American ambassador. Instead, Van Buren got caught up in a ferocious feud between Jackson and Vice President John C. Calhoun. The vice president struck against Jackson, his new adversary, by casting the tie-breaking vote in the Senate to defeat Van Buren's ambassadorial appointment.[11] Van Buren would become a ripe target for Jackson's enemies, for the two men established a close personal and political relationship with each other. When some of Jackson's ostensible allies deserted him under challenging political circumstances, Van Buren stood by the president's side. There were risks in casting his lot with the embattled Jackson, but also great prospects for the advancement of his own political career.

Jackson's first term was mired in an inane controversy over the social status of Margaret "Peggy" O'Neill Eaton, wife of Secretary of War John Eaton. Critics suggested the Eatons' marriage lacked integrity due to past allegations of Mrs. Eaton's adultery and accusations that she failed to sufficiently mourn her late ex-husband before marrying Mr. Eaton. Reflecting the dislike of the couple in Washington, DC, Calhoun's wife Floride and all other cabinet wives refused to socialize with the Eatons. The whole controversy was political fodder for Jackson's opponents to charge that the new president was bringing dishonorable people into government. Jackson and Van Buren sided with the Eatons, but the controversy was so damaging that all cabinet officers, save for Postmaster General William Barry, resigned.[12]

The hullabaloo over the Eatons was only part of a larger process that made Van Buren Jackson's heir apparent while diminishing Calhoun's national influence. The South Carolina tariff nullification crisis, which almost resulted in armed conflict, ended Calhoun's ascendancy within the Jacksonian Democratic regime. Jackson generally favored low tariffs, and he was an advocate for states' rights. He drew the line, however, at Calhoun's theory of nullification: the notion that a state could forcibly resist or refuse to abide by laws it deemed unconstitutional. A standoff ensued, resulting in a significant amount of chest-thumping and Calhoun's resignation as vice president, followed by a quiet compromise to lower the tariff and South Carolina's agreement to abide by the law.

The political consequences were very significant. Jackson, who always placed a high premium on loyalty from his subordinates, was drawn closer to Van Buren on political and personal levels. Calhoun remained an important figure in Southern politics, but nationally his political clout was weakened by his conflict with the Jackson Administration. Van Buren became a top Jackson advisor, particularly on internal-improvement policies. While the two men did not always agree on political strategies and tactics, they shared similar overarching goals.[13] For his own national aspirations, Van Buren would have to overcome Southern apprehensions about his candidacy. Some Southern Democrats were unnerved by Van Buren's inconsistent record on the tariff issue, and they did not fully trust his commitment to federal support for the noninterference of slavery.[14] In search of a new vice presidential nominee to replace Calhoun, the 1832 Democratic National Convention nominated Van Buren as Jackson's running mate on the first ballot. Van Buren captured the nomination with the requisite two-thirds vote from the delegates, but there were some Southern defections in favor of two other candidates. Democrats in five Southern states then proceeded to rally around Virginia federal judge Philip Barbour as the vice presidential nominee instead of Van Buren. Barbour ultimately endorsed the regular Democratic ticket, but the Southern concerns about Van Buren were apparent.[15]

In Jackson's second term, Van Buren remained close to the president, as he fulfilled a role that was unusual for the nineteenth-century vice president. Ever since Jefferson's service under John Adams, many early vice presidents maintained distant or hostile relationships with their presidents. Calhoun and Aaron Burr politically imploded in office. Two vice presidents had already died in office by the time Van Buren assumed the position. The Little Magician used the position to act as a presidential confidant, policy advisor, and political strategist.[16] His place in the administration resembled the vice presidential role that would become common more than a century later. Meanwhile, the New Yorker jockeyed for position in preparation for the 1836 presidential election.

### *The Election of 1836: Reassembling the (Reduced) Jacksonian Coalition*

While Van Buren's path to the presidential nomination was scarcely in doubt, there were challenges along the way. Some elements of Jackson's coalition were restive or hostile, and the 1836 election afforded opportunities for intraparty tensions to worsen. Popular sentiment in Jackson's own Tennessee, where some Jackson men had split with the administration, was ambivalent at best about Van Buren.[17] The nullifiers remained angry, and the Bank War unnerved some Democrats.[18] For his own part, Jackson gave full support to his lieutenant for the nomination and the election, but only within the limits of nineteenth-century presidential practices. For a president of this era to be visibly involved in the campaign of his designated successor was deemed outside of the statesmanlike boundaries of the office. A top member of Jackson's inner circle, Francis Preston Blair, successfully lobbied Democratic National Convention delegates for Van Buren's nomination.[19]

The vice presidential nomination proved to be a little more of a headache. Van Buren understood that a strong Virginia–New York alliance was as important to the Democrats as it had been to the Democratic-Republicans of the previous generation. His first choice for the vice presidency would have been William Cabell Rives of Virginia. Instead, the controversial Colonel Richard Johnson of Kentucky was awarded the nomination. Johnson, who partook in a relationship with a biracial woman, was disliked by Southern Democrats. The nomination provoked a convention walkout by the Virginia delegation.[20] On the other hand, Johnson commanded considerable grassroots support elsewhere in the country as an advocate for the common man.[21]

To a greater degree than Madison in 1808, Van Buren was about to face off with a much better-organized Whig Party opposition. Whigs organized their party around opposition to Jackson during his second term. They denounced Jackson's expansive and populist use of the presidency as dangerous and autocratic, asserting that congressional authority was more democratic and less prone to abuse. Most Whigs favored an active role for the federal government as an agent of economic modernization, including federal support for roads, bridges, and canals. They promoted protective tariffs and sought to return to the Hamiltonian national banking system. Their party included a hodgepodge of mercantilists, slavery opponents, Southern planters, manufacturers, anti-Masons, temperance advocates, Protestant evangelicals, and an assortment of Jackson and Van Buren enemies. Whigs of the mid-1830s lacked the discipline and sophisticated party machinery of the Democrats, and they had trouble coalescing around national leaders. Now the party had the opportunity to capitalize on the vulnerabilities of the Jackson Administration.[22]

The Whig Party, however, was still planting its feet into this new Jacksonian world of political parties based on mass participation. No national party convention was held. The party was respectful of its regional divisions and embraced a strategy of nominating multiple candidates. Each candidate would appeal to the parts of the country where he could be the most viable alternative to the Democrats. Senator Daniel Webster of Massachusetts would deliver his home state. General William Henry Harrison, hero of the Battle of Tippecanoe, would appeal to the North and the Border states. Hugh White, an ex-Jacksonian Democrat from Tennessee, would be the main Southern candidate.[23] Whigs would have a national strategy of mixed messages and multiple messengers. At its best, this approach could have deadlocked the Electoral College and thrown the election to the House.

The Whig strategy revealed weak links in the Jacksonian coalition, but could not overcome the Democrats' superior organizational advantages. Harrison and White were competitive in their respective regions, but Van Buren held the edge. Winning 170 electoral votes, Van Buren showed strength in every part of the country. Whig candidates won 124 electoral votes. In the popular vote, Van Buren won 50.8%, while Whig candidates combined to win just over 49%. The Van Buren victory was decisive, but below the landslide proportions of his predecessor. In the House elections of 1836, Democratic majorities were reduced by 15 seats. In the Senate, however, Democrats gained nine seats.

JACKSON'S THIRD TERM: THE OLD HICKORY ERODES

In his inaugural address, the new president was cognizant of the shadow that loomed over him:

In receiving from the people the sacred trust twice confided to my illustrious predecessor, and which he has discharged so faithfully and so well, I know that I can not expect to perform the arduous task with equal ability and success. But united as I have been in his counsels, a daily witness of his exclusive and unsurpassed devotion to his country's welfare, agreeing with him in sentiments which his countrymen have warmly supported, and permitted to partake largely of his confidence, I may hope that somewhat of the same cheering approbation will be found to attend upon my path.[24]

The administration would be plagued by the worst economic crisis in a generation, a controversial Native American policy, worsening sectional tensions, and disagreements with Mexico. As he had pledged in the campaign, Van Buren followed a mostly Jacksonian track. His stance as Jackson's heir apparent stressed continuity and finishing the unfinished tasks of his predecessor's revolutionary presidency. As the consequences of Jackson's policies mounted, particularly in the economic sphere, Van Buren embraced his role as a custodian of policies that now came under attack from all fronts. He left himself with little room to maneuver, which was made even more problematic by the fact that he lacked his predecessor's heroic reputation and personal popularity. The "cheering approbation" Van Buren hoped for failed to materialize.

### A Panicking Jacksonian America

Only two months after Van Buren's inauguration, he found himself engulfed by a crisis that would consume his presidency. Overwhelmed banks in New York ceased specie payments in May 1837, unleashing a cascade of economic disaster. Banks in other cities either failed or no longer issued specie payments, credit tightened, foreign investment plummeted, internal improvement projects were abandoned, industrial production slowed, and farm prices declined. Unemployment became widespread and Van Buren had on his hands the worst economic depression in American history up to that point.

Fairly or not, Jacksonian policies came under attack. Van Buren listened to the critics and weighed their arguments, but ultimately steered a Jacksonian course, even when addressing the policy errors of his predecessor. The financial community assigned great blame to the Specie Circular order as a cause of the depression. Van Buren considered revising or rescinding the directive. However, after consultation with merchants, his cabinet, other Democrats, and even former President Jackson, Van Buren opted to retain the policy for the time being.[25] A new National Bank of the United States was not even on the table for consideration. Jackson's placement of federal funds into state-chartered banks, however, was a temporary and disruptive measure in search of a more permanent solution.

The new president's first major move was to call a special session of Congress in September. Short-term measures could be taken to address the consequences of some of Jackson's policy excesses, even if only to a limited degree. A written message to Congress detailed Van Buren's proposals, as well as an indictment of the usual Jacksonian enemies (bankers and speculators) for causing the panic.[26] With the surplus revenue long gone, payments to the states were suspended. To loosen the money supply, treasury notes totaling $10 million were released. Hard-pressed mercantilists were also given a reprieve on customs bonds that were due.[27] A Van Buren proposal to create a bankruptcy law aimed at banks and corporations was not adopted by Congress.[28]

The signature Van Buren initiative was the independent Treasury bill, often referred to as the divorce bill. This measure called for moving federal deposits out of the state banks and into a federally run and noncommercial treasury system. While an independent Treasury would achieve the Jacksonian dream of divorcing government from commercial banking, it also arguably strengthened the federal government by centralizing the Treasury under the direct authority of the executive branch. The proposal, which Jackson favored,[29] set off a grueling congressional debate that would persist for nearly three years. Democrats controlled Congress, but lined up into separate factions in either full support, qualified support, or opposition to the measure. Democratic opponents sometimes built an alliance with the opposition party, although Whigs favored a new national bank. Surprising support for the Van Buren policy came from Calhoun, the avowed enemy of Jackson and the current president. Meanwhile, Van Buren's close ally, Senator William Rives of Virginia, led the opposition. Rives argued for refining and improving the existing system of using state banks for federal deposits. This, he argued, would benefit the national economy by financially tying the states to the federal government. Other Democratic opponents feared that the consolidation of federal deposits would only enlarge the federal government and presidential powers at the expense of the states. The Senate passed the independent Treasury bill, but it died in the House, and the special session was soon adjourned.[30] Rejection of Van Buren's leading initiative overshadowed the modest measures approved in the special session.

And prosperity did not return. Modest signs of recovery and easier credit emerged in 1838, and Van Buren and most Democrats did not object when Congress repealed the Specie Circular order that May. The economy double-dipped, however, in the autumn of 1839. Tighter credit, due to developments in Great Britain, set off a chain reaction of plummeting agricultural prices, more bank failures, and widespread economic hardship. Van Buren continued working for the passage of an independent Treasury bill, and the congressional debate was no less difficult and time-consuming. This time, however, Democratic opponents were in a weaker position in Congress, lacking organization and leadership. The measure was enacted in July 1840, but the political and economic damage was done.[31]

Debate continues as to the specific causes of the Panic of 1837 and to what degree government policies were culpable. Future financial crises could be characterized the same way, as the economic impact of actors outside of governmental control should not be underestimated. Long before robust governmental activism in the economy, presidents were held accountable for poor economic performance. Unfortunately for some presidents, economic policies can take far longer than a four-year term to fully reveal their real and perceived consequences. Similar to George Bush and Herbert Hoover in the twentieth century, Van Buren bore the blame for economic problems that had built up during the tenure of his ideological predecessor.

Presidents of the nineteenth century were not constitutionally or politically well equipped to promptly respond to major economic shocks, even if they had the will to do so.

Van Buren employed mixed approaches in his handling of the depression. His continued resistance to a new national bank was a clear example of Jacksonian continuity. Retention of the Specie Circular order was also an exercise in continuity, but Van Buren adopted a corrective approach when he allowed this temporary policy to be repealed. The expansion approach was utilized when Van Buren worked to establish a permanent separation of the federal government from the enterprise of banking, since this was an unfulfilled ideological commitment of the Jacksonian regime. As a practical matter, he was also correcting one of Jackson's foolish policies. As the mop-up man cleaning up after the consequences of Jackson's Bank War, Van Buren was forced into mixed policy formulas that yielded him little political credit. Jackson's course of action on banking issues was driven by ideology and vengeance, with little concern for long-term solutions and consequences. Van Buren's remedies sought to move past Jackson's hasty and temporary banking policies with permanent solutions that would restore investors' confidence in the American economy. Overwhelmed by the depression and political opponents, Van Buren's innovations only further exposed Democratic divisions and revealed the broken Jacksonian economic model. There was now a real policy record of failure and underachievement upon which the Jacksonian Democratic Party could be challenged.

## More Tears: Native American Removal

Similar to their Jeffersonian predecessors, Jacksonian Democrats celebrated the American proliferation of agriculture controlled by whites. Jacksonian Democrats maintained a greater tolerance for urbanization than Jeffersonians, but their common creed stressed the importance of available land and entrepreneurial agriculture as essential for the health of democracy. Native American removal was deemed a key component of this vision because Jacksonian democracy did not hold an equal place for nonwhites. The Van Buren approach to Native Americans followed Jackson's policy trajectory, but not without violent and tragic consequences.

The Indian Removal Act of 1830 was the basis for a series of forced expulsions of Native American peoples during Jackson's tenure. The law called for negotiation of treaties with tribal leaders to facilitate the removal of Native peoples to the West. Congressional debate was fierce.[32] The policy was blasted by Christian missionaries, humanitarian advocates, and Whigs. Jacksonian Democrats argued that the policy would open up lands for white settlers and actually benefit Native Americans by extricating them from potentially violent conflicts with whites. Relocation would be a deadly policy in a nation where travel could still be very dangerous, especially for the elderly, the sick, and children. And the government would not take significant measures to make the relocation process any less hazardous. Native tribes that resisted opened themselves up to forced removals by the government and land thefts by squatters. On Jackson's watch, treaties were signed and removals commenced, beginning with the Choctaw. By Van Buren's inauguration, removal of Chickasaws had taken place, and removal of the Creeks was well underway.[33]

Many Florida Seminoles would not acquiesce to forced removal. Believing that their people had been hoodwinked into a relocation treaty by the Jackson Administration, many Seminole chiefs withdrew their support. Other chiefs refused to sign. Hostilities broke out in late 1835, resulting in a nettlesome seven-year war that would preoccupy Jackson and his successors.[34] Alongside a failing economy, the flagging campaign against the Florida Seminoles only contributed to the image Van Buren was earning for himself as an incompetent manager and a bumbling custodian of Jackson's policies.

Meanwhile, the Van Buren Administration had to complete the removal of the Cherokee people, since they had resisted removal for years, including through the courts. The Treaty of New Echota, ratified late in the Jackson Administration, called upon the Cherokee to move west by May 1838. However, Cherokees were divided among themselves over the treaty, because many did not take part in the

negotiation process. The treaty was deemed illegitimate by Cherokee opponents, who refused to move. Van Buren did not hesitate to
initiate the removal process as the deadline neared. He shared his
predecessor's views concerning Native American civilization and
the need for separation from white society. In April 1838, the army
began assembling the Cherokee for a forced removal to the West.
Approximately 4,000 Cherokee perished on the infamous Trail of
Tears.[35] Following the removal, Van Buren's annual message to Congress brushed aside the loss of life and defended the policy's long-
term capacity for peace and the Westernization of Native peoples.[36]

In this policy arena, Van Buren's approach can be described as
maintaining the Jacksonian trajectory, since there was much unfinished work to be done. The expansion approach was utilized
to complete the long-term objectives of Jackson's Indian removal
policy. When Van Buren's actions met resistance, he employed the
full power of the federal government in an effort to bring the Seminoles and other Native peoples into compliance. Executing a policy
formula that was fraught with conflict and loss of life, Van Buren
received little political credit for his actions.

## Deference to the South

Jackson was able to marginalize the South Carolina nullifiers during his presidency while maintaining mainstream Southern support
for his party. His background as a Tennessean, a slaveholder, and a
states' rights advocate surely helped to preserve his credibility with
other Southern Democrats who were not ready to embrace nullification. As white Southern anxieties over the political and economic
clout of the North grew, a president with Van Buren's New York
background would not command the same level of Southern respect. New York was the center of commerce, industrialization, and
growing antislavery agitation. Southern Democrats continued to be
distrustful of their Northern president, suspecting that he valued
party unity over Southern principles. In spite of his close personal
and political kinship with Jackson, Van Buren would have to constantly prove his commitment to respecting Southern culture and
state sovereignty.

Maintaining the continuity of Jackson's approach, Van Buren usually deferred to the mainstream Southern Democratic preferences of his era. Native American removal was strongly supported in the South, for it freed up lands for white settlement. The administration defended international slave trading in the case of *La Amistad*, a Spanish slave ship. *La Amistad* departed from Cuba and unexpectedly arrived on the American East Coast in August 1839 after a mutiny. The Van Buren Administration argued that the United States was bound by a treaty to return the ship and the slaves to Spain.[37] Southern Democrats applauded. Van Buren also successfully brokered a compensation deal with the British to settle claims over slaves freed in the West Indies. On three separate occasions during the Jackson Administration, American ships carrying slaves were forced to stop in the British-controlled West Indies due to bad weather. Each time the British freed the slaves. After years of negotiating through two administrations, compensation was awarded for freed slaves on two of the ships.[38] A promise was made to protect slavery in the District of Columbia: only with the consent of Southern states would Van Buren sign a bill ending slavery in the nation's capital. An additional promise was made to veto any bill interfering with slavery in Florida, should it someday become a state.[39]

But try as he might, placating all Southern Democrats all the time was not a task that could be easily accomplished. Even Calhoun's reconciliation with Van Buren was of little benefit, as he was a polarizing figure. Nor did all Southern Democrats agree on the independent Treasury, the defining legislative issue of Van Buren's presidency. The depressed economy cast a pall even over debates relating to slavery. The Southern economy was badly damaged by the collapse in cotton prices. On the matter of Texas, Van Buren found that preserving domestic political stability and peace with Mexico was preferable to satisfying Southern Democrats' territorial appetites.

### Not Ready to Mess with Texas and Mexico

Removal of Native Americans and territorial acquisition all came back to a common denominator of expansionism. While sympathetic to this overarching objective, Van Buren was especially sensitive to the implications of hasty territorial growth upon the Jacksonian Democratic coalition. Given his experience as a party leader and builder, Van Buren was keen to the equilibrium-disrupting potential of adding new states and reaggravating sectional anxieties (often concerning slavery). The status of the Republic of Texas presented Van Buren with these concerns, as well as the potential to reaggravate tensions with Mexico.

As vice president, Van Buren urged caution upon Jackson when confronted with the question of recognizing the newly independent republic. As expected, Southern Democrats favored recognizing and eventually annexing Texas, while Northerners worried about the consequences of enlarging the South's national influence. Waiting until after Van Buren's election and with only days left in his own term, Jackson recognized Texas in early March 1837.[40] Accordingly, demands increased upon the new president to start the annexation process, given Texas's strong demographic and cultural connections to the South. In his retirement, Jackson was an annexation supporter.[41] As president in his own right, Van Buren had to assume responsibility over a restive party coalition rife with sectional divisions. Rather than carry forward the Jacksonian commitment to expansion, Van Buren rejected the acquisition of Texas. The administration contended that annexation could be constitutionally problematic, given Texas's status as an independent republic. In addition, argued Secretary of State John Forsyth, there were existing treaties with Mexico that precluded such an option and could provoke war if broken.[42]

Given the demands of the financial crisis, Van Buren was able to minimize the issue for the remainder of his presidency. Democratic momentum for annexation was slowed, but not halted. In his retreat on the Texas matter, Van Buren was also able to achieve a diplomatic resolution to lingering grievances with Mexico. After considerable delay, an international commission was established to resolve outstanding American financial claims upon Mexico. In the process of reaching a settlement, Van Buren walked back some of Jackson's bellicose statements on the matter.[43] By prioritizing a peaceful solution, Van Buren steered a course correction away from a Jacksonian policy that might have led to war.

Native American removal and the independent Treasury matter were both components of more comprehensive and long-term policy visions. At a considerable political cost, Jacksonian policy commitments had already been made by the time Van Buren assumed office. Elected upon a promise to continue these policies, the heir apparent felt significant pressure to act along his predecessor's trajectory. The Texas issue, however, was a relatively newer controversy for the United States. Although Van Buren steered his government away from the position of his predecessor, the Jacksonian Democratic regime did not yet have a deep policy investment in the Texas matter. Nor would an enthusiastic rush into war with Mexico protect any particular Jacksonian policy achievement. As Madison learned with the War of 1812, wars can introduce unpredictable disruptions into the governing party's coalition. Van Buren's moves on Texas and Mexico annoyed some Southern Democrats, but sectional harmony within his party coalition would be preserved.

### The Election of 1840: Whig Populism and Van Buren's Defeat

Whigs celebrated their identity as an upper-crust, business-oriented party. Frowning upon Jacksonian populism as little more than devious demagoguery, Whigs now capitalized on Van Buren's vulnerabilities to mature into a grassroots alternative to the Democratic Party. Whigs in 1836 were hampered by organizational shortcomings and a divided candidate slate. Whigs in 1840, however, tapped into populist frustration with the results of Democratic policies. The opposition party downplayed a substantive ideological critique of the governing party, in favor of a campaign based upon showmanship, spectacle, and gimmickry.

The opposition party bypassed the divisive figure of Henry Clay for its presidential nomination, instead choosing General Harrison for a rematch with Van Buren. This time, Harrison would be the singular nominee of a party unified around its opposition to the administration, even as Whigs remained rather divided on many key issues. John Tyler, a Virginia ex-Democrat who did not share many Whig policy positions, was nominated for vice president.

Unlike the Democrats, Whigs did not produce a party platform in 1840, thereby minimizing internal party divisions and avoiding a substantive issue contrast with their opponents.[44] Pursuant to the Whigs' incoherency, the party chose in Harrison a candidate who held vague and unknown positions on substantive policy issues. While Harrison departed from this era's presidential protocol by giving campaign speeches, he usually remained unspecific. On process issues, however, he contrasted himself to Jackson and Van Buren by advocating congressional supremacy over the executive and limiting himself to one term. Other Whig speakers and literature blasted Van Buren for allegedly abusing his authority. A proposal by Secretary of War Joel Poinsett to consolidate and professionalize the militias was denounced by Whigs as a step toward executive tyranny and the enhancement of patronage.[45]

The Whig campaign was superior and keenly attuned to Jacksonian approaches to political organizing and messaging. Mounting woes during the Jackson and Van Buren years enabled Whigs to use populism as a vehicle to attack Democratic incompetence and hypocrisy. This upper-crust, mercantilist-oriented party could now make a credible economic argument before the downscale voters who had always made up the Democratic political base. Jacksonian hard-money policies could now be depicted as miserly, antiquated, and reckless ideological engineering. Jacksonian commitments to limited government in the economy could now simply be ridiculed as feckless. Far from being the protectors of the working classes, Democrats were now the custodians of a failed economy that produced widespread suffering and unemployment. Meanwhile, Whigs lampooned Van Buren as a clueless lover of luxury amid the depression. A famous speech by Whig Representative Charles Ogle denounced the president's swanky lifestyle and preferences for fancy belongings, ranging from "golden spoons" to "sterling silver" and meticulous landscaping on the Executive Mansion grounds.[46] The speech was hyperbole, but it was an embarrassing characterization for the leader of the party of the workingman. Ogle's mockery also continued a Whig narrative of Jackson and Van Buren as would-be monarchists and ersatz men of the common people.

Part of the Whig appeal to the voters came by way of pithy slogans, songs, parades, rallies, and symbolic gimmicks. Democrats mocked Harrison as an overrated general who was not up for the rigors of the presidency. Referring to an off-the-cuff remark a Whig critic made about Harrison, Democrats suggested that the old general would be content to imbibe a bottle of hard cider and "sit the remainder of his days in his log cabin."[47] In response, Whigs embraced the log cabin and hard cider labels in a colorful campaign. Hard cider became the chief beverage at Whig campaign rallies, while hastily constructed log cabins became the signature campaign prop.[48] Whigs created a campaign narrative that temporarily destroyed Jacksonian Democratic credibility as defenders of ordinary citizens against agents of privilege. There was Van Buren's hypocritical opulence amid a depression and his empty rhetoric about standing up for the common man. Meanwhile, Harrison was depicted as a humble public servant and a frontier hero who would respect the constitutional limitations of the presidency. Harrison was actually born into an elite Virginia plantation family, while Van Buren's family background was very middle class, but these facts were irrelevant in the campaign.

Given their close ties to the business community, Whigs always had the financial resources to fund a robust opposition party to the Democrats. The other necessary ingredients were proper organization and a commitment to the kind of grassroots campaign tactics that defined the Jacksonian Era. Whigs used an impressive network of party-controlled newspapers to disseminate cartoons, anti–Van Buren speeches, slogans, and general partisan rhetoric. Party surrogates fanned out all over the nation to stump for the ticket. Reflecting grassroots anger at Jacksonian Democrats, local pro-Harrison clubs became a source of manpower for Whig campaign rallies. Attendance at Whig rallies rivaled contemporary campaign rallies, with frequently over 10,000 people attending. Whigs in the states built disciplined organizations to challenge Democrats in down-ballot elections, which would enable the party to better compete for national office.[49]

The Democrats nominated Van Buren without controversy, but Vice President Johnson once again created a headache. He had been of little use in the administration, even abdicating Washington, DC, for a time to start a tavern in Kentucky.[50] The Democratic National Convention declined to nominate Johnson, or any other candidate, for vice president. State Democratic parties were empowered to choose their own nominee. Democrats could make no use of what should have been major assets. The party enjoyed the fruits of patronage in several states, as well as an eleven-year-old patronage machine at the national level. Proadministration newspapers still had the capability of loudly carrying the Democratic message. The campaign appeals that Democrats used were equally as colorful, hard-hitting, and populist as those of the Whigs, but they fell flat under the weight of Van Buren's perceived failure in office.

The Whig victory was unambiguous. Popular interest in the election was revealed in a turnout of 80.3% of eligible voters.[51] Showing impressive regional strength all over the nation, Harrison carried 19 states for 234 electoral votes and 52.9% of the popular vote. Van Buren carried only seven states, even losing New York. The president won only 60 electoral votes and 46.8% of the popular vote. Van Buren's popular vote total in 1840 was only 4% less than in 1836, but this time Whigs were able to carry key states by consolidating behind one nominee. Democratic majorities in Congress also collapsed, giving Whigs full control of two branches of the federal government.

## THE JACKSONIAN REGIME: DOWN BUT NOT OUT

On the leading issues of his administration, Native American removal and the Treasury, Van Buren steered a strict Jacksonian track. In the short run, his objectives were accomplished: the Native peoples continued to be steadily removed to the West and the independent Treasury was ultimately enacted. Relocation of Native Americans continued to be controversial and the Seminole War in Florida raged on endlessly. The independent Treasury bill was enacted only after three years of further economic hardship and political bloodletting in Congress. New policies require time to

implement, and even more time for the political and economic results to appear. A worsening depression overwhelmed any possibility for Van Buren to enjoy the political or economic benefits of his
new Treasury policy. Unfortunately for him, he received no credit
for his achievements. Even after Jackson's presidency, the office Van
Buren held was politically and constitutionally limited in its capacity to respond to major crises. To a greater degree than Madison,
Van Buren found heir apparent leadership to be especially difficult,
for there was now a stronger and better-organized opposition party.

The challenges of completing the Native American removal to
the West, as well as a hemorrhaging economy, left little political
value in new commitments to territorial expansion. In his opposition to annexing Texas, Van Buren slowed political momentum
for a process that Jackson began when he recognized the independent republic. Faced with the risks of new sectional strife (including
within his own party) and an escalation of tensions with Mexico,
Van Buren declined to pursue territorial expansion and opted for diplomacy. Jackson's revolutionary brand of politics was followed by
Van Buren's protective instinct for the national Democratic Party
coalition.

Jacksonian Democrats were down and defeated in 1840, but not
out. The depressed economy opened up new lines of attack upon
Democratic credibility and competence. Van Buren's presidency
opened up party divisions and a resurgent opposition. However,
Whigs found it no easier to implement their long-pent-up agenda.
Harrison died a month after his inauguration and President Tyler
defied Clay and his party by opposing signature Whig policies. Van
Buren's independent Treasury law, however, was repealed in 1841.[52]
Democratic resilience persisted for the next two decades, as the
party elected three more presidents prior to the Civil War. Indeed,
James Polk succeeded at completing Jacksonian commitments to
territorial expansion and an independent treasury. The fragile Democratic coalition now had to contend with a well-organized and robust Whig opposition that would persist for more than a decade.

# 5

## ULYSSES S. GRANT: LET US HAVE PEACE AND HARD MONEY

### TAKING THE HEIR APPARENT PRESIDENCY IN A NEW DIRECTION

Madison and Van Buren revealed two examples of presidents who were career politicians, party builders, and close confidants of their predecessors. Both men were groomed for national political leadership. Truman and Bush also demonstrated similar loyalty to their presidential predecessors and worked their way up the party leadership ladder. Ulysses S. Grant's background could not have been more different. Grant was a lifelong military man who disdained politics and never held or ran for public office before becoming president. Nor did he hold a rigid or extreme political ideology. As the first Republican president to succeed Lincoln, Grant could take the heir apparent stance that eluded Democrat Andrew Johnson. Grant assumed office with a level of popularity that eclipsed the heirs apparent noted above. As a national war hero, Grant was the commanding general in the defining crisis that brought the Republican regime to power. As a general, he demonstrated a preference for resolve in accomplishing objectives, as well as a spirit of reconciliation in victory. As president, Grant could steer a course back toward the principles of the Republican regime, while still retaining some authority to compromise and bargain with other power brokers in the political system. In spite of a four-year time difference between their presidencies, the core problems facing Lincoln at the time of his death awaited Grant when he assumed office.

## RECONSTRUCTION AND REPUBLICAN CAPITALISM

Bursting onto the political scene in the mid-1850s, the Republican Party quickly filled the vacuum left by the demise of the Whig Party. In a matter of six years, the new party swept to victory in the Northeast and the Midwest, rapidly capturing statehouses and congressional seats. Democratic vulnerabilities had only multiplied since Van Buren's defeat. Even when Democrats were able to win, escalating controversies over slavery, sectionalism, tariffs, and immigration wore down the Jacksonian coalition through the next two decades. The anti-immigrant American Party (often called the "Know Nothing Party") was overwhelmed by the new party's broader platform on issues. Unlike their Whig predecessors, Republicans had no Southern base of support. However, Republicans consolidated their Northern support from the ranks of former Whigs, Democrats, and Know Nothings. That gave the party the ability to narrowly control the national political balance of power. The House of Representatives fell under Republican control in the elections of 1858. Three years later, Republicans controlled the presidency and both chambers of Congress. Southern secession only strengthened Republican control of the federal government.

Taking the Whigs' place as a business-oriented party, Republicans continued to promote aspects of the defunct party's agenda. Federal sponsorship of internal improvements remained a priority, as well as railway development, free homesteads, and land-grant colleges. Like the Whigs before them, Republicans advocated protective tariffs to keep American industries safe from the unpredictable influences of international markets. Republicans linked industrialization, mechanization, and corporate growth with prosperity, equal opportunity, and freedom. Similar to old school Jacksonian Democrats, Republicans embraced hard-money policies, so as to discourage speculators and promote responsible behavior by economic actors. Except in emergencies like the Civil War, paper money was to be avoided to the greatest extent possible. Unlike Jacksonian Democrats, however, Republicans welcomed corporate growth and a close relationship between the financial industry and the federal government. An activist federal government was welcomed, so long as its primary function was to affirmatively promote capitalist growth, hard money, and industrialization. Regulatory meddling was to be kept to a minimum. Social welfare programs were not yet a major part of American government, with the major exception of the pension program for Union veterans of the war. For decades after the war, Republicans continuously expanded the program and loosened eligibility rules.[1]

The party emerged as an antislavery party, stopping short of endorsing outright abolition. Republicans advocated restricting the practice to where it already existed.[2] Under that approach, slave states and their advocates would be increasingly marginalized as the nation continued to grow along new economic and cultural trajectories. Slavery was not only immoral but also inconsistent with the modern capitalist republic the new party envisioned. The right of a man to sell the product of his labor for whatever price the market would bear should be the basis of a worker's participation in the economy. The Civil War disrupted the Republican calculus on the slavery issue. Slavery opponents gradually convinced Abraham Lincoln to hitch the abolitionist cause to the task of reunifying the nation. In addition, abolition could weaken the Confederacy militarily, if the issue was handled with the appropriate political shrewdness.

Prior to Reconstruction, Republican positions on the status of African Americans and civil rights fell short of a full commitment to equality.[3] During Reconstruction, the goal of racial equality clashed with the goal of reunifying the white South with the rest of the nation. Republicans differed among themselves over how to prioritize these goals. Republicans from the Radical wing valued racial equality and punishment of the white South. Strong affirmative measures from the federal government were necessary to impose racial equality upon the South, but such actions were also liable to provoke political resistance and violent opposition. Other Republicans gave first priority to economic modernization and the integration of the South into the national economy. For these Republicans, forcing racial equality onto the white South would not be worth it if it would only exacerbate sectional tensions and possibly hurt economic growth.

For a generation, Republicans claimed moral authority to govern on the basis of their victorious stewardship of the Civil War. Asserting that they had saved the union from disintegration and states' rights militancy, Republicans positioned themselves as guardians of national unity, stability, and domestic peace.[4] A common tactic Republicans used in opposition was known as "waving the bloody shirt." For decades, Republican orators, politicians, and newspapers would loudly denounce Democrats as subversive and responsible for all the human suffering of the war.[5] In addition, Republicans positioned themselves as protectors of Protestant values, including a general sympathy for the temperance movement.[6] While the central identity of Reconstruction Republicans was Northern, Anglo-Saxon, and Protestant, the party was also the preferred choice of black men and assumed a moderate position on immigration.[7]

Still, the Republican Party that Grant inherited in 1869 faced vulnerabilities. Industrialization and capitalist growth tested party unity as much as or more than Reconstruction policy. Debates over fiscal and monetary issues cut across the Republican cleavage between moderates and Radicals. Other divisions formed around personalities and patronage disputes. The Radical wing was past its prime, as their leader, Rep. Thaddeus Stevens, died in August 1868. Though they failed in their crusade to remove Andrew Johnson from office, Radicals could still exert pressure upon the national party. Radicals preserved their political credibility by backing the more moderate Grant for the presidential nomination.[8] His apolitical history made him a neater fit into the moderate camp of Republicans that placed a high value upon conciliation and pragmatism.

Reconstruction periodically generated violent resistance in the South, testing the patience of Republicans who wanted their party to move past sectional divisions. In addition, Reconstruction-era factions within Republican ranks could be fluid and variable from state to state. Eastern Republicans tended to favor a strict gold standard, while Western Republicans were more likely to be sympathetic to bimetallism and looser monetary policies.[9] The boom-and-bust cycle could be cruel. Rapid economic growth could create enormous wealth and raise standards of living, but when the nineteenth-century economy crashed, there was likely to be a very large thud when the wreckage hit the ground. Grant, like Van Buren, would learn this lesson during his presidency.

## STEERING THE REPUBLICAN REGIME BACK ON COURSE

### *Lincoln, Johnson, and the Republican Party*

Lincoln envisioned a moderate course of Reconstruction: lenient terms for Confederate state readmission and prompt restoration of citizenship rights for most Confederate soldiers and leaders. Deeming it too punitive, Lincoln pocket vetoed the Wade-Davis Reconstruction bill enacted by Congress in July 1864. Only days before his murder, Lincoln declared his support for limited African American suffrage. "I would myself prefer," he said, "that it were now conferred on the very intelligent, and on those who serve our cause as soldiers."[10] Other Republicans resented Lincoln's tardiness on emancipation and racial equality. Radical Republicans had made their displeasure with Lincoln clear long before the war's end. They were mortified that the president would subordinate the eradication of slavery to the objectives of the war and political convenience. In the 1864 election campaign, Radicals backed a third-party campaign against Lincoln. The plan fizzled when their candidate, John C. Frémont, brokered a deal with the president to drop out in September.[11] Like other regime builders, Lincoln was able to suppress and contain internal party friction. The ascendant Civil War Republicans were ultimately united around the objective of military victory and saving the Union from disintegration.

In the interest of wartime bipartisanship, Lincoln chose Tennessee's Andrew Johnson as his running mate in 1864. Johnson was a

Democrat and Union loyalist who disliked the elite planter class of his state.[12] He also held an open contempt for African Americans. Upon becoming president, Johnson brushed aside Radical Republican plans for Reconstruction and finalized his own policies: sweeping amnesties for most ex-Confederates and lenient terms of readmission for the old rebel states. Any semblance of racial equality was not to be found in the Johnson plan. Southern states would be free to enact explicit laws relegating blacks to second-class citizenship. In his annual message of 1866, Johnson warned against an obtrusive federal role in Reconstruction, calling for a return to strict adherence to the Constitution:

> In our efforts to preserve "the unity of government which constitutes as one people" by restoring the States to the condition which they held prior to the rebellion, we should be cautious, lest, having rescued our nation from perils of threatened disintegration, we resort to consolidation, and in the end absolute despotism, as a remedy for the recurrence of similar troubles. The war having terminated, and with it all occasion for the exercise of powers of doubtful constitutionality, we should hasten to bring legislation within the boundaries prescribed by the Constitution and to return to the ancient landmarks established by our fathers for the guidance of succeeding generations.[13]

Radical Republicans in Congress had other plans. Their relationship with Johnson rapidly turned poisonous. Johnson vetoed a civil rights bill twice, but was ultimately overridden. Republicans blocked the seating of Southern members of Congress, contingent upon the legal protections of African American civil rights beforehand. Clashes continued between Johnson and Congress, as Johnson vetoed Reconstruction measures that limited his authority, expanded black suffrage, and imposed strict standards upon the occupied Southern states. Out of Johnson's 29 vetoes, 15 were overridden, a staggeringly high figure for an American president.[14]

Johnson's adversarial relationship with the Radicals should not be considered surprising, given their very different ideologies. On the other hand, Johnson's stubbornness came to alienate all

Republican factions. In August and September 1866, Johnson embarked upon an abrasive public speaking tour to defend his policies and denounce Radicals in Congress. The tour was replete with hyperbole and drunken rants.[15] For a president ostensibly devoted to the reconciliation of North and South, Johnson's rhetoric only made Reconstruction even more of a partisan issue. Republicans did not agree among themselves upon all Reconstruction measures, but Johnson's behavior united them against him.

After the war, the Republican Party was still ascendant. The Democratic opposition was on the defensive, weakened by the federal takeover of the South and delegitimized by the vindication of Lincoln's wartime stewardship. Without a president in the White House, national Republican leadership during this period was instead defined by its congressional factions. A moderate Republican heir apparent to Lincoln would have very likely clashed with Radicals over Reconstruction. On the other hand, matters would have been unlikely to escalate to the level of impeachment because such a president would have commanded support from moderate and conservative Republicans. It is also possible that Radicals would have adopted a more conciliatory stance with a genuinely Republican president.

Johnson was mispositioned to be an heir apparent at this particular point in history. He was a Southern Democrat, the embodiment of the Republican regime's ultimate villain in a political universe defined by the Civil War. The Republican Party during Johnson's presidency was defined by the sectional crisis that preceded the war, the Union cause in the war, the abolition of slavery, and gestures toward racial equality. For a president of Johnson's profile, any moves toward conciliation with the old Confederacy were bound to be viewed as subversive. The fierce passions and loyalties of mid-nineteenth-century party politics were subsumed into the passions of the Civil War and its aftermath. Radicals led a drive to impeach Johnson after the president defied them by removing his war secretary from office. The Senate fell one vote shy of the two-thirds margin needed to convict and remove, because a handful of moderate Republicans voted to acquit Johnson at his trial.[16]

*The Election of 1868: The Delayed Heir Apparent Arrives*

General Grant was forced to tag along with his commander-in-chief while Johnson toured the country in defense of the administration's Reconstruction policies. Writing to his wife Julia, Grant lamented Johnson's embittered speeches. "I look upon them as a national disgrace," he wrote.[17] In fact, many of the spectators appeared at Johnson's speeches to see Grant, who was greeted with much adulation.[18] Grant was the most popular general in the country after the war, having delivered the military victories that eluded previous generals. He was also a Lincoln favorite: "I can't spare this man; he fights," the president said after the Union victory at Shiloh.[19] A year later, Lincoln and Congress arranged for Grant to be promoted to lieutenant general, and eventually supreme commander of all Union armies. Unlike Lincoln, Grant had no history with the Republican Party, but pressure began to mount for him to seek the presidential nomination in 1868. Pragmatic Republicans were becoming exasperated with the Radicals, and with the right candidate, Democrats could take advantage of public anxieties about Reconstruction.

As was normal for nineteenth-century presidential aspirants, Grant was publicly coy about his ambitions, but he made himself available to Republicans who promoted him for the nomination. Less than enamored with Grant, the weakening Radical faction preferred a more seasoned politician who shared their ideological commitments. Grant was, however, a towering figure at this moment in time, and the Radicals' sense of pragmatism won out. No Republican emerged to challenge Grant for the nomination. In the end, there was little drama over the presidential nomination at the party convention in May. Grant was unanimously nominated on the first ballot, an impressive feat when one remembers how common it was for party conventions to be very divisive events in the nineteenth century. Radicals prevailed in securing the vice presidential nod for one of their own, House Speaker Schuyler Colfax.[20]

"Let us have peace," Grant famously pledged, as he accepted the nomination. A Republican who commanded support from all of his party factions might stand a chance at reconciling sectional divisions. The campaign of 1868, however, was hardly harmonious. Scattered acts of politically motivated Ku Klux Klan violence marred the campaign, as Democrats deployed explicitly racist appeals to voters. Black civil rights and political participation were derided. Accusations were made (similar to four years before) that Republicans wanted to promote miscegenation. Rumors were spread that Grant was the father of a girl with a Native American mother. Mockery of Grant's alcoholism resurfaced in the campaign. Finally, in seeking to turn his greatest strength—his military leadership—into a weakness, Democrats held Grant responsible for the carnage of the war.[21]

The Democratic nominee, former New York Governor Horatio Seymour, was not a supporter of Lincoln's war policies. Seymour was also accused of treating New York City draft rioters with sympathy.[22] Using a playbook similar to the one from four years before, Republican orators and publications asserted that Democrats were either uncommitted to national unity or outright seditious. It was all too easy for Republicans to denounce Seymour as an enabler of Southern troublemakers, if not an outright traitor himself. Republican spokespersons lauded Grant as the protector of all the blood and treasure that had been sacrificed on the Union's behalf. In a campaign pamphlet, the Soldiers' and Sailors' National Republican Executive Committee pleaded with Union veterans:

> Let us resolve that we will never give up the fight until the country is reconstructed upon the basis of *equal and exact justice to all men*. Let us swear, by the memory of our three hundred thousand slain comrades, that we will not prove recreant to the cause for which they died, and that their widows and orphans shall not be left to the tender mercies of the *Democratic rebel party*. Let a million of *Boys in Blue* carry the *Stars and Stripes* they have saved high over the head of our brave leader, and place him in the seat where he will be enabled to prove his patriotism and his wisdom by maintaining the Government he was so largely instrumental in rescuing from the bloody grasp of treason and war.[23]

A soldier and a patriot, who would steer Reconstruction in the right direction, Grant would stand against the hasty ambitions of the Radicals, while responsibly protecting black civil rights and stopping violent Southern resistance.

The campaign was divisive and passionate, but Grant commanded a level of unity from his own party that eclipsed Madison and Van Buren in their first presidential campaigns. The margin of Grant's electoral victory was still somewhat more modest than Lincoln's reelection. Showing strength in all regions, Grant won 26 states for 214 electoral votes, while Seymour carried just eight states for 80 electoral votes. The popular vote was somewhat closer: 52.7% for Grant, and 47.3% for Seymour. Three Southern states were still outside of the Union, but Grant's show of force in the South was impressive. African American men decisively chose Grant, as the general won a substantial share of these newly enfranchised voters.[24] In his heir apparent capacity, Grant was most successful at holding this critical bloc of voters for the Republican regime. Congressional coattails for Republicans were constrained, as Southern Democrats began reasserting their national strength. Democrats managed a net gain of 20 seats in the House, while Republicans scored a net gain of five in the Senate.[25] Republican majorities in both chambers were preserved.

## RESTORING THE REPUBLICAN REGIME

Mainstream Republicans once again had full control of the national policymaking process. Four years after Lincoln's death, the fundamental residual issues remained for the new president. Reconstruction and African American civil rights were far from settled matters. Reconstruction would prove no easier, as efforts to secure black civil rights continued to generate violent Southern resistance and eventually Republican exhaustion. A financial panic in Grant's second term cast doubt upon Republican stewardship of the economy, and provoked new battles over currency within the governing party.

## Reconstruction and Civil Rights

With Radicals weakened and Democrats defeated, the Grant Administration could pursue the brand of Reconstruction that Lincoln envisioned, with the political authority as Yankee Republicans to bargain and compromise with Southern power brokers. The overarching objectives of Reconstruction were very incomplete by the time Grant assumed office. This president utilized the expansion approach to build from Lincoln's Reconstruction commitments, so as to place a greater emphasis on black Americans' political rights and the federal government's duty to protect them. During his second term, however, Grant tended to retreat from this approach, as the political costs began to mount.

On the matter of black suffrage, Grant took further steps forward than Lincoln's limited vision. The vote was not a privilege to be granted to selected black men on the basis of military service or the government's vague criteria of who was or was not "intelligent." Rather, black male suffrage should be a right by edict of the Constitution, on equal footing with the abolition of slavery, due process of law, and equal protection under the law. In addition, as the election results revealed, black voters were becoming a Republican constituency. The new president prioritized the proposed Fifteenth Amendment, securing the right of all black male citizens to vote. Similar to the recently adopted Thirteenth and Fourteenth Amendments, Congress would have powers to enforce this measure with legislation that might enhance the federal role in Reconstruction. Grant advocated for the amendment's enactment in his inaugural message.[26] Congress had already passed the measure by the time Grant assumed office, but the new president did his part to obtain the necessary ratifications in the states. Grant successfully urged the governor of Nebraska to call his legislature into session to ratify the amendment. Legislation was also signed compelling proratification votes from four Southern states as a prerequisite for readmittance to the Union and fully seated congressional delegations.[27] Upon the amendment's adoption on March 30, 1870, Grant declared "that the adoption of the fifteenth amendment to the Constitution completes the greatest civil change and constitutes the most important event that has occurred since the nation came into life."[28]

Lincoln used the advancement of African American civil rights to weaken the Confederacy militarily. During the war, Lincoln stopped enforcing the Fugitive Slave Act upon rebel states, invited black men to enlist in the military, and issued the Emancipation Proclamation, which was selectively applicable. Lincoln had never been a supporter of slavery or full racial equality under the law. Saving the Union came first. In the latter months of the war, however, Lincoln began moving away from simply using emancipation as a means to vanquish an enemy. Black Americans were more than just tools to be used to defeat the Confederates. Rather, they were citizens with rights, even if many Americans and their government were slow to recognize that principle. Comprehensive emancipation by edict of the Constitution and limited black suffrage opened new doors to federal commitments to civil rights and equality.

With much difficulty, occasional inconsistency, and setbacks along the way, Grant continued this process. Enforcement Acts followed in 1870 and 1871, giving Grant and the federal government statutory powers to protect rights secured in the Reconstruction amendments. Provisions were included to permit the federal government to monitor Southern elections. The military could also be used as a tool to restore order and suppress organized violence—namely, the Ku Klux Klan. Under extraordinary circumstances, habeas corpus could be suspended.[29] To handle these new federal responsibilities, federal law enforcement matters were consolidated under the new Department of Justice, headed by the attorney general.[30] For eighty years the attorney general served in the cabinet, but without an institutional apparatus behind him, as was the case with the secretaries of state and treasury. In signing these measures, Grant committed the federal government to the affirmative protection of African American civil rights.

Enforcement in practice was another matter entirely. The expansion approach to heir apparent leadership can result in successful or failed policy implementation. Success here, however, does not guarantee political rewards. A president faced with dim prospects and declining political support may choose the course of retreating from grand ambitions. As Grant worked to expand the commitments of his governing regime, Democratic opposition strengthened, while Republican exasperation steadily grew. Grant's second term saw increasing retreats from the ambitious and expansive vision of Reconstruction envisioned early in the administration.

The Klan, the White League, and the Redshirts all maintained ties to the Southern Democratic Party. They terrorized blacks, fought Reconstruction Republican state governments tooth and nail, and aimed for the restoration of Democratic hegemony. In Grant's first term, the Enforcement Acts were used as robustly as limited federal resources would permit. Prosecutions spread throughout the South, although criminal sanctions were not always severe. To halt Klan violence in South Carolina, Grant invoked the Ku Klux Klan Enforcement Act to suspend habeas corpus in nine counties.[31] The Klan was defunct by 1872, but racial violence against blacks remained a part of Southern life.

The White League formed as a consequence of the disputed gubernatorial election in Louisiana in 1872. Grant sent troops to the state to uphold a federal court order giving the election to the Republican candidate. Anarchy spread all over the state for the next two years as political conflicts between state Democrats and Republicans regularly turned violent. In early 1875, troops under Grant's old army subordinate, General Phil Sheridan, restored legitimately elected Republicans to the legislature and suppressed the White League. Congress got involved and brokered a compromise to preserve peace and maintain political stability in the state. It was a costly and short-lived victory for Grant, Republicans, and Reconstruction. Northern public support had soured upon excessive federal meddling in persistent Southern hot spots, and even some administration cabinet secretaries were losing enthusiasm for Reconstruction. The gubernatorial election of 1876 was also marred by violence and a questionable Democratic victory, but this time the Grant Administration declined to get involved.[32]

Mississippi presented another example of flagging support for

Reconstruction. As a state with an especially large African American population, it saw many blacks elected to public office during Reconstruction. If there was any state where Reconstruction had to work to prove its national political credibility, this was it. At the same time, Mississippi was also vulnerable to organized and random acts of violence. White racist mobs instigated violence against pro-Reconstruction politicians, terrorized blacks, and plotted the resumption of white Democratic rule. In early 1875, a black sheriff who had been deposed was reinstalled thanks to federal military intervention in Vicksburg. Later in the year the state held fraudulent, violence-marred elections. Reconstruction Republican Governor Adelbert Ames called for federal military assistance, but reflecting Northern and Republican exhaustion, Grant declined the request. Administration officials believed that the American public was spent from years of constant meddling in persistent eruptions of Southern violence. Northern Republican officials apparently warned Grant that further interjection into the Mississippi morass would produce a Northern voter backlash, including upcoming state elections in Ohio. The Northeast and Midwest were still the flagship regions for Republicans, and national party leaders had to tend to their regional base before concerning themselves with party building in the South. Ames left office, turning the state over to white supremacist Democrats.[33]

The Grant Administration found it increasingly difficult, politically and logistically, to stop the reimposition of Southern white supremacy by way of violent elections and dishonest tactics. State after state was slipping through the fingers of pro-Reconstruction Republicans and into the hands of white Democrats. Georgia fell under full Democratic control by early 1872. Facing an inevitable Republican loss, Grant followed the advice of Attorney General Amos Akerman not to meddle in the state's political affairs. The new Georgia government moved aggressively to curtail the political and economic advancements black citizens had briefly achieved after the war. In 1874, Democrats recaptured Alabama through voter suppression and overtly racist campaign tactics. Democrats badly defeated Texas's reform-minded Republican Governor E. J. Davis for reelection in 1873. That election was rife with dirty tactics, but the Grant Administration stood down. South Carolina's gubernatorial election of 1876 was marred by violence from the Redshirts, a Klan-like organization that openly supported the Democratic candidate, former Confederate General Wade Hampton. After refusing at first, Grant ultimately authorized federal troops to keep the peace in the election, but the violence and voter suppression were overwhelming. Hampton prevailed following a postelection dispute lasting several months.[34]

In Arkansas, Grant limited his involvement in the Joseph Brooks–Elisha Baxter war concerning the state's 1872 gubernatorial election. Brooks and Baxter were Republicans from different party factions, and both claimed to have won the election. The dispute turned violent in the spring of 1874. The administration encouraged both sides to negotiate a settlement, and refused to insert federal troops into the fracas, except as a last resort. With Grant's support, Baxter was allowed to serve as governor, and there was no federal military involvement. Republican divisions in Arkansas opened the door for Democrats to exploit Baxter's politically weakened position, write a new constitution, and win the governorship in a new election that fall.[35]

Still, at a time when Grant and national Republicans were deprioritizing Reconstruction, the president signed into law a new Civil Rights Act in March 1875. On paper, the law extended federal commitments to equality, barring racial discrimination in "accommodations, advantages, facilities, and privileges of inns, public conveyances on land or water, theatres, and other places of public amusement."[36] The prohibition of discrimination in public education was not included in the final bill. A large federal commitment would have been required to make the promises of the law a reality, but this Civil Rights Act went mostly unenforced.[37]

The Grant Administration defended the constitutionality of the Enforcement Acts in court, but suffered a major blow in the cases of *United States v. Cruikshank* and *United States v. Reese* in 1876. The *Cruikshank* ruling stemmed from the massacre at Colfax, an episode that occurred amid the Louisiana gubernatorial election dispute. The Supreme Court limited the reach of the Fourteenth Amendment and, by extension, the Enforcement Act of 1870. The ruling asserted that governments could be expected to uphold equal protection under the law and due process. If, however, private individuals violated those rights upon other people, then it was not the concern of the federal government to intervene. The convictions of the white instigators of the Colfax massacre were thrown out. In the *Reese* ruling, issued the same day as the *Cruikshank* decision, the court also used a restrictive interpretation of the Enforcement Act pursuant to the Fifteenth Amendment. Throwing out large portions of the law, the Court deemed it too vague, and not narrowly tailored to the mandates of the Fifteenth Amendment.[38]

Federal involvement in state and local elections was new to American political and legal culture in the 1860s and 1870s. The conundrum for national Republican leaders was that, on the one hand, military force or quasi force was often required in the South to make racial equality under the law a reality. Southern Democratic resistance to Reconstruction was violent, unlike the political opposition Van Buren faced from Whigs and the nuisance opposition Madison faced from weakened Federalists. On the other hand, the repeated use of force seemed counter to the national reconciliation that was so valued by moderate and pragmatic Republicans. The Republican *New York Tribune* exclaimed: "There can be no question that the old reconstruction policy has been a disastrous failure. The rule of the bayonet and the deputy-marshal, the tyranny of carpet-bag, legislatures, the incessant interference of intimidation laws, the management of elections from Washington, and the supervision of the counting by agents of the Custom-house—all these heroic devices have served merely to aggravate the disorders of the unhappy South."[39] To carry out Reconstruction, the Grant Administration relied upon the Justice Department, the army, and unstable Southern Republican state governments. The Freedmen's Bureau was created by Lincoln in 1865 to help freed slaves start new lives. The Grant Administration could have rehabilitated the Bureau, following years of being undermined and underfunded by the Johnson Administration. By the time Grant assumed office, the Bureau had lost political support and was labeled as a welfare agency for blacks.[40] The remains of the Bureau were closed down by 1872. The elimination of the Freedmen's Bureau meant that African Americans would lack an institutional base within the government solely dedicated to advancing their economic interests.

For an heir apparent to expand upon the commitments of his ideological predecessor, other actors within the governing regime must be willing to bear the political risks and costs. Grant found that support eroding in his second term, especially as the interests of all Americans became mired in an economic depression. As a consequence, public support for Reconstruction waned and Grant's willingness to take political risks in this arena diminished. As the administration retreated from the expansion approach, Grant became associated with a Reconstruction policy that failed to live up to expectations. The president's attention was now divided between Reconstruction and an economic calamity.

### Let Us Have Hard Money

The new Republican regime restored central banking. To bring a greater centralization to the nation's currency, Lincoln and Congress created a national banking system. The National Bank Acts of 1863 and 1864 provided for a network of privately owned national banks with federal charters. Elsewhere, the imperatives of the Civil War demanded that Republicans depart from their own fiscal and monetary doctrines. An income tax was enacted for the first time in American history. Strict adherence to the gold standard was abandoned in light of the financial needs created by mobilization for total war. The federal government also issued bonds and greenbacks (paper money).[41] Lincoln held the political authority to brush aside Republican orthodoxies concerning hard money in pursuit of the higher objective of winning the war. Union victory in the war was the organizing basis behind the Republican Party to a far greater extent than their principles about currency.

Grant began the process of moving the nation back toward the economic policies Republicans normally favored in peacetime.

Similar to Van Buren, Grant sought to steer economic policy back onto a permanent footing that was consistent with the orthodoxies of his governing regime. Here Grant played a corrective policy role, although not as a repudiation of the Lincoln Administration. This new Republican administration worked to shift their regime's economic policies away from the emergency-based approach of the Civil War. The wartime income tax was reduced in 1870 and phased out by 1872,[42] but most significantly, Grant wanted a sound currency. Inflationary approaches to monetary policy were to be phased out, meaning less emphasis upon paper money and, ultimately, even less emphasis upon silver as well.

In his inaugural address, the new president asserted that wartime debts must be repaid upon hard money principles: "The payment of this, principal and interest, as well as the return to a specie basis as soon as it can be accomplished without material detriment to the debtor class or to the country at large, must be provided for. To protect the national honor, every dollar of Government indebtedness should be paid in gold, unless otherwise expressly stipulated in the contract."[43] Grant also denounced "repudiationists" who favored repayment of debts in greenbacks. Rebuilding the nation's credit rating was part of Reconstruction, and a sound monetary standard was essential to maintaining the confidence of investors. Republicans insinuated that advocates of greenbacks (who were usually Democrats) were somehow not serious about rebuilding a strong postwar America.[44]

Congress and the president got right to work. In March 1869, the Public Credit Act was enacted into law. The measure largely met Grant's objectives by compelling payment of bonds in gold. Similarly, the law also called for redemption of greenbacks, thus beginning the process of winding down the use of paper money. In the Treasury Department, Secretary George Boutwell prioritized paying down the national debt and improving the efficiency of his department. Just as the administration's new monetary policy was getting off the ground, Grant and Boutwell had to break up a scheme by two speculators to corner the gold market. Grant directed the release of $4 million of gold into the market. Panic selling followed, but the plotters were thwarted. The stock market plunged, investor confidence was shaken, and the overall economy suffered.[45]

Debates over currency could often break down along class and cultural lines, potentially threatening the Republican Party's national political coalition. While Grant was a firm believer in hard money and paying down the national debt, he would make some concessions to advocates of greenbacks and looser money. Western and Southern Republicans pushed for passage of the National Bank Currency Act. Enacted into law in July 1870, the measure kept the greenback supply at current levels and circulated another $54 million in notes from the national banks. These new bank notes would replace $45 million in "3 percent certificates,"[46] which would be retired from circulation. Finally, the law called for most of the new national bank notes to circulate in Southern and Western states. This legislation had a minimal inflationary effect on the currency and built up the legitimacy of the national banking system created during the Civil War.[47]

Movement toward an exclusive gold standard continued. In February 1873 Grant signed the Coinage Act, which passed Congress by an overwhelming margin. Most significantly, the law demonetized silver. Much of Europe was already in the process of moving away from silver currency, but the policy was unpopular in the silver-rich West, where it was excoriated as the "Crime of '73."[48] Grant's policy was responsive to Republican financiers who favored an anti-inflationary policy and the winding down of Lincoln's Civil War–era economic framework. As silver became increasingly inflationary, hard-money Republicans shifted more of their emphasis to gold.[49] Periodic political clashes between supporters of the gold standard and supporters of bimetallism would continue for more than 20 years.

Republican economic policies were tested with the onset of the Panic of 1873. The sudden collapse of Jay Cooke & Company, a powerful Philadelphia bank, set off a cascade of bank failures, plunging markets, contractions of credit, and job losses. Cooke was largely responsible for helping to fund the federal government's Civil War mobilization. The institution also financed the railroad industry with visions of transcontinental expansion, but Cooke's investment in the Northern Pacific Railroad went awry and the bank became insolvent.[50] The economy now sank into a depression, creating vulnerabilities for Republican economic orthodoxies and weakening elite and public support for Reconstruction.

Grant was not opposed to all measures to expand the money supply, but he refused to abandon his long-term plans for an American economy based upon tight money and the gold standard. In the early months after the crash, the administration authorized a limited release of greenbacks and the redemption of bonds. However, advocates of a looser money supply, including some Republicans, went on the offensive. In April 1874, Congress sent Grant a measure that was casually labeled the Inflation Bill. The legislation would have pumped the money supply upward through new greenbacks and currency backed by specie. Republicans from the West tended to support the legislation, while Eastern Republicans were mostly in opposition. Grant contemplated what to do for the next few days, receiving mixed advice from his cabinet and hearing ferocious opposition from Eastern financiers. The president chose to veto the Inflation Bill, repeating his preference for a steady return to the gold standard, and warning against damaging the international credit of the United States.[51]

In Grant's annual message in 1874, the president asked Congress to approve "by legislation a method by which we will return to specie."[52] The culminating achievement that followed was the Specie Payment Resumption Act, enacted in January 1875 by a lame-duck Congress. The law was gradual and facilitated the final transition to a gold standard over the next four years. Greenbacks were to be further reduced through retirement and their redemption in gold beginning in 1879.[53] The economy remained in a depressed state for the rest of Grant's presidency, but his long-term policy goal was achieved, even at a large political cost. At a slow but certain pace, Grant restored the Republican regime's orthodox principles of monetary policy.

### The Election of 1872: Suppressing the Liberal Republican Revolt

Popular support for Reconstruction was already beginning to erode even before the economic crash. Even within the old Radical faction, support for confrontational and transformative Reconstruction policies was softening. With all Southern states back in the Union—at varying levels of federal supervision—Democrats could try to capitalize upon flagging Republican enthusiasm for Reconstruction. Scandals and allegations of political favoritism in the Grant Administration were starting to surface. While personally very popular, Grant was increasingly vulnerable to charges of incompetency and mismanagement.

Grant was easily renominated for a second term, but a faction of Republican dissidents began plotting a separate effort to defeat the president. The Liberal Republicans were a diverse group of anti-Grant Republicans that favored civil service reform, reducing the tariff, and a more lenient brand of Reconstruction. Civil rights for blacks were not a priority, as the Liberals viewed such policies as disruptive to national unity. Their presidential nominee was the editor of the *New York Tribune*, Horace Greeley, a onetime Radical Republican who was now a harsh critic of Grant. Greeley disagreed with numerous Liberal Republican issue positions and priorities. With little debate, the Democratic Party's convention chose to endorse Greeley on a fusion ticket. It was a strange alliance: a party still defined by its Southern base joining forces with a socially awkward Northern Republican who held issue positions that were inconsistent with his new party and inconsistent with his own political past.[54]

The Amnesty Act was signed into law in May 1872, reenfranchising most Confederate veterans. This measure probably cost Grant Southern white votes, but he did not need them. A better candidate may have been able to run a competitive race against Grant, but Republicans could still activate partisan feelings rooted in postwar sectional loyalties. Greeley was vulnerable to much mockery for his shifting political stances and his personal traits. A public speaking tour in the closing months of the campaign did him no good. Grant easily maintained the Republican coalition to win reelection. With significant help from black voters, Grant carried eight old Confederate states. Grant swept the rest of the country, save for three border states. The incumbent won 55.6% of the popular vote and 286 electoral votes, an improvement on both counts from four years before. Republicans maintained large congressional majorities, posting healthy gains in the House and losing nine in the Senate.[55]

## The Democrats and the South Rise Again

The governing party was left in a weaker position by the end of Grant's presidency. Mounting scandals, a depressed economy, and an unpopular congressional pay raise created many headwinds for Republicans in the 1874 midterm elections. The Democrats' Southern base was fully reconstituted, as federal supervision was on the decline and subject to growing resistance. Picking up 94 seats through gains all over the nation, Democrats won control of the House for the first time since 1856. Republicans retained solid control of the Senate, but Democrats gained nine seats.[56]

The presidential election of 1876 revealed the extent to which Democrats had reconstituted themselves as a robust agent of opposition at a national level. Democratic nominee and New York Governor Samuel Tilden won the popular vote over Republican nominee Rutherford B. Hayes, the governor of Ohio. The election outcome was mired in controversy for several more weeks. Democrats agreed to stand down and allow Hayes to prevail after a grand bargain was achieved that ended what was left of Reconstruction. The remaining federal occupation troops would end their Reconstruction mission and Hayes would invite a white Southern Democrat into his cabinet. Hayes and national Republicans also agreed to recognize Democratic victories in the disputed gubernatorial elections in Louisiana and South Carolina.[57]

Republicans usually held the upper hand, but the next 20 years featured very close electoral competition between both major parties. To rally their political coalition, Republicans continued to claim moral authority to govern on the basis of the achievements of the Civil War. Republicans also positioned themselves as confident stewards of capitalist growth, modernization, and industrialization. Subsequent Republican presidents took up the causes of antitrust regulation and civil service reform. White Democratic control of the South would now be entrenched for the next 90 years, thereby strengthening the party at a national level. The advancement of black civil rights dropped out of mainstream political debate.

## GRANT AND THE RETURN OF POLITICAL EQUILIBRIUM

Grant's presidency exemplified the heir apparent's dilemma because he was the first Republican to hold the White House after Lincoln. Lincoln's vice president, Democrat Andrew Johnson, was poorly suited to play the heir apparent role. And Johnson was not received by the ascendant governing regime as a legitimate successor to Lincoln's revolutionary presidency. Johnson's poor political skills were unhelpful to his presidency, but his prospects for serving as an heir apparent to Lincoln were constrained by his pedigree as a Southern Democrat at the start of Reconstruction.

In the heir apparent capacity, Grant followed mixed approaches. His administration endeavored to expand the Reconstruction commitments of the Republican regime, but increasingly retreated from this approach. Grant expanded upon Lincoln's commitment to black male suffrage and pursued a mostly vigorous pattern of federal enforcement of Reconstruction during his first term. During his second term, federal enforcement waxed and waned, but generally declined as Southern resistance intensified and Republican political will eroded. Adopting a corrective approach, Grant gradually restored traditional Republican principles of economic policy. Hard-money policies were phased in, even as the economy plunged into a depression. Republicans were not always united around hard-money policies, but Grant followed a steady trajectory toward the approaches favored by the Eastern financial wing of his party.

As a governing regime passes from its nascent years into the hands of an heir apparent, political headwinds mount up and weaken the capacity for revolutionary policy measures to materialize. As a national hero and the beneficiary of a suppressed Southern Democratic base, Grant won two landslide elections. His Republican Party, however, was weakened by the economic depression and the concurrent controversies over Reconstruction policy. Republican economic orthodoxies clearly prevailed, but the party's commitments to equality and civil rights tumbled under the political costs of enforcement. The mutually reinforcing phenomena of a rising Democratic Party and a collapsing Reconstruction policy restored equilibrium to the political system.

# 6

## HARRY TRUMAN:
## FAIR DEAL DEMOCRAT

### POST-DEPRESSION AND POSTWAR NEW DEAL POLITICS

Franklin Roosevelt's successor inherited a national state that had expanded to previously unprecedented levels. The Great Depression and the Second World War created conditions that demanded major redefinitions in the domestic social contract, as well as America's role in international affairs. Subsequent presidents would now sit atop an administrative apparatus with sweeping responsibilities over the economy, social welfare, national defense, and foreign policy. Harry Truman's tasks were to redirect this governmental machinery toward a peacetime domestic economy and to establish America's place in a new postwar world order. As a loyal disciple of the governing Democratic regime, Truman had to legitimize the new liberal order beyond the towering presidency of Roosevelt.

Roosevelt called his economic approach the New Deal.[1] Empowered by a major Democratic landslide in the election of 1932, as well as the worst economic crisis in American history, New Deal political philosophy was not always coherent in practice. Early in the Roosevelt Administration, New Deal programs often took on an improvised and haphazard form. In 1933, legislation was commonly rushed through Congress without the careful and deliberate crafting of lawmakers. Accordingly, Congress was very compliant with Roosevelt's initiatives in 1933 and 1934. The remainder of

Roosevelt's first and second terms included many significant New Deal policies, but the Supreme Court also struck down major initiatives in 1935 and 1936. In Roosevelt's second term, passage of New Deal legislation in Congress became more challenging.[2]

Experimentation in government was held to be a virtue. As Roosevelt said in the campaign in 1932, "Say that civilization is a tree which continually produces rot and dead wood. The radical says: 'Cut it down.' The conservative says: 'Don't touch it.' The liberal compromises: 'Let's prune.'"[3] New Deal Democrats believed in proactively using the machinery of government to improve human welfare and smooth out irregularities in the business cycle. If left to their own devices, economic markets could create prosperity and rising standards of living, but they were also prone to gross inefficiencies, contractions, and uncertainties. Building off of elements from the Progressive Era, New Deal Democrats embraced positive liberalism and a far greater faith in central state action than their party had ever previously advocated. The federal government must serve as a regulatory counterweight to powerful economic actors like banks, corporations, and the Wall Street community. Direct social welfare could preserve families and human productivity, lest citizens fall into an abyss of destitution.

Workers needed more than just social welfare. They also required empowerment, lest they be left to the whims of a cruel marketplace. Minimum wage laws, maximum hours legislation, and prohibitions on dangerous and excessive child labor were extended throughout the American workforce by way of the Fair Labor Standards Act. The right to form labor unions was guaranteed by the National Labor Relations Act, although Roosevelt and New Dealers did not initially prioritize this measure. The federal government would now regulate a labor system rooted in collective bargaining and mediation. Union membership surged as organized labor quickly evolved into a major partner within the New Deal Democratic coalition.[4]

At the same time, while many liberal Democrats frowned upon government-sanctioned racism, the early New Deal philosophy tolerated the existence of state-sponsored segregation. New Dealers' commitments to social justice and economic security did not extend to any kind of challenge to state-sanctioned racial segregation, discrimination, or voter disenfranchisement. The New Deal was born out of the Depression, and national Democrats prioritized the economic crisis during the nascent years of this governing regime. In addition, the New Deal electoral coalition was highly dependent upon the South (where blacks were generally disenfranchised), and Southern Democratic committee chairmen wielded disproportionate clout over Congress.[5] Any legislation that could have had a potential effect upon racial segregation in institutions and in public life would have had to clear powerful congressional committees that were often dominated by Southerners. Indeed, many Southern Democrats saw no conflict between support for New Deal programs (often very economically beneficial to their region) alongside support for Jim Crow policies.

Accordingly, New Deal programs of the 1930s and 1940s frequently discriminated on the basis of race, either explicitly or in practice. Segregation and discrimination were common in the Civilian Conservation Corps. Statutes forbidding racial discrimination in New Deal programs were frequently flouted by program administrators. The administration did not make a habit of challenging local administrators who chose to maintain local customs of discrimination. The Agricultural Adjustment Act was economically harmful for black sharecroppers and poor farmers. Social Security initially excluded domestic servants and agricultural workers, leaving out many black Americans. Industry codes under the National Recovery Act often maintained discriminatory practices against black workers.[6] Even the GI Bill of Rights, enacted in 1944, contained no mandate upon participating colleges and universities to integrate.[7] Roosevelt, however, did sign an executive order barring racial discrimination in defense industry employment.[8]

Millions of black Americans benefited from New Deal social welfare programs, as well as wartime industrial employment. In the 1936 election, Roosevelt and the Democrats absorbed these voters into the New Deal coalition, creating a political alliance with white Southerners that would be hard to maintain.[9] After the war, important institutions and industries continued to function on a segregated basis, limiting or outright closing opportunities for blacks. The private sector was generally free to discriminate on the basis of race. Unpunished violence against black citizens, including war veterans, continued to occur.[10]

The thrust of the New Deal after World War II was a centrally administered social welfare and regulatory state. Work relief programs were generally phased out as the nation moved toward a war footing. Full employment was achieved due to the most massive military mobilization in American history. Social Security remained in place as a contributory pension program with a far more limited reach than exists today. Infrastructure programs such as the Tennessee Valley Authority and the Rural Electrification Administration continued and established client constituencies. Farm subsidy programs continued through a revised Agricultural Adjustment Act. The Securities and Exchange Commission and the Federal Deposit Insurance Corporation continued in their roles as vital regulators in the financial industry.

The transition out of the World War II economy was disruptive. Millions of newly empowered union workers in industry after industry launched strikes, demanding higher wages. Defense contractors began laying off workers. The economy was beset by inflation and periodic shortages of electrical power and common household groceries. Millions of men were returning home from the war only to find that some cities were running short on housing. Fears abounded that Depression-era conditions would return in the absence of wartime public investment.[11]

New Deal Democrats mostly embraced an internationalist foreign policy. Even before American combat involvement in the war, Democrats strongly supported the Lend Lease policy to aid the Allies.[12] From that point and beyond in the war, New Dealers asserted that the United States should maintain an active and engaged foreign policy, backed by credible military muscle. An international defense of what Roosevelt called the "four freedoms"—freedom of speech and worship, as well as freedom from want and fear—was linked to the success of American democracy.[13] Roosevelt died shortly before the war's victorious end, and his successor would be charged with establishing the postwar American role vis-à-vis the Soviet Union.

Harry Truman, like another heir apparent before him, Ulysses S. Grant, was tasked with charting a reconstructive role for the United States following a very consequential war. In both cases, the federal government had to assume significant responsibility over securing the peace, enforcing postwar obligations upon defeated foes, and rebuilding infrastructure. For Grant, reconstruction was a strictly American policy, while Truman's reconstructive mandate occurred on an international stage. Europe and Japan had to be rebuilt. The international balance of power was rapidly moving toward a bipolar state of affairs between the United States and the Soviet Union. The existence of nuclear weapons, and their inevitable proliferation, brought a new urgency and delicacy to relations between the two superpowers.

## "MILD ABOUT HARRY": THE ACCEPTABLE NEW DEALER

Harry Truman's appearance on the 1944 national Democratic ticket was the product of a compromise between party power brokers as Roosevelt sought an unprecedented fourth term in office. The vice presidential nomination had often served as a sort of bargaining chip before and during political party conventions of the nineteenth and early twentieth centuries. Roosevelt agreed to demands from conservative Democrats and party leaders that the eccentric and very liberal Vice President Henry Wallace be removed from the ticket. For his own part, Truman did not seem to have much interest in the vice presidency, but the Missouri senator was the most acceptable compromise candidate amid a long list of contenders. Roosevelt was physically weakened, with political insiders musing openly that he might not survive a fourth term. While attending the 1944 Democratic National Convention, Truman received a phone call from the president, who appealed to the Missourian's sense of party loyalty. Amid a convention with many private negotiations between party power brokers, Truman agreed to run. Wallace, still commanding significant support from liberals, refused to drop out of the race, but Truman's support from Roosevelt and party bosses secured the nomination for the Missourian.[14]

Truman appeared to be a perfect fit for the New Deal coalition. He embodied many of the fractious coalition partners that held the Democratic Party together. The Missouri senator was a loyal but practical New Dealer. He was a border stater with Southern views on racial issues, but gradually moved toward support for black civil rights during his political career. A protégé of Kansas City's Democratic boss Tom Pendergast, Truman was the product of big-city machine politics, yet he steered clear of official misconduct. Indeed, the Senate committee led by Truman was credited with rooting out wartime graft and waste in defense contracts. Organized labor supported him for the vice presidential nomination, but then cooled on him early in his presidency. As with other coalition partners, Truman would have to win back labor's support for the 1948 campaign.[15]

As the vice presidency was still an office of limited stature, Roosevelt did not deem it important to inform Truman of the atomic bomb project. Distance between presidents and vice presidents remained common. Roosevelt respected his future successor, but the two men were not close on personal or professional levels.[16] Truman's pathway to the heir apparent presidency did not come by way of close association with his predecessor, as had been the case with Madison and Van Buren. Nor was he a national hero, as Grant was. The new president worked his way up the Democratic ladder, and reluctantly made himself available to national power brokers positioning their party for a post-Roosevelt political landscape. Critics of Truman lamented his mediocrity and simplicity, in contrast to Roosevelt's rhetorical panache and towering political influence. Skeptics would say, "We're just mild about Harry."[17]

### Forging Ahead: The 21 Point Plan and the Fair Deal

In the heir apparent role, Truman deployed all three approaches in the domestic policy arena. First, he made a robust defense of his predecessor's policies throughout his tenure. Even under several years of low job approval ratings and strong Conservative Coalition opposition in Congress, Truman continued to advocate for New Deal prescriptions to social and economic problems.[18] The 1948 presidential campaign was a venue for Truman to make these arguments. Playing an ultimately unsuccessful defense, Truman in his stand against the Taft-Hartley Act affirmed his regime's principles on the rights of organized labor. Second, Truman embraced the expansion approach by hitching New Deal principles to his 21 Point Plan and Fair Deal agenda. These policy proposals built off of existing New Deal programs and agencies. Efforts to chart newer commitments to housing found success with Congress, while universal health care and civil rights succumbed to congressional opposition. Third, in the corrective stance, Truman was tasked with revising his predecessor's wartime policies. Like Van Buren and Grant, Truman had to address temporary policy measures that were now outdated. Truman performed this task, not as a repudiation of Roosevelt's record but to retool the federal government away from a temporary wartime footing. Since this was a disruptive process and the international landscape remained tenuous, Truman urged a cautious approach to reconversion.

Roosevelt's annual message in 1944 called for an ambitious commitment to domestic social welfare once military victory was achieved overseas. He asserted that all citizens enjoyed basic rights to a job, a decent standard of living, decent housing, health care, and education. Roosevelt framed these commitments as part of a "second Bill of Rights under which a new basis of security and prosperity can be established for all regardless of station, race, or creed."[19] Even amid a world war, Roosevelt reminded Congress and the nation that Depression-era commitments to economic security should not waver, and that much work remained to be done.

The new president envisioned a domestic agenda that affirmed these principles. Only a few days after the formal Japanese surrender, Truman addressed Congress. Enjoying very high job approval ratings, Truman proposed a 21 point agenda for the postwar domestic order.[20] Numerous proposals built off of the social welfare and regulatory framework of the New Deal, revealing an aggressive effort to engage in the expansion approach. Other measures were aimed at improving administrative efficiency and facilitating an orderly transition away from an economy based upon total war. Truman's plans were ambitious, but the results he achieved were more modest.

Proposals included a higher minimum wage, which should cover more occupations. Unemployment insurance benefits should be expanded, but public policy should aim for an active governmental commitment to full employment. "The objectives for our domestic economy which we seek in our long-range plans were summarized by the late President Franklin D. Roosevelt over a year and a half ago in the form of an economic bill of rights. Let us make the attainment of those rights the essence of postwar American economic life," Truman asserted.[21] Accordingly, public works projects should be expanded. Government should actively assist small businesses and farmers. Veterans' benefits should be enhanced. The housing shortage should be addressed through a large federal investment and commitment. The pay scale for federal employees should be revised and made more attractive to prospective workers.

Other proposals were frank acknowledgments of the need to conduct the postwar transition with cautious speed. Here Truman engaged in a slow corrective approach, calling for a renewal of some federal war powers over the economy, and warning that wartime agencies should be wound down by way of an orderly process and without haste. Military demobilization would also have to be carried out responsibly in light of America's new international responsibilities. Voluntary enlistments should be encouraged and eligibility expanded, while the draft must continue to maintain military personnel quotas. Some tax reduction could be enacted, but as Truman noted, "a total war effort cannot be liquidated overnight."[22] Truman's corrective approach here was not a repudiation of his predecessor, but rather a careful effort to steer his governing regime away from the emergency footing of World War II.

Roosevelt's adversaries in Congress had a stronger hand by the time Truman reached the White House. As early as Roosevelt's second term, a coalition of Republicans and Southern Democrats was often able to collaborate in opposition to New Deal legislation. This Conservative Coalition, as it was called, frequently succeeded at defeating or watering down social welfare and regulatory proposals from Democratic presidents from Roosevelt through Jimmy Carter.[23] Worried that larger federal commitments in economic and social welfare arenas would set precedents for new civil rights legislation, Southern Democrats became more cautious about Roosevelt's and Truman's initiatives, if they did not outright oppose them. The Republican capture of Congress in the 1946 congressional elections only further darkened Truman's legislative prospects.

Unemployment insurance expansion was not enacted. Nor did Congress immediately move on his other social welfare proposals. Truman, however, was not left empty-handed, for his administrative reorganization measures were passed. A six-month extension on wartime price controls was enacted. Taxes were also reduced, though to a somewhat greater extent than Truman had requested.[24] In 1946, elements of Truman's proposals found their way into legislation that was enacted. For example, most federal workers got a 14% pay raise with passage of the Federal Employees Pay Act.[25] There was legislation to build hospitals and aid the mentally ill.[26] Amendments to the Social Security Act also ensured that veterans' dependents could qualify for survivor benefits.[27] Although it came without appropriations to directly create jobs, passage of the Employment Act made full employment the official policy goal of the federal government. The legislation included new presidential responsibilities to monitor the economy and consult with the Council of Economic Advisors.[28]

After his election to a full term, Truman employed the expansion approach to advocate for an enhanced social welfare and regulatory state. Calling his overarching agenda the Fair Deal, Truman proposed new initiatives in his annual message in 1949. The Fair Deal included measures to curtail inflation, raise the minimum wage, promote full employment, and enhance rural electrification and housing legislation. In addition, the president advocated an expanded Social Security program, as well as "a system of prepaid medical insurance which will enable every American to afford good medical care." Truman would be the first in a long list of mostly Democratic presidents to call for a national commitment to universal health insurance. To pay for it all, and to hold down inflation, Truman bluntly called for tax increases on individuals, estates, and corporations.[29]

Refusing to weaken the National Labor Relations Act, Truman attempted to practice the continuity approach by vetoing the Taft-Hartley Act. Congress overrode him in June 1947. Facing long odds, Truman then called upon Congress to repeal the law. Posing a major challenge to organized labor's continued growth, the law further regulated union activities, outlawed the closed shop, and permitted individual states to create "right to work" laws. The Taft-Hartley Act became an organizing issue around Truman's electoral campaign in 1948, rallying the labor community back to his cause. Not since Andrew Jackson's National Bank veto of 1832 had a president so skillfully used a veto as a means by which to galvanize his political base of supporters. In his veto of the Taft-Hartley Act, Truman struck a flexible tone concerning action against abusive activity by labor unions, but stood stoutly against fundamentally weakening trade unions. Indeed, he saw trade unions as healthy for democracy itself: "One of the major lessons of recent world history is that free and vital trade unions are a strong bulwark against the growth of totalitarian movements. We must, therefore, be everlastingly alert that in striking at union abuses we do not destroy the contribution which unions make to our democratic strength."[30]

Once again, Truman's ambitions eclipsed his results with Congress. The Conservative Coalition continued to wield large influence and block the core of the Fair Deal program. National health insurance was brushed aside, the Taft-Hartley Act remained fully intact, and Truman's visions of a greatly expanded New Deal welfare state were scaled back. A minimum wage increase was enacted, but the most significant legislation to emerge from Congress was the Housing Act. The bipartisan measure increased public housing commitments, provided aid to communities for slum clearance, and enhanced the roles of the Federal Housing Administration, an agency created during the New Deal.[31]

Truman's expansion approach to Social Security met with some success. Enhancements to Social Security were not trivial, but they also fell short of Truman's ambitions. With the Social Security Amendments of 1950, the administration solidified and further entrenched a key New Deal achievement, as the program became more generous and universal. Higher payroll taxes were phased in and overall benefits were increased by 77%. Millions of previously excluded workers from a variety of occupations would now be brought under coverage. Approximately 10 million additional people would now partake in Social Security, laying the groundwork for its constituent base to grow.[32]

If Truman's proposals fell short of his ambitions, the Fair Deal did establish a link between the New Deal and subsequent Democratic presidents. The founding principles and institutional infrastructure of the New Deal would be building blocks for subsequent endeavors to enhance commitments to social justice. Seeking to reach constituencies and social problems left behind by the New Deal, Truman, Kennedy, Lyndon Johnson, and Carter all envisioned their own policy contributions. Unlike his Democratic successors, Truman had to govern in Roosevelt's immediate aftermath, alongside a revitalized Republican opposition. Truman's ambitions in the domestic arena left little room to go far beyond established New Deal formulas. When he attempted to do so, there were political consequences.

Prior to Truman's presidency, the New Deal regime had only existed in the context of crisis: the worst economic depression in American history, followed by the biggest war in human history. Truman presided over a government that was tasked with maintaining prosperity and a rising middle class, as well as protecting millions of new veterans, and that had all the responsibilities of superpower leadership in the world. Liberal critics of the New Deal, however, argued that the New Deal's general omission of civil rights constituted a major deficiency in an overarching agenda ostensibly devoted to social justice.[33] Truman took the first noteworthy steps toward addressing this problem.

## A New Deal for the Civil Rights Agenda

Included among Truman's Fair Deal proposals were measures to legislatively address civil rights. A presidentially chartered commission submitted a series of recommendations in October 1947. Their report, *To Secure These Rights*, advocated a federal response to lynching and unpunished violence against blacks. Other recommendations included elimination of the poll tax, voting rights legislation, integration of the federal workforce and the military, and an end to discrimination in public accommodations and government services (at state, local, and federal levels). The federal government, the report said, should erect permanent institutions to regularly protect civil rights.[34] In contrast, Roosevelt Administration commitments to civil rights were not institutionalized throughout the federal government and policies were irregularly enforced.

In a special message to Congress on February 2, 1948, Truman affirmed his support for the central principles in the commission's report. He implored Congress to act on civil rights legislation. With an election looming and in response to white Southern denunciations, Truman proclaimed just one month later that he would deprioritize his civil rights agenda during the 1948–1949 congressional session.[35] Executive action was another matter entirely. Two executive orders were issued on July 26, 1948, both concerning discriminatory policies under the direct authority of the federal government. Executive Order 9980 aimed at integrating the federal government's workforce, backed by a Fair Employment Board to enforce the directive. Executive Order 9981 aimed at integrating the armed forces. Both policies brought about integration gradually, and not without setbacks along the way. Southern Democrats were outraged, but Truman secured the black vote for the upcoming election.[36] In addition, shortly after passage of the Housing Act, the administration disqualified new properties from FHA funds if owners practiced racial discrimination.[37] In the courtroom, the Truman

Administration assisted in the civil rights cause by supporting lawsuits challenging Jim Crow policies. The Justice Department filed pro-desegregation amicus briefs in Supreme Court cases concerning university systems, rail travel, and racially discriminatory property covenants.[38] Jim Crow at state and local levels remained robust, but Truman had set the federal government on a trajectory away from federally sanctioned segregation.

"The government has still other opportunities—to help raise the standard of living of our citizens. These opportunities lie in the fields of social security, health, education, housing, and civil rights," Truman told Congress at his annual message in 1949.[39] After his victorious election in November, Truman once again asked Congress to pass the same civil rights legislation it had spurned in 1948. Now Truman packaged civil rights with his Fair Deal proposals. A far cry from Roosevelt's occasional and sparsely enforced commitments to ending discrimination, Truman was the first president to hitch the cause of civil rights to a broader social welfare agenda. Truman's program would not only build off of the institutions, policies, and principles of his predecessor's agenda, but also make the machinery of government fairer to some of the Americans left behind by the New Deal. Subsequent Democratic presidents, most notably Johnson, followed Truman's lead by fusing civil rights with broader commitments to economic security, upward mobility, and combating the root causes of poverty.

Truman practiced the expansionist approach on the civil rights issue, but major legislation on this front died once again during his second term. Similar to Grant, Truman faced defeat on civil rights, and his vigor in pressing the issue with Congress waned in the final years of his presidency. Never straying from his public position in opposition to segregation, Truman started the process of bringing the principles of the civil rights agenda closer to the New Deal regime's commitments to social justice. Discrimination in employment, military service, housing, and education all produced economic consequences for black Americans. Addressing the graduates of predominantly black Howard University in June 1952, Truman said, "Some of us are denied opportunity for economic reasons.

Others are denied opportunity because of racial prejudice and discrimination. I want to see things worked out so that everyone who is capable of it receives a good education."[40] If civil rights were not yet a top priority of the New Deal regime, it was no longer treated as a trivial afterthought.

### Custodian of the New World Order

Reconversion on the home front was bound to be every bit as unpredictable and disruptive as the task of transitioning American foreign policy into a postwar world order. While the United States emerged from the war with a superpower status, how that power was to be deployed left Truman with considerably more options than his domestic agenda yielded. As the presidency has always provided more leeway for independent action in foreign affairs, as compared to domestic matters, Truman enjoyed greater opportunities—and risks—to chart a course that would distinguish himself from his predecessor. The new president pivoted from America's postwar standing to create a proactive, internationalist foreign policy that was backed by military strength. Similar to George H. W. Bush at the end of the Cold War, Truman was tasked with crafting a foreign policy in the aftermath of a transformative presidency that had produced major changes to international balances of power. This phenomenon is not unique in American presidential history, but there are additional risks when both presidents share the same political party and principles.

Truman practiced a foreign policy that mostly employed the expansion approach to heir apparent leadership. While Truman expanded upon Roosevelt's internationalist commitments, he did move in a corrective direction by stepping away from the wartime alliance with the Soviet Union. A Cold War foreign policy evolved quickly. Stopping the spread of communism could be easily adapted to the principles that had undergirded American participation in the war. To a greater degree than Roosevelt, Truman was distrustful of Soviet motives, but cautiously optimistic about a peaceful coexistence.[41] Within two years of the war's end, Soviet actions, as well as the counsel of his own advisors, convinced Truman that the United States had a duty to stand against the Soviets' expanding influence.[42] In addition, the Red Scare was already spreading into domestic politics. Unlike many politicians of his time, Truman viewed the communist threat on the home front as overblown, but he did institute a loyalty program for federal employees. As early as the 1946 congressional elections, Republicans began attacking Democrats as soft on communism, a campaign tactic the GOP would use for the next forty years.[43]

The first major move toward a comprehensive and enduring postwar foreign policy was the formation of the so-called Truman Doctrine in response to the Greek civil war. Communist rebels threatened to topple the Greek regime and subject another Eastern European nation to Soviet influence. In addition, the Soviets wanted joint control of Turkish waterways. Undersecretary of State Dean Acheson warned of the creeping influence of the Soviets into these two countries and beyond. In short, Acheson was arguing a domino theory: the notion that a communist takeover in one nation would create the conditions for a similar outcome in a neighboring nation.[44]

Great Britain, the previous benefactor of these two countries, was financially unable to continue aid. On March 12, 1947, Truman appeared before Congress to ask for $400 million in aid to Greece and Turkey. Truman told Congress that Greece was "threatened by the terrorist activities of several thousand armed men, led by Communists, who defy the government's authority at a number of points, particularly along the northern boundaries." Toward the end of the speech, he confidently embraced a proactive American stance in the new world order: "The free peoples of the world look to us for support in maintaining their freedoms."[45] With bipartisan support, the appropriation quickly passed Congress.[46]

Employing the expansion approach, Truman built from Roosevelt's commitments and followed his predecessor's lead in embracing a robust and proactive role for the United States on the international stage. Both presidents governed in a tenuous and fluid international environment. Roosevelt's task was to completely defeat Nazism, fascism, and Imperial Japan. First, Truman had to finish these unfinished goals. Next, his longer-term task was to maintain stability and balances of power in a bipolar world. Enactment of the Truman Doctrine steered the United States toward a stance of containment, a principle that underlay actions ranging from the Berlin Airlift to American participation in the Korean War. American aid would be sent to nations for the purpose of pushing back against the expansion of communism and Soviet-supported movements. The United States would not, however, seek the active overthrow of communist states. Foreign policy would be largely shaped through the prism of maintaining American strength vis-à-vis the Soviet Union. What was now called the Cold War would dictate alliances with other nations, foreign aid appropriations, defense policy, and even some domestic policies.[47]

Also part of Truman's expansion approach was the European Recovery Program. The aid package, popularly known as the Marshall Plan, aimed at revitalizing the European infrastructure and economy. While all European nations were invited to participate, Eastern Bloc nations under Soviet influence chose not to do so. By promoting economic cooperation within Europe, as well as generating optimism within participating countries, Truman saw the Marshall Plan as an antidote against the conditions that would allow communism to spread. The Soviet Union, Truman asserted, was "interested only in their own plans and were coldly determined to exploit the helpless condition of Europe to further Communism rather than cooperate with the rest of the world."[48] At a cost of over $13 billion, the plan was given bipartisan approval in Congress and signed into law on April 3, 1948.[49] The administration would proactively use foreign aid to strengthen economic alliances with noncommunist European nations.

Under Harry Truman, the president's role as chief administrator of national security institutions grew in concert with the Cold War. The expansion of commitments is likely to result in administrative growth, reorganization, and redirection. The administration's governmental reorganization reflected the demands of the new world order. The large national defense establishment was consolidated. Priorities included major peacetime commitments to military strength, intelligence gathering, and round-the-clock monitoring of national security threats. Postwar demobilization was to be redirected toward a policy of containment, collective security agreements with allies, and vigilant military preparedness. A new conscription law was enacted in June 1948. The National Security Act of 1947 consolidated the nation's previously diffused armed forces into a single Department of Defense. The law also gave birth to the Central Intelligence Agency and the National Security Council, both of which would regularly report to the president.[50] In war or peace, Truman and his successors would preside over a very significant defense and national security establishment. The president was still the final arbiter on the big decisions, but he would now be surrounded by a permanent corps of professional specialists in the national security arena. In its advisory role, the National Security Council produced a lengthy report in April 1950 calling for containment to be backed by military superiority. The report, known as NSC-68, recommended higher defense budgets, more sophisticated intelligence gathering, and a sustained campaign to undermine the Soviet system. Truman gave his approval to NSC-68 later that fall.[51]

*The Election of 1948: An Inch Wide and a Mile Deep*

In most of his first term as president, Truman had a difficult enough time maintaining the New Deal coalition in the absence of the galvanizing crises Roosevelt governed under. Truman's support from organized labor was soft amid a proliferation of postwar strikes, all of which irritated the new president. Union leaders resented Truman's proposal to conscript striking railroad workers into the military.[52] Liberal groups like Americans for Democratic Action were lukewarm at best toward the president. He also had not yet earned the support of black voters, as Truman had not previously been known as an ally of the civil rights cause.[53] As Truman made ever more overtures in favor of black civil rights, Southern Democrats grew more restive and hostile. Other Democrats were aggravated by Truman's generally hawkish foreign policy and the major defense commitments it required. Some Democrats openly advocated dumping Truman and drafting General Dwight Eisenhower as the party's presidential candidate.[54]

In addition to the simmering tensions within the New Deal coalition, Truman faced a resurgent Republican opposition. Republicans had scored well in the congressional elections of 1938 and 1942 under Roosevelt, but not enough to put them in the majority. Congressional elections in 1946 produced sweeping victories for Republicans, propelling the party into control of both chambers of Congress for the first time since 1930. Even before civil rights emerged as a major issue of contention, the New Deal coalition was showing signs of lost vigor amid postwar anxieties and a post-Roosevelt leadership vacuum.

As Truman positioned himself for the campaign in 1948, he set about the task of holding the New Deal coalition together, albeit with a few bits and pieces falling off the wagon along the way. The Democratic National Convention in July was badly divided. Furious over Truman's overtures toward civil rights, as well as the party's civil rights platform plank, four Southern state delegations marched out of the convention hall.[55] Democrats from these four states led the drive behind the States' Rights candidacy of South Carolina Governor Strom Thurmond. The splinter party was organized around the single issue of support for segregation. The Dixiecrats, as they were also known, did not compete outside of the South and the border states. Meanwhile, dissatisfied liberals rallied to the Progressive Party candidacy of Henry Wallace, the former vice president who had also been dismissed from Truman's cabinet. Wallace called for speedier action on civil rights and a conciliatory relationship with the Soviet Union. Truman denounced the insurgent party as consisting of "crackpots" and "communists."[56]

The campaign became Truman's venue to defend the legacy of the New Deal, now a decade and a half long, and charge by implication that Republicans sought to dismantle it.[57] In his convention acceptance address, Truman chastised the Republican Congress for its inaction. Then he announced that he would be calling Congress into a special session, challenging Republicans to pass laws to halt rising prices, to meet the housing crisis—which they are saying they are for in their platform. At the same time I shall ask them to act upon other vitally needed measures such as aid to education, which they say they are for; a national health program; civil rights legislation, which they say they are for; an increase in the minimum wage, which I doubt very much they are for; extension of the social security coverage and increased benefits, which they say they are for; funds for projects needed in our program to provide public power and cheap electricity.[58]

Congress did just what Truman expected. The special session was completely unproductive, and Truman hit the road in full denunciation of the "do-nothing Congress." In a level of personal campaigning that was unprecedented for an incumbent president (over 21,000 miles and 275 speeches),[59] Truman barnstormed the nation, making harsh attacks upon the opposition party. Often campaigning by whistle-stop, Truman became a crowd favorite. In contrast to the aristocratic tinge of Roosevelt's rhetoric, Truman's style was blunt, flat-accented, and even angry at times. Democrats waved their own bloody shirt from the past, reminding voters of Hoover and the Depression, and asserting that Republicans' real goal was the total repeal of the New Deal. As Truman told the delegates to the Democratic National Convention:

In 1932 we were attacking the citadel of special privilege and greed. We were fighting to drive the money changers from the temple. Today, in 1948, we are now the defenders of the stronghold of democracy and of equal opportunity, the haven of the ordinary people of this land and not of the favored classes or the powerful few. The battle cry is just the same now as it was in 1932.[60]

New York Governor Thomas Dewey, the Republican nominee, ran a risk-averse campaign, for public opinion polls showed him with a very comfortable lead. Thurmond never attracted significant support outside of the four states controlled by Dixiecrats. Truman's civil rights initiatives were not popular among white Southerners, but he also did not prioritize these policies to the high degree that would later come from Lyndon Johnson. A cautious approach would enable Truman to hold the support of all but the most adamantly segregationist Southern states, at least for this election. As for Wallace, the support he was expecting from union workers, liberals, and black voters evaporated by Election Day. The ADA endorsed Truman and frequently criticized Wallace as a spoiler candidate who was soft on communism. The Taft-Hartley veto helped to rally the labor community behind Truman, while civil rights leaders also endorsed the president.[61] Truman did more than maintain black voter loyalty to Democratic candidates. He actually brought these voters into the party in greater numbers. Surpassing Roosevelt's success with blacks, Truman won an estimated 77% of their votes. Surveys also revealed that a majority of blacks now identified with the Democratic Party, in contrast to the two-party parity that existed during the Roosevelt years.[62]

While Truman's victory in 1948 was smaller than any of Roosevelt's four electoral victories, he successfully maintained the New Deal coalition, sans some of the more ideologically extreme elements. In the popular vote, Truman fell just short of a majority, winning 49.55%. In the Electoral College, Truman won 303 votes. Both of these numbers were lower than the victorious totals Roosevelt earned in his four elections. Dewey won just over 45% of the popular vote and 189 electoral votes, the latter number representing a sizable improvement for Republicans over the previous four presidential elections. All of the Northeastern states voted for Dewey, save for Massachusetts and Rhode Island. The Wallace vote was insignificant at a national level, but the high total he won in New York may have helped to swing that state to Dewey. Dewey also showed strength in the Great Plains states, a region Democrats would very rarely carry in subsequent presidential elections. Save for Michigan and Indiana, the Midwest was solidly for the president, while the West was almost entirely pro-Truman.

An argument could be made that Truman's victory was an inch wide, but a mile deep, as his coattails seemed larger than his own victory. Democrats recaptured Congress, which Truman openly targeted in his campaign. Given the modesty of the Truman victory, Democratic congressional gains were astonishing: 75 seats in the House and nine in the Senate.[63] On the one hand, the election's outcome revealed the New Deal regime's staying power in spite of Roosevelt's absence, a resurgent Republican Party, and Democratic divisions. On the other hand, while Truman prevailed, the Wallace and Thurmond defections were a harbinger of future problems within the New Deal coalition.

As heir apparent, Truman charted important new courses of his own that would endure beyond his own presidency. He continued and expanded the New Deal Democratic commitments to social welfare. He also nudged the New Deal regime toward a commitment to civil rights, setting the table for Kennedy and Johnson to further fuse the cause of racial equality to economic justice. Kennedy and Johnson also followed Truman's generally hawkish Cold War foreign policy. There were, however, long-term political costs to these policy choices. By the late 1960s, Democrats were bitterly divided over the war in Vietnam, as well as the fundamental principles that shaped American foreign policy. Civil rights, as well as any other issue that could be easily conflated with race, continued to wear down white Southern support for the national Democratic Party. By the late 1960s, these racial anxieties became more of a national dilemma for Democrats, and not just an exclusively Southern problem.

## TRUMAN'S MODERN PRESIDENCY AND HARDER TIMES FOR NEW DEAL DEMOCRATS

There would be no dramatic upset favoring New Deal Democrats in 1952. The war in Korea had stalled and become unpopular.[64] In spite of administration policies, communist adversaries all over the world remained formidable. The administration was also beset by a bribery scandal in the Bureau of Internal Revenue.[65] After losing the New Hampshire Democratic primary, Truman opted not to run for a third term. Unable and unwilling to convincingly distance himself from Truman's policies, Democratic presidential nominee Adlai Stevenson was badly defeated by Republican Dwight Eisenhower. Even more remarkably, Republicans captured control of both chambers of Congress, giving them unified control of Pennsylvania Avenue for the first time in 22 years. Leaving office with his party in a weaker condition, as well as a resurgent opposition party, Truman followed the same heir apparent trajectory as Van Buren, Grant, and Bush.

Like other men in the heir apparent context, Truman struggled to create and implement new policies of his own. In the end, this president was able to achieve fairly substantial policy changes. First, however, Truman had to complete the unfinished business of his ideologically affiliated predecessor: winning the war. Next he had to address the consequences of a postwar international landscape. In this capacity, Truman had to act as the builder and custodian of a new world order, as well as the architect of an even more interventionist American foreign policy. Truman broadened the tenets of American liberalism to include an assertive anticommunism and a moderate commitment to civil rights. His Fair Deal agenda met with limited success in Congress, but it did build off of the policies and principles of the New Deal.

The office that Truman inherited in 1945 was significantly more powerful and influential than the presidencies that were bequeathed to his predecessors. The tools of the modern presidency began to appear during the terms of Theodore Roosevelt and Woodrow Wilson, and were fully in place by the time Truman entered the White House. Accordingly, the stakes of presidential success and failure also grew with the stature of the office. Presidents now enjoyed an ability to set a particular agenda of their own and creatively sell their vision to Congress and the American people. Aggressive marketing was now essential for presidents, including press conferences, radio addresses, and public speeches. The modern presidency of the twentieth century also enabled a chief executive to establish some distance between himself and his party, albeit with possible political costs. Truman took advantage of these characteristics of his office, even as some of his actions brought about serious divisions within the Democratic Party. Moving out of Roosevelt's shadow into a presidential identity of his own, Truman expanded the commitments of the New Deal regime while opening up points of vulnerability for Democrats in the future.

# 7

# GEORGE H. W. BUSH AND THE STALLING OF THE REAGAN REVOLUTION

## AMERICAN CONSERVATISM'S MOMENT

A backlash against liberalism had been building momentum since the late 1960s. By the late 1970s, the postwar economic boom was over and an energy crisis was contributing to inflation. Advancements in civil rights and gender equality produced a negative reaction from some of the same constituencies that supported New Deal Democrats. Cultural conservatives attracted support from Americans who were unnerved by the youth counterculture of the 1960s and early 1970s. Evangelical Christians and conservative Catholics mobilized politically in opposition to the growing secularization of American culture. Republicans embraced these activists, who denounced legalized abortion, homosexuality, pornography, casual drug use, and the blurring of traditional gender roles.

Failure to achieve victory in the Vietnam War generated skepticism about the muscular foreign policy both parties embraced during the first 20 years of the Cold War. Americans were being held hostage by Iranian revolutionaries in Tehran, the Soviet Union had invaded Afghanistan, and President Jimmy Carter rebuked the "inordinate fear of communism" that drove policymakers to support dictatorial governments around the world.[1] Defense budgets drifted downward after the American withdrawal from Vietnam.[2] Public distrust of the FBI and CIA mounted amid revelations of a long campaign of illegal surveillance and sabotage against American citizens, all in the name of stopping communist espionage.[3]

For many years, conventional wisdom held that a Republican as conservative as Ronald Reagan was not electable at a national level.[4] Reagan's primary challenge to President Gerald Ford came up slightly short in 1976. After defeating Ford later that fall, Jimmy Carter sought to steer his party away from the New Deal and Great Society liberalism of his Democratic predecessors. Carter's approach did little to mollify the many factions of his party and only further exposed the vulnerabilities of liberalism to energetic conservative activists. Reagan easily won the Republican presidential nomination in 1980, steering his party sharply to the right on foreign policy, economic policy, and social issues.

The election of 1980 was far more decisive than predicted.[5] Not only did Reagan win a landslide victory, but Republicans won control of the Senate for the first time in 26 years, and reduced the Democratic majority in the House. Republicans remained far behind in state governments and a plurality of voters continued to identify as Democrats.[6] While liberalism was on the defensive in the 1980s, Reagan embarked upon a revolutionary conservative agenda that met with mixed success. Congressional Democrats and their interest group allies mounted a mostly successful defense of social welfare programs throughout Reagan's presidency. Reagan did achieve success with passage of his major tax cut legislation in August 1981.[7] Administration initiatives to build up the armed forces were also generally successful in Congress.[8] Elsewhere, Reagan generally loosened the regulatory tentacles of the federal government, but he also faced robust opposition from environmentalist organizations who fought the administration in Congress, in the courts, and through the media.[9]

The new conservative Republican regime confidently embraced the business community as an essential ingredient to prosperity. Cumbersome government regulation stifled entrepreneurial initiative and bogged down workers and managers in a morass of unnecessary red tape. Most of the time, the judgment and wisdom of business leaders were to be trusted over the regulation-minded politicians and Washington bureaucrats. Labor unions undermined workers' individualism, creativity, and free choice. Taxes should be lowered across the board and simplified as a matter of moral principle: government does not have the right to take too much of the money that people earn. For Reagan Republicans this was also an economic theory. Through an approach known as supply-side economics, lower tax rates, especially for the wealthy, were thought to stimulate so much economic activity that higher revenues would actually pour into the federal treasury.

Social welfare programs dating back to the New Deal and beyond should be viewed with suspicion, for such policies were prone to waste, fraud, and abuse. An overly active social welfare state undermined individual initiative, a strong work ethic, and personal responsibility. The federal government should limit public assistance programs to only the most helpless and vulnerable. Policymakers should aim to balance the budget if at all possible, with an emphasis upon trimming twentieth-century social programs. Governments at state and local levels, as well as private charities, could better administer social services.

Reagan's conservative Republicans favored a more active federal government in the foreign and defense policy arenas. Their worldview unapologetically asserted American exceptionalism and the role of the United States as an agent for spreading freedom around the world. Capitalism was held to be the natural extension of democracy and free will. Military spending was to be dramatically increased so as to achieve an advantage over the Soviet Union. Then the United States could bargain with its adversary from a position of strength. Stepping somewhat away from the Cold War policy of containment, these conservatives called for active efforts to undermine communist states and pro-Soviet governments. Similar to Cold War policymakers in previous administrations, Reagan Republicans called for supporting anticommunist governments in the name of the higher objective of weakening the Soviet Union. The Carter Administration's emphasis on human rights was dismissed, except when this angle could be used to criticize the Soviets and their allies.

Government could also be an agent for upholding traditional standards of morality and acceptable rules of personal conduct. In the arena of social and cultural policies, Reagan Republicans disapproved of the proposed Equal Rights Amendment and disliked the emerging gay rights movement. They built an alliance with conservative Catholics and evangelicals and, accordingly, opposed legal abortion and called for stricter laws against pornography and drug use. Reagan and other social conservatives called for the restoration of organized prayer in public schools and denounced other rulings from the liberal Warren Supreme Court that had strengthened the wall of separation of church and state.

Reagan was overwhelmingly reelected to a second term, but there was no guarantee that the Republican ascendancy would continue. Democrats recaptured the Senate in 1986, and there were noteworthy Republican vulnerabilities for Democrats to exploit. Tensions with the Soviets were easing as Reagan pursued arms control agreements in his second term, but other events threatened to undermine Republican credibility in foreign affairs. Beginning in late 1986, the administration became mired in the Iran-Contra scandal, a complex affair involving the sale of arms to Iran in exchange for American hostages and the illegal diversion of profits to Nicaraguan Contra rebels. Administration policies in the Middle East and Central America remained controversial.

At home the economy was growing, producing low levels of unemployment and inflation. At the same time, disparities between rich and poor were growing as the nation began moving toward a postindustrial and service-oriented economy. Cities were becoming plagued by homelessness, and a growing Acquired Immune Deficiency Syndrome (AIDS) epidemic was causing considerable consternation. In spite of existing civil rights laws, racial tensions persisted and frequently spilled over into political debates over crime and welfare. Budget deficits threatened to spiral out of control, due to the unsustainable formula of tax cuts and high spending on defense and domestic programs.

## GEORGE H. W. BUSH: A LEADING FOLLOWER IN THE REAGAN REVOLUTION

George Bush was a loyal Republican all his life. His association with Reagan and the New Right conservatism of the 1980s was more tenuous. A native New Englander and the son of a US Senator, Bush served two terms as a Texas congressman, but came up short in two Senate campaigns. But Bush built a presidential résumé that gave him executive experience, as well as expertise in foreign affairs and national security. His quest for the 1980 presidential nomination was quickly overwhelmed by Reagan's momentum. Bush was not the favorite of social conservatives, as their issues did not define his political career. Nor was Bush's heart in supply-side economics: he mocked Reagan's economic plans as "voodoo economics" during the primary campaign.[10] Similar to Madison and Van Buren, Bush was an experienced party leader. During the trying years of the Watergate scandal, he chaired the Republican National Committee. In this assignment, Bush worked in more of a damage control position, as opposed to working on party-building activities. In contrast to Bush, Reagan was thin on foreign policy experience. Similar to Truman and other vice presidential selections, Bush was chosen to plug weaknesses in the Republican ticket and broaden electoral appeal.

### The Election of 1988: Winning One for the Gipper

The popularity of Ronald Reagan remained stronger than the overall appeal of his political party. His job approval ratings began recovering in 1988, as the debacle of the Iran-Contra affair regressed from the news.[11] Still, Democrats were confident and not all Republicans were immediately convinced that Bush deserved a free pass to the presidential nomination. Nor was the vice presidency the strongest stepping-stone. Hubert Humphrey was overwhelmed by the Johnson Administration's troubles with the Vietnam War and urban riots. Richard Nixon was unable to capitalize on Eisenhower's popularity. Numerous past vice presidents were not even considered presidential material in the first place. Van Buren was the last incumbent vice president to be promoted to the top job. As for Bush, he lacked his predecessor's charisma and doubts about his involvement in the Iran-Contra affair lingered. One influential magazine mused that the vice president was a "wimp."[12]

Reagan himself did not publicly take sides in the 1988 Republican primaries, abiding by what he called "an Eleventh Commandment" to "not speak ill of any fellow Republican."[13] Reagan maintained a good professional relationship with his vice president, but he was also respectful of the primary process that put the choice of party nominees in the hands of Republican voters, not party bosses. Other party factions and enterprising Republicans were to be respectfully given a fair hearing. Reagan lunched frequently with his vice president and Bush was especially active on foreign policy matters.[14] However, the Reagan-Bush relationship did not match the highly personal relationship and deep political alliance Jackson and Van Buren had formed over 150 years ago.

Bush recovered after losing the Iowa caucus and easily dispatched his party rivals, Senate Minority Leader Robert Dole and television evangelist Pat Robertson. Transitioning into the general election campaign, Bush faced a large gap in the polls against Democratic nominee Michael Dukakis, the governor of Massachusetts.[15] In two elections, Reagan had performed well with a sizable number of working-class Democrats.[16] However, these so-called Reagan Democrats were not yet sold on the Republican nominee. The selection of Dan Quayle for the vice presidential nomination pleased social conservatives, but invited ridicule elsewhere, amid allegations that the Indiana senator was inexperienced and lacking in intellect.[17] Reagan did offer an unequivocal endorsement of his vice president at the Republican National Convention, imploring Bush to "go out there and win one for the Gipper."[18]

Bush found his voice in the 1988 campaign by hitching himself to the tax policy of the Reagan Administration. The Republican nominee pledged to protect Reagan's sweeping tax cuts from the Democratic titans who controlled Capitol Hill. Implicitly suggesting that Democratic control of Congress was a given, Bush made one of the most famous campaign promises in American political history when he accepted the Republican nomination at the party convention:

> I'm the one who won't raise taxes. My opponent now says he'll raise them as a last resort, or a third resort. When a politician talks like that, you know that's one resort he'll be checking into. My opponent won't rule out raising taxes. But I will. The Congress will push me to raise taxes, and I'll say no, and they'll push, and I'll say no, and they'll push again, and I'll say to them, "Read my lips: no new taxes."[19]

Four years after Democratic presidential nominee Walter Mondale had embarrassingly promised to raise taxes at his nationally televised party convention acceptance address, Democrats remained vulnerable on this issue. Reagan's revolution was largely defined by dramatic reductions in federal income taxes. The tax issue was a potent political weapon for Republicans to flay Democrats as the party of big government and fiscal irresponsibility. Large budget deficits and intractable Democratic majorities in Congress may have made future tax cuts unlikely, but Bush could stake his claim to the Reagan legacy by pledging to be the loyal defender of his predecessor's signature economic policy. Nonetheless, the tax promise was bound to complicate the task of governing in an environment of large budget deficits, as Bush's future Office of Management and Budget Director Richard Darman had warned. Bush's political advisors, led by speechwriter Peggy Noonan and communications strategist Roger Ailes, insisted on making the pledge a centerpiece of Bush's campaign message.[20]

The vice president's successful campaign also included familiar Republican appeals to the usual menu of issues that established GOP dominance of presidential elections between 1968 and 1988:

law and order, patriotism, national security, and family values. The Democrats, by comparison, were accused of offering the same old discredited liberalism: soft on crime, weak on defense, vacillating foreign policy, and moral permissiveness. Bush's victories in the popular and electoral vote were impressive, but fell short of Reagan's 1984 landslide reelection. Polling 53.4% of the popular vote and 426 electoral votes, Bush carried 40 states, including a full sweep of the South and a strong showing in all other regions. The Reagan Democrats came back to the Republican candidate on Election Day, although in reduced numbers from 1984.[21] Coattails were nowhere to be found, as Democratic congressional majorities remained ironclad. Republicans actually lost three seats in the House and the party balance of power in the Senate was unchanged.[22] Bush, like Madison, Van Buren, Grant, and Truman before him, met the heir apparent's challenge of reassembling his predecessor's electoral coalition, albeit by a less impressive margin.

## REPORTING FOR POST-REAGAN CUSTODIAL DUTY

Valuing personal loyalty above and beyond loyalty to conservative doctrines, the new president asked for the resignations of Reagan appointees by Inauguration Day. Some Reagan appointees who had close ties to Bush, like James Baker, III, were asked to stay in the administration. Baker was installed as secretary of state. The nomination of former senator John Tower for secretary of defense was rejected when controversy arose due to his alleged alcoholism and womanizing. The younger and more active Bush committed to being a more hands-on president than Reagan, who had maintained a more delegation-centered approach.[23]

Revolutionary political action costs money, whether it comes in the form of war, new social programs, laws to protect civil rights, tax cuts, regulation, or deregulation. Bush and other heirs apparent found that prospects for continuing down this innovative path are likely to be limited by tighter budgets, policies that do not function as anticipated, and diminishing political will within the president's party. With some success and some failure, Bush would be more of a custodian and less of a revolutionary reformer. A custodian is responsible for being a caretaker, making repairs, and cleaning up messes. Unlike Reagan, as well as the other heirs apparent covered here, Bush was boxed in by a Congress fully controlled by the opposition party for his entire presidency. Democratic leaders had little appetite to cooperate in another round of activist conservative reforms. Bush found himself in the corrective leadership role very frequently, given the scarcity of allies he found among other domestic political actors. Warning against the costs of a return to New Deal/Great Society liberalism or new conservative tax cut plans, Bush proclaimed in his inauguration that "we have more will than wallet."[24]

### Cleaning Up the S & L Thrifts

Staring the new president in the face were the mounting costs of the Savings and Loan debacle. The deregulation-minded Reagan Administration had pushed through legislation to loosen federal rules upon S & L institutions (sometimes referred to as thrifts). Congressional support was bipartisan for the Garn-St. Germain Act of October 1982. Home mortgages had been the predominant arena of S & Ls, but the new rules would permit these institutions to diversify into commercial loans. In the absence of regulation, reckless and even criminal behavior followed. S & Ls began collapsing at an alarming rate. The cost of insuring depositors meant that taxpayers were on the hook for a growing amount of money that finally ballooned to several hundred billion dollars.[25]

The S & L crisis forced Bush into the corrective policy approach. Whether or not the Garn–St. Germain Act was the most important factor behind the S & L crisis, Bush now embraced a reorganization and enhancement of the regulatory machinery that supervised these institutions. The congressional response came in August 1989 with the Financial Institutions Reform, Recovery, and Enforcement Act. The legislation met most of Bush's objectives and stepped away from Reagan-era deregulation. However, the high cost of closing down the failed S & Ls and the bailout of depositors created additional budgetary pressures at a most inconvenient time.[26] Boxed in by a Democratic Congress with little interest in unconditionally cutting domestic social programs, a slowing economy, and budget deficits already at high levels, Bush's sacrosanct tax promise was in jeopardy.

### Yes, New Taxes

The famous "no new taxes" pledge was a campaign promise of continuity, but Bush's actions were a clear exercise in the corrective policy approach. From the beginning, signs were everywhere that Bush's tax promise would be hard to keep. The president and his economic team continued to publicly pledge their commitment to the promise of no new taxes throughout 1989, but by 1990, these assurances began to weaken. Complicating matters was a budgetary statute from the Reagan Administration, the Gramm-Rudman-Hollings Act. This bipartisan measure provided for a phased-in plan toward balancing the budget. Mandatory deficit reduction targets would have to be met to eliminate the deficit by 1993. Under this law, failure to meet the targets would trigger automatic and across-the-board spending cuts. Amid an environment of divided government on Pennsylvania Avenue, failure to reach a budget agreement by the statutory deadline would result in a shutdown of federal agencies, the furlough of many federal workers, and the suspension of all government activities deemed "nonessential."[27]

Bush gradually softened and eventually abandoned his tax promise throughout 1990, as crucial budget negotiations with congressional Democrats took place. Early in the year, Bush expressed an openness to methods of raising revenues that stopped short of higher income taxes. Federal taxes and fees upon consumers and voluntary users of products and services could be raised. Taxes on the purchase of airline tickets could be raised. Fees could be levied upon commodity transactions, and an existing temporary tax upon telephone usage could be made permanent.[28] As a bipartisan budget deal came together in September, Bush endorsed increased taxes on gasoline, a "broad-based energy tax; and a 10 percent tax on such luxury items as expensive automobiles, boats and electronic equipment."[29] Congressional Democrats demanded an increase in the top marginal income tax rate, while Bush advocated a capital gains tax cut.

As it became clear that Bush's tax promise was about to be broken, conservative opinion leaders rebelled. "Bush simply has no stomach for confrontation, and every day the budget process drags out, he paints himself further and further into a corner," the *National Review* lamented.[30] Rising stars in the Republican Party saw their opportunity to lead the antitax rebellion. Minority Whip Newt Gingrich led a faction of activist conservatives in the House who preferred confrontation over cooperation with the Democratic majority on Capitol Hill. In opposition to Bush and the congressional leaders of his party, Gingrich publicly denounced the budget deal. A majority of House Republicans voted against the package, and liberal Democrats grumbled over the reductions in domestic spending. The House rejected the agreement, and Bush would not agree to a continuing resolution to keep the government running past the statutory deadline to pass a budget. A short government shutdown followed.[31]

Meanwhile, Democrats in Congress were emboldened to challenge Republicans on the tax issue in ways that would have been more difficult under President Reagan. During the 1980s wealthy Americans saw their incomes and household wealth grow enormously, and they were also the biggest beneficiaries of Reagan's tax cuts.[32] For eight years, Democrats had tried to make an issue out of the economic fairness of Reagan's policies, but with little success. Reagan's economic agenda was new and revolutionary in the early 1980s, a popular reaction against almost two generations of liberal governance. After nine years of Republican stewardship of the budget and the economy, there was now a long policy record upon which their party's performance could be judged. Policy results were now more important than mere policy principles. By 1990, deficits were higher and public anxiety was on the rise as the economy sputtered toward recession. Bush skillfully used the tax issue to great populist effect in the campaign in 1988. In a governing environment, however, Bush was unable and unwilling to make populist appeals to the country on behalf of Reagan's economic principles.

Even Reagan himself had increased Social Security payroll taxes and closed several tax loopholes and shelters throughout his presidency.[33] He did not pay a political price for these compromises with congressional Democrats. As the builder of a new governing regime, Reagan enjoyed a flexibility with the application of principles into public policy. This flexibility eluded Reagan's successor, as Bush was elected to protect and defend his predecessor's policy achievements in the tax arena. For Bush, the abandonment of his campaign's defining promise meant that Republicans would give up political credibility, even if only temporarily, on an issue that was key to the ascendancy of Reagan and conservatism in the 1980s. The tax issue would be unavailable for Republicans to use in the next presidential campaign, even as Democrat Bill Clinton promised additional tax increases on the wealthy.

As a final budget deal came together, Bush did not put up much of a fight. The Omnibus Budget Reconciliation Act of 1990 contained the various excise tax increases Bush supported. His capital gains tax cut proposal was not included. Most notably, the package also raised top marginal income tax rates from 28% to 31%, leaving no doubt that the "no new taxes" pledge was officially broken.[34] Bush signed a budget deal that congressional Republicans opposed 25–19 in the Senate and 126–47 in the House.[35] Economic conservatives were furious, but the political damage was delayed as the nation's attention turned to a looming war in the Middle East.

### The Persian Gulf War: Bush's Hollow Triumph

As budget negotiations wore on, the military of Iraq invaded the neighboring nation of Kuwait on August 2, 1990, as a result of long-running disputes over oil and drilling. Under the Reagan Administration, Iraq had been a nominal ally. Iraqi leader Saddam Hussein was a brutal dictator, but American policymakers viewed his generally secular government as a counterweight to the Islamic theocracy of

Iran. During the eight-year Iran-Iraq war, a closer relationship with Iraq was established. Formal diplomatic ties were instituted, along with a pipeline of economic and military aid. The Reagan Administration cleared the way for Iraq to receive agricultural commodity credits and intelligence information "while also permitting the sale of American-made arms to Baghdad." Aid continued into the Bush Administration.[36]

The extent to which American aid dangerously strengthened a future enemy of the United States is not a debate that will be taken up here. Circumstances demanded that administration policy promptly shift to a corrective approach in response to the invasion. Bush quickly condemned Iraq's actions and deployed American forces to Saudi Arabia to assume a defensive position. As Saudi Arabia was a major oil producer, an Iraqi invasion and takeover would rattle markets and dramatically shift the balance of power in the Middle East. An embargo was imposed to evict Iraq from Kuwait by way of economic pressure. While the United States committed the most military resources, an international coalition was mobilized against Iraq. Bush and Secretary Baker worked to assemble military, financial, and political support around the world, as well as United Nations authorization to engage in an offensive mission. To prepare for that possibility, the number of American troops deployed to Saudi Arabia escalated to over 500,000.[37]

The likelihood of a war was not in doubt by the winter. Nor was its outcome. On January 17, 1991, American-led coalition forces initiated Operation Desert Storm to eject Iraq from Kuwait. The mission was completed within a month and a half, resulting in an overwhelming victory and remarkably low coalition casualties. Hussein was allowed to stay in power, as the authorizing UN resolution did not give coalition forces the authority to depose the Iraqi dictator. In addition, Bush and his national security team had no appetite for turning a short and victorious military campaign into a war of occupation inside Iraq. Iraqi forces promptly proceeded to set Kuwaiti oil fields on fire as they were chased out of the country. Bush's rhetoric also implied that there would be American assistance in the event of an Iraqi uprising against Hussein, but no such help materialized. Kurdish and Shiite rebellions within Iraq were brutally repressed. In the short run, Bush paid little price for the postwar fallout. The United States was awash in patriotic fervor and Bush's job approval rating surged to 89%.[38]

For a nation not long removed from the turmoil of the Vietnam War, the Gulf War posed risks to Bush and Republicans. Republicans long enjoyed large public opinion advantages on issues relating to foreign policy and national security. On the other hand, patience remained thin for high American casualties, lengthy commitments, and expensive overseas military operations. Rather than try to overcome these post–Vietnam War phenomena, Bush confidently worked within their limitations. Bush minimized his political risks by constructing an international coalition, using overwhelming force, and refusing to extend the mission into new domains.[39] Although Congress held spirited debates over a resolution authorizing military force, the measure was approved with a respectable level of bipartisan support.[40] Antiwar demonstrations did take place throughout the nation, but failed to generate substantial political momentum. Republican unity was remarkable before and during the war, save for a small band of paleoconservatives, led by commentator and former Reagan communications director Patrick Buchanan.

In spite of the Cold War's end, Bush continued to share his predecessor's view that the United States should remain militarily strong and act assertively on the international stage in defense of American interests. The post–Cold War world order demanded different assessments of international situations, and Bush's actions in the Persian Gulf War utilized two approaches employed by heir apparent presidents. He corrected and reversed the embarrassing Reagan-Bush policy of supporting Saddam Hussein, but he also built off of and expanded upon Reagan's principles on foreign and defense policy. In the context of the Cold War, Reagan built up the military and steered the United States toward a more hawkish stance vis-à-vis the Soviet Union. The Bush Administration's approach suggested that even after the Cold War, American leadership, backed by military muscle, was necessary to vanquish new enemies that threatened international stability and American interests.

## *A New World Order—Again*

Bush was an active player in building a new world order and building up American institutions in response (mainly in the national security arena). Eastern European communist governments began rapidly collapsing in 1989, followed by the Soviet Union itself in 1991. Bush's most immediate task was not to build up institutions, but rather to manage the post–Cold War transition without overly hasty policy choices and political grandstanding. Vigilance was no less important in an increasingly multipolar world. Alliances and bases of power would now be more fluid, and old ethnoreligious hatreds threatened to erupt into violence. At home, conservatives claimed vindication for Reagan's hawkish polices. Liberals demanded a "peace dividend" from reduced defense budgets and a renewed emphasis on domestic ills.

Bush had little interest in pursuing a highly ideological or confrontational course of action. It is in the nature of politicians to claim credit for achievements and positive developments, but Bush refrained from gloating as the Berlin Wall was torn down and Germany reunified soon afterward. In this environment, Bush departed from the assertive Cold War rhetoric that defined much of Reagan's early presidency. The muscular rhetoric of Reagan vis-à-vis the Soviet Union was seldom to be found. In this respect, Bush's approach was a correction from his predecessor. In addition, while Bush welcomed the crumbling of the Eastern Bloc, he would not make the United States a partner in anticommunist movements or revolutions. If Reagan took American-Soviet relations beyond containment with a new assertiveness, Bush wound down the Cold War with modesty and a protective emphasis on the dangers that could come from power vacuums in ex-communist countries.

Reagan placed more emphasis upon diplomacy with the Soviets in his second term, and Bush followed this approach as president. Bush nurtured his relationship with Soviet leader Mikhail Gorbachev, a reformer who was open to the Soviets loosening their control over the Eastern Bloc. Gorbachev and Reagan had established good working relations during the latter's second term. Bush sought to expand and build off of that cooperative relationship. Good relations with Gorbachev could actually facilitate a smoother transition in Eastern Europe, especially if Soviet hard-liners remained marginalized. Some conservative Republicans expressed annoyance at the close relationship. Gorbachev's use of force to suppress Lithuania's secession from the Soviet Union did not generate a ferocious response from Bush. Bush responded to the cascade of seceding Soviet republics with caution. Conservatives mocked a speech Bush delivered on August 1, 1991, in Ukraine as "Chicken Kiev" for its allegedly tepid support for the secessionist movements. Nor did Bush respond to the failed Soviet coup with belligerent rhetoric or actions. As he managed the American exit from the Cold War, Bush adopted an approach toward the Soviet Union that expanded upon Reagan's second-term formulas, but with a softer rhetoric. By the time the Soviet Union dissolved at the end of 1991, Bush was having trouble getting political credit and Americans' attention was turning to the economy.[41]

Other loose ends from Reagan's Central American policies had to be addressed. Acting in a corrective stance, Bush redirected American policy concerning the Nicaraguan Contra rebels, who were fighting the leftist Sandinista government of that country. Congress had terminated Reagan's controversial policy of military aid to the Contras due to their poor human rights record. Bush and Baker chose not to continue pursuing military aid and instead secured a nonmilitary aid package from Congress in April 1989. The administration pushed for democratic elections and reforms in Nicaragua. While the aid package won large bipartisan approval, some conservatives denounced the new policy. "The hope of freedom is gone. The dark curtain of the Sandinista Gestapo has descended on Nicaragua," claimed the hawkish Congressman Duncan Hunter (R-CA).[42] Elections were indeed held in February 1990, resulting in the Sandinistas' defeat.

Panama presented another unsolved problem from the Reagan Administration. Bush would act according to the corrective approach by authorizing the removal of a troublesome former Reagan Administration ally. Dictator Manuel Noriega had established a long relationship with the CIA going back decades, and he had assisted the Reagan Administration in aiding the Contras. Noriega was also deeply involved in drug trafficking, a point of embarrassment for Reagan and Bush, as both of their administrations were ostensibly dedicated to fighting the illegal drug trade. Not until Reagan's second term did the United States begin distancing itself from Noriega. In May 1989 Noriega refused to honor elections that revealed his defeat, after which there was a violent crackdown on his political opponents. A Panamanian coup attempt in the fall did not receive strong support from the administration, making Bush look feckless. After a series of episodes where Noriega's forces assaulted a handful of American military officers, a furious Bush ordered an invasion to remove the dictator in December. In what was called Operation Just Cause, American forces promptly deposed Noriega and installed the democratically elected president of Panama. After a standoff of several days, Noriega surrendered and was transferred to American civilian authorities to face multiple criminal charges.[43]

### Kinder, Gentler Steps away from the Reagan Revolution

Common criticisms of Reagan's policies revolved around claims that the machinery of government was being steered away from protecting the vulnerable and assisting the less fortunate. Opponents charged that tax cuts, deregulation, reducing the social welfare state, and antiunion policies would only benefit the rich at the expense of the working class. Liberals openly worried that Reagan's conservative vision was nothing short of a declaration of war upon all of the twentieth century's advancements in civil rights, environmental protection, social welfare, and economic fairness.[44]

Reagan's charisma and communicative talents were valuable tools for him when critics attacked his policies. Additionally, even Reagan himself was unable or unwilling to always govern along the ideological lines demanded by his supporters. Lacking Reagan's personal attributes, but still commanding much public respect, Bush gingerly stepped away from revolutionary movement conservatism. This heir apparent would implicitly address some of the perceived flaws of his predecessor's policies and ideologies, while stopping short of a full-scale repudiation. Asserting that he wanted "a kinder, gentler nation," Bush implied that his presidency would prioritize the plight of the disadvantaged, revealing an openness to corrective approaches to some of Reagan's policies.[45] A retreat was sounded on various battlefronts of the Reagan Revolution. Bush's most noteworthy domestic policy achievements were not defining commitments of Reagan's conservative agenda. Negotiations with the solidly Democratic Congress produced legislation to expand the use of government to regulate industries, protect the environment, safeguard civil rights, and expand educational opportunities. These achievements marked a corrective policy course away from some of the perceived harsh edges of Reagan's conservatism.

Liberal Democrats would not get the "peace dividend" from the end of the Cold War that they had envisioned. While hardly repudiating Reagan's military buildup, Bush would allow reasonable trimmings to the Pentagon's budget in the aftermath of the Cold War. The budget deal in 1990 called for reductions in the defense budget. Bush and Secretary of Defense Richard Cheney also agreed to the politically thankless task of closing unnecessary military bases. Military bases were the source of thousands of jobs and fiercely protected by their respective members of Congress, but the process was carried out to its conclusion.[46]

In the arena of civil rights, Bush signed into law the Americans with Disabilities Act in July 1990. The law was "the most sweeping anti-discrimination measure to be approved since the Civil Rights Act of 1964."[47] The ADA barred employment discrimination and phased in requirements that public accommodations be accessible. The legislation commanded widespread bipartisan support in Congress, but Bush's allies in the business community grumbled about the costs of compliance and expressed fears of lawsuits.[48] Federal commitments to civil rights protections were also enhanced when

Bush signed the Civil Rights Act of 1991. The legislation clarified provisions in existing civil rights laws and provided new rights of due process for people bringing claims of employment discrimination.[49] The previous and more robust version of the bill was vetoed, however, with Bush claiming that the legislation would force businesses into adopting racial hiring quotas.[50]

The Bush Administration addressed other policies of concern to liberal activists, but not to their satisfaction. While the Reagan Administration was accused of neglecting the AIDS epidemic, the Bush Administration took more aggressive action. Funding for research and other AIDS-related programs was steadily, but not dramatically, increased.[51] Bush signed into law the Ryan White Care Act in August 1990, which opened up treatment for AIDS patients who did not already have adequate health care services.[52] However, Bush continued to be a greatly distrusted figure within the AIDS activist community, given his close ties to Reagan. While he made more money available to fight the disease, Bush was rebuked by members of the National Commission on AIDS for failing to use his office to publicly make fighting AIDS a national priority.[53]

Environmental protection was another arena where Reagan was accused of inaction, neglect, and preferential treatment of polluters. The Reagan Administration's Environmental Protection Agency was marred by scandals. Bush had a background in the oil industry and his promises to be the "environmental" president were widely ridiculed. Yet he prioritized a reauthorization of the Clean Air Act and cooperated with Congress to get it done. The new Clean Air Act was enacted in November 1990 and it enhanced the federal government's regulatory role. The new law called for stricter auto emission standards, tougher smog controls, promotion of cleaner gasoline, and new commitments to combating acid rain. Environmentalist organizations, who had long been skeptical of Bush, praised the president's actions.[54]

Ridicule was also directed toward Bush when he promised to be the "education" president. The Reagan Administration had openly called for the abolition of the federal Department of Education, believing that state and local governments should be the primary policy actors in this arena. Bush downplayed this stance and was not opposed to a national education strategy. Still, an administration proposal to reform education by emphasizing testing and higher standards went nowhere due to a lack of budgetary support.[55] However, some existing federal commitments dating back to Johnson's Great Society were expanded. Funding for Head Start was solidly increased, and eligibility for the Pell Grant college financial aid program was expanded to include more part-time students.[56]

Bush generally followed his predecessor's notably nonconservative footsteps when it came to immigration policy. Just as Reagan signed a fairly expansive amnesty for illegal immigrants in 1986, Bush cooperated with liberal Democratic Senator Edward Kennedy on comprehensive reform legislation in November 1990. Expanding upon commitments in the law from 1986, legal immigration numbers were increased, provisions were included to promote family unification, and extensions of time were given to some people still applying for amnesty. Another provision lifted the existing ban on homosexual immigrants.[57]

### The Election of 1992: Momentum Is a Stubborn Thing

The sky-high approval ratings Bush enjoyed after the Gulf War scared off a lot of top Democratic prospects from running for the 1992 presidential nomination. Job ratings of over 70% or 80% are unsustainable for any president given the many politically polarizing choices they must make on a regular basis. Presidents are also always bound to be the top targets of ambitious journalists, activist critics, and adversarial politicians. As party leaders, regime managers, and agenda setters, it is unreasonable for any president to expect to persistently maintain job approval ratings that transcend the nation's fundamental ideological and partisan divisions.

A major wakeup call for Republicans came in a special Pennsylvania US Senate election in November 1991. A vacant Senate seat from that state had been filled by way of the Democratic governor's appointment. The Democratic incumbent, Senator Harris Wofford, was expected to be little more than a temporary placeholder. The

Republican candidate in the special election was Richard Thornburgh, a former Pennsylvania governor and former Bush Administration attorney general. As expected, Thornburgh began the campaign with a wide lead in the polls, but Wofford drilled away at voters' anxieties on the economy and the growing problem of Americans without access to health care. In a stunning reversal revealing deep concerns about domestic issues, Wofford won the election with 55% of the vote.[58]

Bush, however, continued to be slow in getting his reelection campaign off the ground. Preoccupied by events in the Soviet Union and the aftermath of the Gulf War, Bush did not use 1991 to begin establishing the strategic themes that would define his reelection campaign, much less a second term. Bush had always said that he was not much interested in what he mocked as "the vision thing,"[59] preferring to focus on steady administration, pragmatic compromises, and stability in world affairs. Meanwhile, Democrats asserted that Bush's heavy emphasis on foreign affairs was evidence that he had little interest in domestic issues.[60]

By early 1992, not only were Democrats confident, but Bush was being challenged on his Republican right flank by Pat Buchanan. A charismatic orator because of his past profession as a speechwriter, Buchanan loudly denounced Bush's record on all fronts. Buchanan carried the flag for conservatives who regarded the tax increase as a betrayal and attacked Bush for his tepid support of social conservative causes. In particular, Bush was accused of allowing federal funding for pornography by way of the National Endowment for the Arts. Buchanan's appeals also served as a sort of throwback to the isolationism and protectionism some Republicans embraced in the early twentieth century. In this respect, Buchanan represented a divergence from Reagan Republican orthodoxy. Denouncing Bush's internationalism and free trade policies, Buchanan pledged to "put America first." In the New Hampshire Republican primary, Buchanan embarrassed Bush by taking more than 37% of the vote. In other states (Georgia, Colorado, Maryland, Florida, and Rhode Island), Buchanan embarrassed Bush again by taking 30% or more of the Republican primary vote. Although he failed to win a single primary or caucus with his lightly funded campaign, Buchanan had exposed Bush's vulnerabilities within the Republican base.[61]

Circumstances in 1992 seemed to point to a certain Democratic victory, but after losing five out of the last six presidential elections, the party was taking nothing for granted. Some Democratic office holders and political consultants had been working since the mid-1980s to remedy their party's inherent disadvantages in national elections. The probusiness Democratic Leadership Council aimed to steer the party toward centrist economic and social welfare policies. The DLC frowned upon the interest group liberalism and identity politics that defined the party in the 1960s and 1970s. The Democrats' emphasis on retooling their message and ideas followed the pattern of previous parties who stood in opposition to an heir apparent president.

The Democratic nominee, Arkansas Governor Bill Clinton, was a product of the DLC. His centrist policy stances and populist appeal were advantageous for Democrats, but his personal background presented numerous problems. Clinton was beset by allegations of dodging the draft during the Vietnam War, womanizing, and smoking marijuana (he claimed he "didn't inhale"). While the Bush campaign did not explicitly raise the matter of infidelity, Clinton's peccadilloes and evasive explanations were folded into a collective issue concerning the governor's character.[62] Here Republicans could deploy their old campaign playbook, depicting the Democrats as the party of permissiveness and hostility to the military.

Elsewhere, Bush was challenged by an independent candidate who threatened the Republican electoral coalition. Ross Perot, a Texas billionaire, was the product of a nationwide ballot petition drive. His signature issue was the budget deficit, a continued area of vulnerability for Reagan Republicans and their claims of fiscal responsibility. Most of Perot's attacks during the campaign targeted Bush, supplementing Clinton's criticisms with a centrist-to-conservative critique of the president's handling of the budget and the economy. Bush's reelection prospects would now be further undermined by a candidate who did not carry the liabilities of the Democratic Party and the political left. Perot did not handle media scrutiny very well, but he attracted rave reviews with his thirty-minute televised informercials on public policy issues and performed well in televised debates.[63]

The Bush campaign was forced to spend the spring and summer rallying the Republican base. As Clinton's campaign worked to address their candidate's image problems, the Bush team dug themselves into a deeper hole. Vice President Quayle made a speech denouncing Murphy Brown, the titular character in a television sitcom about a news anchor who chose to have a baby out of wedlock. Quayle sought to initiate a national debate about fatherhood and family values, but the speech also attracted much ridicule. At the party convention, Pat Buchanan stole the show with a divisive prime-time speech that celebrated Republican cultural conservatism and excoriated Bill and Hillary Clinton's values.[64]

Matters improved little during the fall campaign, as Bush's belated attempts to position himself as a reformer were unconvincing. Clinton's lead in the polls narrowed somewhat, but no major reversal of momentum took place. At one televised town hall debate, Bush was caught looking at his watch and he appeared confused by a woman's question about the economy. Bush's efforts to claim credit for the end of the Cold War fell flat from an electorate preoccupied with the economy and other domestic issues. A hastily thrown together grab bag of old administration policy proposals (called the "Agenda for an American Renewal") did nothing to alter the fundamentals of the campaign. Bush's efforts to duplicate Truman in 1948 by loudly blaming Congress for inaction went nowhere. Even the robust economic growth rates in the third and fourth quarters of 1992 came too late to save the president from defeat.[65]

Clinton won 370 electoral votes, showing wide strength in all regions. Bush won 168 electoral votes, performing best in the South and the Great Plains states. Ross Perot carried no states, but won an impressive 18.9%, thereby holding down the popular vote for Clinton and Bush. Indeed, Perot had no spoiler effect on the election, as these voters told exit pollsters that they would have split evenly, 38% for Bush and 38% for Clinton in a hypothetical two-way race.[66] Clinton won only 43% of the popular vote, while Bush's 37.5% was the lowest popular vote percentage for any incumbent president in eighty years. Support from Reagan Democrats eroded, as Bush won only 10% of self-identifying Democrats. Meanwhile, 17% of Republicans voted for Perot and 10% for Clinton. In Congress, Republicans gained nine seats in the House and scored no net change in the Senate. In both chambers, however, Republicans remained well entrenched into the minority.[67]

## THE REAGAN REVOLUTION TAKES A PAUSE

George Bush followed a common heir apparent presidential trajectory with worsening divisions and vulnerabilities in his party, as well as a stronger opposition party that eventually defeated him. As Bush left office, the Republican Party was in its worst shape in more than a decade. The Democrats not only held commanding control of Congress, they had also broken the Republicans' dominance of presidential elections. On Bush's watch, the Democrats retooled and addressed the problems that had so greatly complicated their efforts to win the White House for many years. Republicans were divided between different factions emphasizing various issues, while Newt Gingrich was calling for a more activist brand of conservatism within the House.[68]

Bush's domestic achievements frequently stepped away from conservative Republican orthodoxies, yet this yielded little political credit from normally Democratic constituencies. Indeed, he performed worse with Democratic voters than his predecessor. In a clean-up custodial role, Bush also frequently departed from or altered his predecessor's policies. Deregulation of Savings and Loan institutions forced Bush to endorse reregulation and a costly bailout, both of which yielded him little political credit. High budget deficits forced him to abandon a sacrosanct campaign promise on taxes, producing an intraparty revolt. He continued to support the Nicaraguan Contra rebels, but through nonmilitary means. Reversing Reagan's support for Saddam Hussein, Bush led a victorious international coalition in the Persian Gulf War. Former ally Manuel

Noriega was removed and replaced. In a final act of unfinished business from the Reagan years, pardons were issued in December 1992 for several men who had been indicted or convicted of crimes relating to the Iran-Contra scandal.[69]

The end of the Cold War and the end of the Soviet Union itself consumed much of Bush's time, but yielded him virtually no domestic political credit in the early 1990s. As this process was unfolding, Bush abjured feisty rhetoric, overconfident crowing, and hasty decisions. Although some foreign policy conservatives were annoyed by his approach, Bush acted with an emphasis on stability and an orderly post–Cold War transition. While conservatives claimed vindication for Reagan's foreign and defense policies, Bush would be more of a supportive facilitator and less of a partner in the process of unraveling Soviet and Eastern European communism. The end of the Cold War also deprived Republicans of a powerful domestic political issue. In three elections, Reagan and Bush could successfully depict the Democrats as weaklings and appeasers in foreign policy. By 1992, these campaign barbs lost resonance. Not until the post-9/11 congressional elections of 2002 could Republicans effectively use foreign policy as a national campaign issue.

The Reagan Revolution, while chastened, was not over. It took on new form during the Clinton Administration. Only two years after Bush's defeat, Republicans rebounded to win control of both chambers of Congress for the first time in 40 years. Republican gains in the statehouses were similarly impressive, including a net gain of 10 governorships. Clinton's failed efforts to overhaul health care policy served as a reminder that the political climate of the 1990s was not hospitable to major expansions of the social welfare state. As the new House speaker, Gingrich initially pursued an activist conservative agenda, but lacking a presidential partner in the White House, he was forced to retreat. Meanwhile, Clinton redirected his presidency to reflect the limitations of a generally conservative political landscape.[70] Republican objectives such as welfare reform, deregulation of various industries, free trade, and lower capital gains taxes were accomplished with Clinton's cooperation.

By the time George Bush's son became president, the nation was almost evenly divided politically. To sustain itself, a national governing coalition must endure demographic, economic, and cultural changes over a period of many years. Twenty-first-century Republicans continued to use tax cuts, deregulation, and privatization as defining issues. Social conservative issue agendas remained essential to vital Republican constituencies. Assertiveness in foreign policy also reemerged as an organizing issue when the United States embarked upon a long-term campaign against terrorism. The new challenge for Republicans was to reconcile their Reagan-era commitments with a nation that had become significantly more diverse.

# 8

# CONCLUSION

## THE PERILS OF INHERITANCE

Political context and environment matters as much or more than an individual president's talents and skill. Jefferson, Jackson, Lincoln, Roosevelt, and Reagan presided over ascendant parties that represented revolutionary departures in governance. Their policies were new and different. Hence, the opposition party was unable to capitalize on the policy consequences of these presidents while they were in office. By the time their heirs apparent arrived in office, the opposition party was better equipped to challenge the governing party. A more extensive policy track record had built up by the time the heir apparent assumed office.

Assuming the presidency in the heir apparent role would seem to present many advantages. In part, these presidents are elected as a ratification of their predecessors' records. Upon entering the White House, an established governing coalition is in place and there is a policy record upon which to build. These presidents, stewards of a repeatedly victorious party, can claim popular support for their principles and agendas. The opposition party, having lost successive elections, appears disorganized and dispirited. Divisions within the governing party exist, but seem to be contained as their presidencies begin.

As the impact of their predecessors still looms very large, heirs apparent will have to navigate a political environment that grows increasingly hostile. Depending upon the issue or set of circumstances, heirs apparent will choose between three approaches. All three approaches serve a purpose and sometimes the lines between different pathways can be blurry. Because every course carries risks and rewards, presidents will be prone to oscillating between approaches as political circumstances dictate. In response, critics can say with some credibility that presidents who frequently switch between approaches are ideologically incoherent, lacking in core principles, and overly concerned with short-term political calculus.

First, heirs apparent can pursue continuity, maintaining their predecessors' policies and defending against attacks by hostile political actors. New heir apparent presidents are likely to promise a significant degree of continuity. The heir apparent's first election campaign will feature robust defenses and pledges to protect and defend the predecessor's record. If the predecessor is the builder of a new governing regime, this tactic is likely to be successful for getting an heir apparent elected. The new president will win by rebuilding the predecessor's electoral coalition, although with a reduced margin of victory.

Unfortunately, the heir apparent also inherits the policy problems, political baggage, and political enemies of the predecessor. Within a short period of time, these challenges will outweigh any advantages the new president may have initially enjoyed. Amid signs of a stronger opposition party, the new president may practice continuity as a form of resistance. The veto pen can be a useful tool to stop legislation that attacks the predecessor's policy record and the principles of the governing regime. There may be great rewards for adhering to continuity in an election campaign or early in a presidency. However, as the months and years of an heir apparent's term go by, continuity becomes more difficult to practice. Existing policies may become outdated and obsolete, and the national and international political environments may change. An heir apparent who clings too rigidly to a controversial policy from the predecessor's tenure runs the risk of being depicted as stubborn and too wedded to ideology. Bush was widely criticized for breaking his tax promise, but few have considered the political quagmire he would have likely found himself in had he dogmatically stuck to his guns.

Maintaining strong credentials as a disciple of a governing regime will also require more than just carrying out a predecessor's policies, for presidents need to be more than just custodians. They need to be independent executives. The second course of action heirs apparent can choose is to expand commitments, vowing to build from their predecessors' policies, expanding existing programs, and striving to complete unfinished agendas. Coalition partners will also be demanding action on new issues and agendas that went unaddressed during the predecessor's tenure. Domestic crises will demand more independent courses of action. A new foreign policy landscape will also present new demands for independent action, as Truman and Bush both experienced. An heir apparent, like any other president affiliated with a governing regime, will find it necessary to prove his worth by acting on ideological commitments, even when the interpretation of those principles is up for debate. As they seek to chart their own course, heir apparent presidents will root their actions in the principles of their governing regime.

Third, an heir apparent will have to adopt the corrective approach to repair flaws in the policies of the governing regime. To protect their regime's legitimacy and credibility in the long run, these presidents will have to do much of the dirty work of sacrificing elements of their predecessors' policy records. Any governing regime must be willing to refine, repair, and even repudiate unworkable or unwanted policies. Failure to do so will ultimately erode legitimacy to govern and public perceptions of competence. Through this corrective pathway, an heir apparent will claim to be acting in concert with the ideological and programmatic principles of the governing regime. Not all coalition partners, however, will agree, and the president will be accused of betraying the predecessor's hard-won achievements. Long-simmering intraparty tensions will start to intensify, foreshadowing even more serious divisions in years to come.

Democrats in the 1980s continued to hammer away at the big budget deficits under Reagan and Bush. To preserve the credibility of conservative Republicans as fiscal stewards of the economy,

Bush chose to abandon his tax promise to close the deficit. While most of Reagan's tax cuts remained in place after the budget deal in 1990, Bush could never escape the short-term political damage from his own party. Van Buren and the Democrats were mired in a depression in the late 1830s. Although it yielded him no political credit and his party was divided on their policy response, Van Buren phased out Jackson's bank deposit scheme. To replace it, an independent treasury was implemented, but it was repealed soon after Van Buren left office. The independent treasury formed the basis for James Polk's subsequent policy and represented the Democrats' alternative to the Whigs' national banking plans. At a bare minimum, Van Buren had at least ended a Jacksonian policy that was risky and unstable.

Sensing vulnerabilities around multiplying crises and the president's contradictory courses of action, the opposition party will strengthen. Now that the governing party has a long record in office, its competence can be critiqued and its policies are more vulnerable to political attacks. In Madison's case, the Federalist comeback was temporary and regionally limited in this era of a weaker political party system. Subsequent presidents in the heir apparent category either experienced outright electoral defeat or otherwise left office with their party holding a weaker command of the American political landscape. In each case the party still rebounded in subsequent elections, allowing presidential successors to resume the fight for agendas that did not come to fruition under the heir apparent.

## THE STRAIGHTJACKET PRESIDENCY

To assert that all presidents encounter unexpected problems in office is hardly a novel suggestion. Presidents of all calibers will have moments of failure. Yet there are likely to be differences between each president's ability to wield political authority under trying circumstances. In response to mistakes and dysfunctional policies, the political system will also be more forgiving of some presidents than others. The heirs apparent covered here governed in the backdrop of political eras defined by their very transformative predecessors. Memories of a recent revolution in American politics remain very fresh when the heir apparent assumes office. These presidents are strictly expected to follow an established policy trajectory and an established ideological framework. Accordingly, their ability to act independently will often be limited to attempting to finish their predecessors' unfinished policy agendas and unfulfilled ideas. Similarly, an heir apparent's independent actions may include efforts to enlarge policies and programs created during the predecessor's tenure. Independent actions that genuinely represent departures from the predecessor's policies will be fraught with more risks. Even as the president claims to be acting out of pragmatism or a particular interpretation of the governing regime's principles, intraparty critics will surely push back.

## THE INDEPENDENT FOLLOWER

The examples covered here concerned heirs apparent who governed in the shadows of the most transformative presidents. Regardless of the political context, presidents who assume office in the heir apparent category will have to choose how closely to hew to the record of their party's predecessor. Regardless of any consideration of regimes or governing coalitions in American politics, an heir apparent will find some limitations and opportunities due to the choices made by the predecessor. If a president is popular and perceived as being successful, it should not be surprising to see an heir apparent who promises continuity and to build off of the outgoing administration's record.

In the rare circumstances where an unpopular, failed, or disgraced president is followed into office by a successor of the same party, the heir apparent label may be an albatross. James Buchanan, for example, found it unhelpful to succeed Franklin Pierce, a fellow Democrat. In a hypothetical scenario like this, it would be advisable for the new president to establish as much distance from the predecessor as is feasible. It is also possible, however unlikely, that there could be major ideological differences between two successive presidents of the same party, in which case the heir apparent label would not be appropriate. What is most common for presidents in the heir apparent category is to pursue a zigzagging mixture of approaches as it concerns the relationship between the current and predecessor administrations.

The modern presidency of the twentieth century and beyond makes it possible for effective communicators to carve out a formidable public identity of their own. On the other hand, just as the office is more powerful, so too are the forces that can make a presidency fail. As the office has moved to the center of American political and governmental life, presidents are always under attack, prone to isolation, and subject to the demands of constantly evolving communications technology. For any president in the heir apparent category to be successful, a careful and skillful departure from the predecessor will be necessary. Leaders who lack individuality and initiative are unlikely to command respect from other actors. Presidents who do not take the risks of independent action may find that political power and authority gravitate to other actors and institutions.

Political momentum always slows down. It is probably unrealistic for an aspiring heir apparent to promise the continuation of a predecessor's revolutionary brand of politics. Fortunately, a president does not need to be a revolutionary to have a successful administration. As all presidents must be keenly aware of the political landscape they are inheriting, presidents in the heir apparent capacity should disabuse themselves of notions that they will be another Jefferson, Jackson, Lincoln, Roosevelt, or Reagan. Such an outcome is not impossible, but it is unlikely. To enhance prospects for success, a variety of tactics and personal attributes will serve a contemporary heir apparent well.

Measuring the success of a president in the heir apparent capacity demands answers to three major questions. First, did this president win election to a second term? Election to a first term functions as a validation of the predecessor's tenure, as well as the quality of the heir apparent's campaign skills. When the heir apparent faces the voters for a second term, the new president will have moved out of the predecessor's shadow to at least some degree. Such an election will serve as a referendum upon this president's handling of heir apparent leadership, and upon how well these multiple approaches are comprehensively employed. Madison, Grant, and Truman won second terms and earned the opportunity to move further out of their predecessors' shadows.

Second, did this president establish original and successful policy agendas that endured well beyond his years in the White House? Here, a mastery of the expansion approach is required. While heirs apparent may find it worthwhile and politically advantageous to expand specific programs that are rooted in the predecessor's tenure, political credit may be hard to obtain on this front. An impressive expansion of Social Security was an achievement for Truman, but this will always be recognized as Roosevelt's program. Truman's integration of the armed forces, however, was a genuinely independent action that could be hitched to the New Deal's principles of social justice. This was also a policy that has proved to be remarkably successful. Departing from the shadow of an imposing predecessor demands more than charisma and positive personal attributes. Rather, an heir apparent's job is to establish a clear record of independent action, tempered with a respect for the longer-term principles that the predecessor worked so hard to legitimize.

Third, how well does the heir apparent handle the thankless task of correcting the consequences of his predecessor's policies that didn't work out as promised? Political credit will be unlikely to materialize while the heir apparent is performing these duties, but successful presidencies (regardless of how we categorize them) require skillful responses to unanticipated crises and policy malfunctions. The problem for heirs apparent is that their political kinship will complicate their ability to claim credit. They will always own the policy failures they may actually work so hard to correct. Rather than getting credit for his skillful cleanup of the S & L crisis, Bush was more likely to be tarred by association with the excesses of Reagan's deregulation policies. Madison, meanwhile, made a bad situation worse with his remedies to Jefferson's embargo policy.

Because the corrective approach is likely to be a short-term political loser, these presidents must also have an aggressive agenda that is uniquely their own, so as to give them the chance to move out of their predecessor's shadow in a positive way.

## COMING OUT OF THE SHADOW THE RIGHT WAY

First, an effective communications operation will be necessary for any president to carve out an individual identity. Amid all the noise of American politics, a politician who is in the shadow of a predecessor will need to be a good messenger on his or her own behalf. The days when presidents could rely on their parties to act as surrogate messengers are long gone. While being a good rhetorician is surely an asset, it is just as important to run an effective White House communications operation to define the president's agendas. If the predecessor masters one mode of communication to reach the American people, the heir apparent should seek a new and unique method of messaging to burnish his or her own individuality. For example, while Reagan excelled in formal televised addresses, Bush held dramatically more press conferences.[1]

Second, facing a political landscape with more intraparty critics and a stronger opposition party, heirs apparent must be skilled at playing defense. Under attack from many fronts, they cannot afford to passively let intraparty critics define the party's commitments and principles. Similarly, a retooled and revitalized opposition party may present itself as a viable alternative to voters if the president is not actively defending the administration. Truman personally used the campaign in 1948 as a venue to defend his administration and the New Deal legacy. Bush, on the other hand, ran a lackadaisical reelection campaign and made himself look indecisive when he repudiated his own tax increase.[2]

Third, as the opposition party is prone to gaining strength, the president will have to look for opportunities for bipartisan cooperation. A bickering governing party may force the president to look for elements of the opposition to build bipartisan support in Congress.

While some intraparty critics will respond by labeling this course of action a betrayal, presidents who build a record of legislative achievement will operate from a greater position of strength, as opposed to coming up empty-handed. In Bush's case, Democrats dominated Congress and he had little choice of doing anything other than working with the hand he was dealt. Truman, for all of his loud denunciations of Congress, achieved bipartisan support for the Housing Act and much of his foreign policy legislation.

Fourth, competing factions within the governing party must be managed. In the interest of precluding any unnecessary friction, efforts should be made to make at least some concessions to all elements of the governing party coalition. Concessions may concern public policy, appointments, or party strategies and tactics. In all likelihood, these presidents will find that legislative achievements come by way of different congressional coalitions on issue after issue. An adversary on one issue may be an ally on the next issue. If all factions have a vested stake in the White House, presidents will at least have a fighting chance to develop intraparty working relationships. At the same time, choices will have to be made concerning the overarching thrust of the administration. The president will have to steer toward specific commitments and favored factions, while respectfully brushing aside the agendas being advocated by other elements of the party.

Finally, presidents in the heir apparent category are best served by proposing an ambitious agenda, even at the risk of being unsuccessful with Congress. Indeed, presidents who set low expectations will get low results. Creating an individual presidential identity demands more than just effective messaging and communications. As heirs apparent are vulnerable to being viewed with less respect than their predecessors, it is important that a comprehensive, proactive, and original agenda be set at the start of the administration. Compromises can be made and priorities can be set as events and political developments dictate. Planks may include a mixture of approaches that continue, expand, or repudiate the predecessor's policies. Truman followed the ambitious agenda-setting approach, succeeding with some items and falling short in other arenas. Still, he advanced ideas that formed the basis for Democratic ideology and commitments in years to come. Bush may have been limited by a Democratic Congress, but he could have used his post–Gulf War popularity to pursue a domestic agenda that was uniquely his own.

Truman stands out among these heirs apparent as the only one who did not ascend to the presidency by way of election. He must also be considered the most successful of the five presidents covered here. He won a second term in spite of frequently low job approval ratings, a revitalized Republican opposition, and two different splinter factions coming out of the Democratic Party. The circumstances under which Truman inherited the office were daunting, but also presented significant opportunities to establish his own individual accomplishments and earn credit for them. He clung closely to the New Deal policies of his predecessor, expanding them where he could, and further legitimizing his regime's approaches to the economy and social welfare. He also charted limited new paths forward on civil rights and social welfare, creating foundations upon which subsequent presidents could build. It was in the foreign policy arena, however, where Truman marked his most significant and enduring independent achievements. With American power at its apex, the international landscape presented opportunities and risks for the president to build the framework of a new world order. The postwar spirit of foreign policy bipartisanship was high, enabling Truman to win broad support for his plans. By creating the general framework for American Cold War foreign policy, Truman could lay claim to establishing the United States's significant place on the international stage for the next forty years.

The other four presidents in the heir apparent category also had their moments of success. Often they failed to earn credit for their achievements, and in two cases they were defeated for reelection. On other occasions, they were overwhelmed by failures of their own making, a hostile political environment they could not master, or adverse circumstances they simply could not control. Presidents of the twentieth century and beyond, however, have more tools at their disposal to set agendas, sell their ideas to the American people, and take unilateral executive actions without consulting other political actors. Bush had many of these tools available, but failed to use them promptly and effectively. Nineteenth-century presidents, on the other hand, were constrained by a political system that often frowned upon independent presidential action. Madison, Van Buren, and Grant would have found it hard to drastically depart from the norms of nineteenth-century presidential behavior, especially coming after the Herculean figures that preceded them. The presidency of the twentieth and twenty-first centuries, on the other hand, has demanded a greater degree of independence. Faced with the dilemmas of being an heir apparent, a contemporary president in this category has a fighting chance of being successful.

Assuming the mantle of leadership in the aftermath of a larger-than-life leader requires pragmatism, flexibility, and a reduced ego. Ambition can also be a useful attribute, if it is tempered with a realistic assessment of the facts. Political allies are bound to be more transient and less reliable. Political enemies are more likely to multiply than to diminish. Persistent choices will have to be made between independent actions and a brand of leadership that follows the trail blazed by the predecessor. While the first leader is skilled at the art of leading a political revolution, the successor's tasks are equally important, but less glamorous.

# NOTES

## CHAPTER 1. INTRODUCTION

1. Special to the *New York Times*, "Walsh Resigns as Coach and Seifert Replaces Him," *New York Times*, January 27, 1989.

2. Cover story, "Bob Eaton Is No Lee Iacocca—but He Doesn't Need to Be," *Business Week*, November 8, 1992.

3. Alexander Hamilton, *Federalist Papers* Nos. 67–77, March 11–April 4, 1788, Library of Congress, http://thomas.loc.gov/home/histdox/fedpapers .html.

4. On the president's post–New Deal powers of persuasion, see Richard E. Neustadt, *Presidential Power and the Modern Presidents: The Politics of Leadership from Roosevelt to Reagan* (New York: Free Press, 1990); on the potentially dangerous growth of presidential powers and isolation, see Arthur M. Schlesinger, Jr., *The Imperial Presidency* (New York: First Mariner, 2004); on the revival of the imperial presidency, see Andrew Rudalevige, *The New Imperial Presidency: Renewing Presidential Power after Watergate* (Ann Arbor: University of Michigan Press, 2006).

5. Hamilton, *Federalist Paper* No. 72, March 21, 1788, http://thomas.loc .gov/home/histdox/fed_72.html.

6. Sidney M. Milkis, *The President and the Parties: The Transformation of the American Party System since the New Deal* (New York: Oxford University Press, 1993), 171–172.

7. Robert W. Merry, *A Country of Vast Designs: James K. Polk, the Mexican War, and the Conquest of the American Continent* (New York: Simon & Schuster, 2009).

8. Stephen Skowronek, *The Politics Presidents Make: Leadership from John Adams to Bill Clinton* (Cambridge, MA: Belknap Press of Harvard University Press, 1997), 235; Jeffrey K. Tulis, *The Rhetorical Presidency* (Princeton: Princeton University Press, 1987), 97–110.

9. Michael Duffy and Michael Scherer, "The Role Model: What Obama Sees in Reagan," *Time*, January 27, 2011.

CHAPTER 2. SECOND IN LINE IN POLITICAL TIME

1. See, for example, Joseph Califano, Jr., *The Triumph and Tragedy of Lyndon Johnson* (New York: Simon & Schuster, 1991).

2. This is a core argument of Stephen Skowronek, *The Politics Presidents Make: Leadership from John Adams to Bill Clinton* (Cambridge, MA: Belknap Press of Harvard University Press, 1997), 8–15.

3. Abraham Lincoln, "Second Annual Message," December 1, 1862, ed. Gerhard Peters and John T. Woolley, *American Presidency Project*, www.presidency.ucsb.edu/ws/?pid=29503.

4. On the Clinton health care bill fiasco, see Haynes Johnson and David S. Broder, *The System: The American Way of Politics at the Breaking Point* (Boston: Little, Brown, 1997).

5. Skowronek, *The Politics Presidents Make*, 49–52, 58.

6. Ibid., 36–43.

7. Bruce Ackerman, *We the People*, vol. 1, *Foundations* (Cambridge, MA: Harvard University Press, 1991), 58–67. Ackerman's "holistic approach" (59) acknowledges and embraces the importance of politics in the evolution of constitutional regimes. The three constitutional regimes he identifies overlap to some degree with the regimes identified by Skowronek. See also Ackerman, *We the People*, vol. 2, *Transformations* (Cambridge, MA: Harvard University Press, 1998); and Ackerman, *We the People*, vol. 3, *The Civil Rights Revolution* (Cambridge, MA: Harvard University Press, 2014). On the creation, conceptual framework, and limitations of regimes, see Andrew J. Polsky, "Partisan Regimes in American Politics," *Polity* 44, no. 1 (January 2012): 51–80.

8. Skowronek, *The Politics Presidents Make*, 52–58.

9. Ibid., 30, 49–52.

10. Ibid., 36–39.

11. Ibid., 41–43.

12. Ibid., 39–41.

13. Ibid., 43–45. A more thorough treatment of these presidents, including the Whig presidents, Andrew Johnson, Grover Cleveland, Woodrow Wilson, Dwight Eisenhower, Richard Nixon, Gerald Ford, and Bill Clinton can be found in David A. Crockett, *The Opposition Presidency: Leadership and the Constraints of History* (College Station: Texas A & M University Press, 2002).

14. Skowronek, *The Politics Presidents Make*, 409–413.

15. Donald A. Zinman, "Passing the Torch through Political Time: Heir Apparent Presidents and the Governing Party," *White House Studies* 9, no. 1 (2009): 51–65.

16. Joel H. Silbey, *Martin Van Buren and the Emergence of American Popular Politics* (Lanham, MD: Rowman & Littlefield, 2002), 59–63.

17. Mark O. Hatfield, ed., with the Senate Historical Office, *Vice Presidents of the United States, 1789–1993*, intro. Mark O. Hatfield (Washington: US Government Printing Office, 1997), 411–419; David McCullough, *Truman* (New York: Simon & Schuster, 1992), 282, 308–309.

18. Biographer Geoffrey Perret notes that Grant had "comparatively little interest in politics"; in 1856 he voted for Democratic presidential nominee James Buchanan out of personal dislike toward the Republican nominee, John C. Frémont. Geoffrey Perret, *Ulysses S. Grant: Soldier & President* (New York: Random House, 1997), 117. See also pp. 383–384 on Grant's "disdain" for the normal business of political parties.

19. Walter Dean Burnham, "The Legacy of George Bush: Travails of an Understudy," in *The Election of 1992*, ed. Gerald M. Pomper (Chatham, NJ: Chatham House, 1993), 1–38. On how the minority party can exploit vulnerabilities in the majority party's governing coalition for electoral victory, see David A. Crockett, *Running against the Grain: How Opposition Presidents Win the White House* (College Station: Texas A & M University Press, 2008).

20. Charles W. Calhoun, *Conceiving a New Republic: The Republican Party and the Southern Question, 1869–1900* (Lawrence: University Press of Kansas, 2006), 45–46.

21. Anthony Leviero, "Truman Declares Democrats Design Better Life in U.S.," *New York Times*, October 22, 1948; R. W. Apple, Jr., "Bush, in Rousing Finale, Vows More Jobs but Never a Tax Rise; Backs Quayle despite Dispute," *New York Times*, August 19, 1988; Zinman, "Passing the Torch through Political Time," 54.

22. Brooks D. Simpson, *The Reconstruction Presidents* (Lawrence: University Press of Kansas, 1998), 143–145; Stephen B. Oates, *With Malice toward None: The Life of Abraham Lincoln* (New York: Harper & Row, 1977), 424–425.

23. Skowronek, *The Politics Presidents Make*, 41–43.

24. Ibid., 20, 56.

25. George McJimsey, *The Presidency of Franklin Delano Roosevelt* (Lawrence: University Press of Kansas, 2000), 144–145.

26. Clerk of the U.S. House of Representatives, H.R. 1 (2009), http://clerk.house.gov/evs/2009/r011070.xml; U.S. Senate, H.R. 1 (2009), www.senate.gov/legislative/LIS/roll_call_lists/roll_call_vote_cfm.cfm?congress=111&session=1&vote=00064.

27. John F. Manley, "The Conservative Coalition in Congress," *American Behavioral Scientist* 17 (November 1973): 223–247.

28. Jefferson saw conflict with so-called Old Republicans, Jackson battled John C. Calhoun and the nullifiers, Lincoln was not fully trusted by Radical Republicans, and Roosevelt developed a tense relationship with Southern and conservative Democrats: Skowronek, *The Politics Presidents Make*, 80–81, 144–148, 224–227, 313–314, 316.

29. Ross Perot won 17% of the Republican vote in the 1992 general election. Roper Center Public Opinion Archives, www.ropercenter.uconn.edu/elections/how_groups_voted/voted_92.html.

30. McCullough, *Truman*, 468–469.

31. On Theodore Roosevelt as the articulator of the Republican regime, see Skowronek, *The Politics Presidents Make*, 228–259.

32. John Adams to Abigail Adams, January 20, 1796, Massachusetts Historical Society, www.masshist.org/digitaladams/aea/cfm/doc.cfm?id=L17960120ja.

33. Ray Raphael, *Mr. President: How and Why the Founders Created a Chief Executive* (New York: Alfred A. Knopf, 2012).

34. Alexander Hamilton, *Federalist Paper* No. 71, March 18, 1788, Library of Congress, http://thomas.loc.gov/home/histdox/fed_71.html.

35. Ackerman, *We the People*, 1:68.

36. Jeffrey L. Pasley, *First Presidential Contest: 1796 and the Founding of American Democracy* (Lawrence: University Press of Kansas, 2013).

37. On the early hostility to political parties, and their gradual emergence and acceptance, see Richard Hofstadter, *The Idea of a Party System: The Rise of Legitimate Opposition in the United States, 1780–1840* (Berkeley: University of California Press, 1969).

38. Sidney M. Milkis and Michael Nelson, *The American Presidency: Origins and Development, 1776–2011*, 6th ed. (Washington, DC: Congressional Quarterly Press, 2012), 92.

39. Ronald P. Formisano, "Federalists and Republicans: Parties, Yes—System, No," in *The Evolution of American Electoral Systems*, ed. Paul Kleppner (Westport, CT: Greenwood Press, 1981), 33–76.

40. Milkis and Nelson, *The American Presidency*, 93–94.

41. Implementation of the Jay Treaty resulted in a standoff between Washington and the House, most notably concerning Washington's refusal to surrender papers from the treaty's negotiation process. Washington took the stance that Congress, especially the House, enjoyed no constitutional authority to meddle in the treaty-making process. Ibid., 88–90.

42. Curt Nichols and Adam S. Myers, "Exploring the Opportunity for Reconstructive Leadership: Presidential Responses to Enervated Political Regimes," *American Politics Research* 38, no. 5 (2010): 806–841, esp. 821–827.

43. For example, Roosevelt took an active and public role in securing the passage of the Hepburn Act of 1906. For a president to take such a visible and aggressive role in the legislative process was unprecedented. For a thorough coverage of Roosevelt and the Hepburn Act, see Jeffrey K. Tulis, *The Rhetorical Presidency* (Princeton: Princeton University Press, 1987), 95–116.

44. Edmund Morris, *Theodore Rex* (New York: Random House, 2001), 534–535.

45. Paolo E. Coletta, *The Presidency of William Howard Taft* (Lawrence: University Press of Kansas, 1973), 80–82.

46. Ibid., 67.

47. Ibid., 154–164.

48. Miller Center of Public Affairs, "American President: William Howard Taft," Domestic Affairs, http://millercenter.org/president/taft/essays/biography/4.

49. Lewis L. Gould, *The William Howard Taft Presidency* (Lawrence: University Press of Kansas, 2009), 25, 90–91.

50. On Taft as an administrator, see ibid., 121–137.

51. Milkis and Nelson, *The American Presidency*, 234–239.

52. Ibid., 237.


CHAPTER 3. JAMES MADISON

1. Thomas Jefferson to Spencer Roane, September 6, 1819, Library of Congress, www.loc.gov/exhibits/jefferson/137.html.

2. On the enactment and enforcement of the embargo, see Forrest McDonald, *The Presidency of Thomas Jefferson* (Lawrence: University Press of Kansas, 1976), 142–152.

3. Garry Wills, *James Madison* (New York: Times Books, 2002), 86.

4. Robert Allen Rutland, *The Presidency of James Madison* (Lawrence: University Press of Kansas, 1990), 198, 200.

5. Ibid., 199–200.

6. Ibid., 20, 37, 199–200.

7. Ralph Ketcham, *James Madison* (Charlottesville: University of Virginia Press, 1971), 306–315, 319–323.

8. Ibid., 345–347.

9. Ibid., 327–333.

10. Wills, *James Madison*, 40–41; Ketcham, *James Madison*, 331.

11. Andrew Burstein and Nancy Isenberg, *Madison and Jefferson* (New York: Random House, 2010), 337–341.

12. Ketcham, *James Madison*, 411–412.

13. Donald A. Zinman, "The Heir Apparent Presidency of James Madison," *Presidential Studies Quarterly* 41, no. 4 (December 2011): 721, 724.

14. David A. Crockett, *Running against the Grain: How Opposition Presidents Win the White House* (College Station: Texas A & M University Press, 2008).

15. Wills, *James Madison*, 69.

16. Ibid.

17. Rutland, *The Presidency of James Madison*, 12–13. The author refers to this faction as the "Invincibles."

18. John S. Pancake, "The 'Invisibles': A Chapter in the Opposition to President Madison," *Journal of Southern History* 21, no. 1 (February 1955): 17–37.

19. Rutland, *The Presidency of James Madison*, 10–17.

20. Noble E. Cunningham, Jr., *The Jeffersonian Republicans in Power: Party Operations, 1801–1809* (Chapel Hill: University of North Carolina Press, 1963), 110–112.

21. Ibid., 116. See also the formal protest of John Randolph published in the *National Intelligencer*, March 7, 1808.

22. Ketcham, *James Madison*, 467. Clinton was overwhelmingly renominated for the vice presidency by the same caucus.

23. Cunningham, *The Jeffersonian Republicans in Power*, 118–121.

24. Paul F. Boller, Jr., *Presidential Campaigns* (New York: Oxford University Press, 1984), 23–24.

25. Ketcham, *James Madison*, 449.

26. Ibid., 467–468.

27. Ibid., 468.

28. Walter Dean Burnham, *Voting in American Elections: The Shaping of the American Political Universe since 1788* (Palo Alto, CA: Academica Press, 2010), 59.

29. Ronald P. Formisano, "Federalists and Republicans: Parties, Yes—System, No," in *The Evolution of American Electoral Systems*, ed. Paul Kleppner (Westport, CT: Greenwood, 1981); Richard Hofstadter, *The Idea of a Party System: The Rise of Legitimate Opposition in the United States, 1780–1840* (Berkeley: University of California Press, 1969), 90, 122–124.

30. Madison, "Veto Message," February 21, 1811, ed. Gerhard Peters and John T. Woolley, *American Presidency Project*, www.presidency.ucsb.edu/ws/?pid=65921.

31. Madison, "Veto Message," February 28, 1811, ed. Gerhard Peters and John T. Woolley, *American Presidency Project*, www.presidency.ucsb.edu/ws/?pid=65922.

32. Rutland, *The Presidency of James Madison*, 203; Madison, "Eighth Annual Message," December 3, 1816, ed. Gerhard Peters and John T. Woolley, *American Presidency Project*, www.presidency.ucsb.edu/ws/?pid=29458.

33. Madison, "Veto Message," April 3, 1812, ed. Gerhard Peters and John T. Woolley, *American Presidency Project*, www.presidency.ucsb.edu/ws/?pid=65940.

34. Rickie Longfellow, "Back in Time: The National Road," US Department of Transportation, www.fhwa.dot.gov/infrastructure/back0103.cfm.

35. Madison to Congress, February 1, 1812, "The Cumberland Road Project," www.cumberlandroadproject.com/federal/cumberland-road-contracts1.php.

36. Rutland, *The Presidency of James Madison*, 198.

37. Ibid., 205–207.

38. Madison, "Veto Message," March 3, 1817, ed. Gerhard Peters and John T. Woolley, *American Presidency Project*, www.presidency.ucsb.edu/ws/?pid=65899.

39. Zinman, "The Heir Apparent Presidency of James Madison," 720.

40. James Madison, "Seventh Annual Message," December 5, 1815, ed. Gerhard Peters and John T. Woolley, *American Presidency Project*, www.presidency.ucsb.edu/ws/?pid=29457.

41. Rutland, *The Presidency of James Madison*, 68–69; Ketcham, *James Madison*, 506.

42. The Jefferson Administration even presided over the openings of three new National Bank branches: Hofstadter, *The Idea of a Party System*, 159.

43. Wills, *James Madison*, 75–77.

44. Rutland, *The Presidency of James Madison*, 69–70.

45. Wills, *James Madison*, 77.

46. J. C. A. Stagg, *Mr. Madison's War: Politics, Diplomacy and Warfare in the Early American Republic, 1783–1830* (Princeton: Princeton University Press, 1983), 438–453.

47. Madison, "Veto Message," January 30, 1815, ed. Gerhard Peters and John T. Woolley, *American Presidency Project*, www.presidency.ucsb.edu/ws /?pid=65980.

48. Stagg, *Mr. Madison's War*, 451.

49. Ibid., 440–441.

50. Madison, "Seventh Annual Message," December 5, 1815, ed. Gerhard Peters and John T. Woolley, *American Presidency Project*, www.presidency .ucsb.edu/ws/?pid=29457.

51. Rutland, *The Presidency of James Madison*, 197.

52. McDonald, *The Presidency of Thomas Jefferson*, 79–80.

53. Ibid., 41, 52, 131.

54. Norris W. Preyer, "Southern Support of the Tariff of 1816: A Reappraisal," *Journal of Southern History* 25, no. 3 (August 1959): 306–322.

55. George Dangerfield, *The Awakening of American Nationalism, 1815–1828* (New York: Harper & Row, 1965), 14–16; Norman K. Risjord, *The Old Republicans: Southern Conservatism in the Age of Jefferson* (New York: Columbia University Press, 1965), 164–165.

56. Rutland, *The Presidency of James Madison*, 39.

57. Wills, *James Madison*, 84–85.

58. Ibid., 62.

59. Ibid., 87–88.

60. Rutland, *The Presidency of James Madison*, 60–62, 67–68.

61. Wills, *James Madison*, 77–79.

62. Rutland, *The Presidency of James Madison*, 67–68.

63. Ketcham, *James Madison*, 529–533.

64. Stagg, *Mr. Madison's War*, 79, 143–144.

65. Mark Pitcavage, "United States Army," in *James Madison and the American Nation, 1751–1836: An Encyclopedia*, ed. Robert A. Rutland (New York: Simon & Schuster, 1994), 413.

66. James C. Bradford, "United States Navy," in Rutland, *James Madison and the American Nation*, 415.

67. Rutland, *The Presidency of James Madison*, 185–189.

68. The House vote was 79–49. The Senate spent two weeks debating before voting 19–13 in favor: ibid., 102.

69. Zinman, "The Heir Apparent Presidency of James Madison," 725; Madison, "Special Message," June 1, 1812, ed. Gerhard Peters and John T. Woolley, *American Presidency Project*, www.presidency.ucsb.edu/ws/?pid=65936.

70. Rutland, *The Presidency of James Madison*, 95–96.

71. Wills, *James Madison*, 96; Risjord, *The Old Republicans*, 143, 146.

72. Leland R. Johnson, "The Suspense Was Hell: The Senate Vote for War in 1812," *Indiana Magazine of History* 65, no. 4 (1969): 247–267.

73. William D. Adler and Jonathan Keller, "A Federal Army, Not a Federalist One: Regime Building in the Jeffersonian Era," *Journal of Policy History* 26, no. 2 (2014): 167–179.

74. Ibid., 180–181. In addition, Andrew J. Polsky has shown that Lincoln dispensed officer commissions to some Democrats as a means of building

bipartisan support for the Union war effort: Polsky, "Mr. Lincoln's Army Revisited: Partisanship, Institutional Position and Union Army Command, 1861–1865," *Studies in American Political Development* 16 (Fall 2002): 176–207.

75. Rutland, *The Presidency of James Madison*, 195.

76. Ketcham, *James Madison*, 606.

77. Russell F. Weigley, *History of the United States Army* (New York: Macmillan, 1967), 566.

78. Bradford, "United States Navy," 416.

79. Zinman, "The Heir Apparent Presidency of James Madison," 721–724.

80. United States House of Representatives, "Party Divisions of the House of Representatives," http://history.house.gov/Institution/Party-Divisions/Party-Divisions/; United States Senate, "Party Division in the Senate, 1789–Present," http://www.senate.gov/pagelayout/history/one_item_and_teasers/partydiv.htm.

81. Zinman, "The Heir Apparent Presidency of James Madison," 721–724.

82. David Hackett Fischer, *The Revolution of American Conservatism: The Federalist Party in the Era of Jeffersonian Democracy* (New York: Harper & Row, 1965), 97–109.

83. Zinman, "The Heir Apparent Presidency of James Madison," 721.

84. Stagg, *Mr. Madison's War*, 106–107.

85. Boller, *Presidential Campaigns*, 26–27; Ketcham, *James Madison*, 544–545.

86. Burnham, *Voting in American Elections*, 60.

87. Investopedia, "Bear Market Rally," www.investopedia.com/terms/b/bear-market-rally.asp.

88. Rutland, *The Presidency of James Madison*, 184–187.

## CHAPTER 4. MARTIN VAN BUREN

1. David A. Crockett, *Running against the Grain: How Opposition Presidents Win the White House* (College Station: Texas A & M University Press, 2008), 58–59.

2. Joel H. Silbey, *Martin Van Buren and the Emergence of American Popular Politics* (Lanham, MD: Rowman & Littlefield, 2002), 91–93.

3. Charles Sellers, *Market Revolution: Jacksonian America, 1815–1846* (Oxford: Oxford University Press, 1991), 343–344.

4. Silbey, *Martin Van Buren*, 115.

5. James C. Curtis, *The Fox at Bay: Martin Van Buren and the Presidency, 1837–1841* (Lexington: University Press of Kentucky, 1970), 65–67.

6. This is the recurring theme in Sellers, *Market Revolution*.

7. Ibid., 403.

8. Jules Witcover, *Party of the People: A History of the Democrats* (New York: Random House, 2003), 161–162.

9. Ted Widmer, *Martin Van Buren* (New York: Times Books, 2005), 46–47.

10. Silbey, *Martin Van Buren*, 44–49.

11. Major L. Wilson, *The Presidency of Martin Van Buren* (Lawrence: University Press of Kansas, 1984), 30.

12. The Eaton matter is a recurring theme in Jon Meacham, *American Lion: Andrew Jackson in the White House* (New York: Random House, 2008).

13. Wilson, *The Presidency of Martin Van Buren*, 32–34.

14. Silbey, *Martin Van Buren*, 42, 52–53, 76, 105.

15. William J. Cooper, Jr., *The South and the Politics of Slavery, 1828–1856* (Baton Rouge: Louisiana State University Press, 1978), 17–22.

16. Widmer, *Martin Van Buren*, 87; Wilson, *The Presidency of Martin Van Buren*, 31–37.

17. Meacham, *American Lion*, 307–309.

18. Silbey, *Martin Van Buren*, 91–93.

19. Meacham, *American Lion*, 309.

20. Paul F. Boller, Jr., *Presidential Campaigns* (New York: Oxford University Press, 1984), 60.

21. Silbey, *Martin Van Buren*, 101–102.

22. The authoritative modern narrative of the Whig Party is Michael F. Holt, *The Rise and Fall of the American Whig Party: Jacksonian Politics and the Onset of the Civil War* (Oxford: Oxford University Press, 1999).

23. A second Southern candidate, North Carolina Senator Willie Person Mangum, was promoted in South Carolina. This state was the last to continue with the practice of awarding electoral votes by way of the state legislature, in lieu of the voters. Mangum only won the South Carolina electoral votes and no popular votes.

24. Martin Van Buren, "Inaugural Address," March 4, 1837, ed. Gerhard Peters and John T. Woolley, *American Presidency Project*, www.presidency.ucsb.edu/ws/?pid=25812.

25. Curtis, *The Fox at Bay*, 67–71.

26. Martin Van Buren, "Special Session Message," September 4, 1837, ed. Gerhard Peters and John T. Woolley, *American Presidency Project*, www.presidency.ucsb.edu/ws/?pid=67234.

27. Silbey, *Martin Van Buren*, 118–119.

28. Wilson, *The Presidency of Martin Van Buren*, 73, 77.

29. Curtis, *The Fox at Bay*, 83.

30. Ibid., 77–78, 108–109; Wilson, *The Presidency of Martin Van Buren*, 76–77.

31. Curtis, *The Fox at Bay*, 129–130, 142–151.

32. Meacham, *American Lion*, 141–145.

33. Wilson, *The Presidency of Martin Van Buren*, 181.

34. Ibid., 181–185.

35. Meacham, *American Lion*, 318; Wilson, *The Presidency of Martin Van Buren*, 185–187.

36. Martin Van Buren, "Second Annual Message," December 3, 1838, ed. Gerhard Peters and John T. Woolley, *American Presidency Project*, www.presidency.ucsb.edu/ws/?pid=29480.

37. Silbey, *Martin Van Buren*, 132–133.

38. Wilson, *The Presidency of Martin Van Buren*, 153–154. Negotiations stalled over the third ship, the *Enterprise*, but a compensation agreement was reached in 1853.

39. Ibid., 201.

40. Curtis, *The Fox at Bay*, 152–156.

41. Wilson, *The Presidency of Martin Van Buren*, 149–150.

42. Alvin Laroy Duckett, *John Forsyth: Political Tactician* (Athens: University of Georgia Press, 1962), 201–202.

43. Curtis, *The Fox at Bay*, 160–169.

44. On the Whigs' strategies and tactics as an opposition party in 1840, see Crockett, *Running against the Grain*, 30–31, 65–67, 93–97.

45. Holt, *American Whig Party*, 110; Wilson, *The Presidency of Martin Van Buren*, 196–197.

46. Holt, *American Whig Party*, 107; Widmer, *Martin Van Buren*, 133–136; Wilson, *The Presidency of Martin Van Buren*, 196–197.

47. Holt, *American Whig Party*, 106.

48. Boller, *Presidential Campaigns*, 66–67. Ever careful not to offend protemperance voters, who were important to the Whig electoral coalition, Harrison rallies also provided nonalcoholic cider.

49. Curtis, *The Fox at Bay*, 190; Holt, *American Whig Party*, 105–106.

50. Widmer, *Martin Van Buren*, 120.

51. Walter Dean Burnham, *Voting in American Elections: The Shaping of the American Political Universe since 1788* (Palo Alto, CA: Academica Press, 2010), 69.

52. Holt, *American Whig Party*, 135.

## CHAPTER 5. ULYSSES S. GRANT

1. The Civil War pension program is a major theme in Theda Skocpol, *Protecting Soldiers and Mothers: The Political Origins of Social Policy in the United States* (Cambridge, MA: Harvard University Press, 1992).

2. The 1860 party platform asserted, "We deny the authority of Congress, of a territorial legislature, or of any individuals, to give legal existence to slavery in any territory of the United States": Republican Party Platforms, "Republican Party Platform of 1860," May 17, 1860, ed. Gerhard Peters and John T. Woolley, *American Presidency Project*, www.presidency.ucsb.edu/ws/?pid=29620.

3. See Lewis L. Gould, *Grand Old Party: A History of the Republicans* (New York: Random House, 2003), 3–41.

4. A recurring theme in John Gerring, *Party Ideologies in America, 1828–1996* (Cambridge: Cambridge University Press, 1998), chap. 3.

5. Gould, *Grand Old Party*, 56–67, 207.

6. Gerring, *Party Ideologies in America*, 101–111.

7. The party platform of 1868 stated, "Foreign immigration, which in the past, has added so much to the wealth, development of resources, and increase of power to this nation—the asylum of the oppressed of all nations—should be

fostered and encouraged by a liberal and just policy." Republican Party Platforms, "Republican Party Platform of 1868," May 20, 1868, ed. Gerhard Peters and John T. Woolley, *American Presidency Project*, www.presidency.ucsb.edu /ws/?pid=29622. "We urge continued careful encouragement and protection of voluntary immigration," the platform of 1872 noted: "Republican Party Platform of 1872," June 5, 1872, ed. Gerhard Peters and John T. Woolley, *American Presidency Project*, www.presidency.ucsb.edu/ws/?pid=29623.

8. Geoffrey Perret, *Ulysses S. Grant: Soldier & President* (New York: Random House, 1997), 376–377.

9. Gould, *Grand Old Party*, 59.

10. Abraham Lincoln, "Last Public Address," April 11, 1865, in *Collected Works of Abraham Lincoln*, vol. 8, http://quod.lib.umich.edu/1 /lincoln/linc oln8/1:850?rgn=div1;singlegenre=All;sort=occur;subview=detail;type=simple; view=fulltext;q1=april+11+1865.

11. Stephen B. Oates, *With Malice toward None: The Life of Abraham Lincoln* (New York: Harper & Row, 1977), 398.

12. Albert Castel, *The Presidency of Andrew Johnson* (Lawrence: University Press of Kansas, 1979), 6–8.

13. Andrew Johnson, "Second Annual Message," December 3, 1866, ed. Gerhard Peters and John T. Woolley, *American Presidency Project*, www.presi dency.ucsb.edu/ws/?pid=29507.

14. This number includes regular vetoes and pocket vetoes. "Presidential Vetoes," ed. Gerhard Peters and John T. Woolley, *American Presidency Project*, www.presidency.ucsb.edu/data/vetoes.php; David A. Crockett, *The Opposition Presidency: Leadership and the Constraints of History* (College Station: Texas A & M University Press, 2002), 80–86.

15. Among many of Johnson's rhetorical masterpieces were his self-comparisons to Jesus Christ, denunciations of Radical Republicans and abolitionists as traitors, and claims that his political enemies wanted him assassinated. Johnson's tour, known as the "Swing around the Circle," is a major topic in Jeffrey K. Tulis, *The Rhetorical Presidency* (Princeton: Princeton University Press, 1987), 87–93.

16. Castel, *The Presidency of Andrew Johnson*, 187–194.

17. Jean Edward Smith, *Grant* (New York: Simon & Schuster, 2001), 426–427.

18. Ibid., 427; William S. McFeely, *Grant: A Biography* (New York: W. W. Norton, 1981), 251–252; Perret, *Ulysses S. Grant*, 370.

19. Smith, *Grant*, 205.

20. Perret, *Ulysses S. Grant*, 375–379.

21. Ibid., 378–379; Paul F. Boller, Jr., *Presidential Campaigns* (New York: Oxford University Press, 1984), 124–125; Eric Foner, *Reconstruction: America's Unfinished Revolution, 1863–1877* (New York: Harper & Row, 1988), 340–343.

22. Boller, *Presidential Campaigns*, 124–125; Josiah Bunting, III, *Ulysses S. Grant* (New York: Times Books, 2004), 83.

23. "Out of Their Own Mouths Shall They Be Condemned," *Soldiers and Sailors, Look to Your Interests*, Grant and Colfax, published by the Soldiers' and Sailors' National Republican Executive Committee, Washington, DC,

1868, Library of Congress, http://memory.loc.gov/cgi-bin/query/h?ammem /rbpebib:@field%28NUMBER+@band%28rbpe+2050310b%29%29.

24. Boller, *Presidential Campaigns*, 125; Bunting, *Ulysses S. Grant*, 85.

25. Party Divisions of the House of Representatives, http://history.house .gov/Institution/Party-Divisions/Party-Divisions/; Party Division in the Senate, www.senate.gov/pagelayout/history/one_item_and_teasers/partydiv.htm.

26. Ulysses S. Grant, "Inaugural Address," March 4, 1869, ed. Gerhard Peters and John T. Woolley, *American Presidency Project*, www.presidency.ucsb.edu /ws/?pid=25820.

27. William Gillette, *The Right to Vote: Politics and the Passage of the Fifteenth Amendment* (Baltimore: Johns Hopkins University Press, 1965), 98–103, 146.

28. Ulysses S. Grant, "Special Message," March 30, 1870, ed. Gerhard Peters and John T. Woolley, *American Presidency Project*, www.presidency.ucsb.edu /ws/?pid=70628.

29. Foner, *Reconstruction*, 454–459.

30. McFeely, *Grant*, 368.

31. Foner, *Reconstruction*, 456–459.

32. Ibid., 550–555, 569–570, 577.

33. Ibid., 558–563.

34. Ibid., 423–424, 549, 552–553, 574–575; McFeely, *Grant*, 439; Brooks D. Simpson, *The Reconstruction Presidents* (Lawrence: University Press of Kansas, 1998), 157, 168.

35. Foner, *Reconstruction*, 528; Simpson, *The Reconstruction Presidents*, 171, 180.

36. Sec. 1, Civil Rights Act of 1875, "Civil Rights Cases," Legal Information Institute, Cornell University, www.law.cornell.edu/supremecourt/text /109/3.

37. Simpson, *The Reconstruction Presidents*, 181; McFeely, *Grant*, 418. The Supreme Court declared the measure unconstitutional in 1883 in the five *Civil Rights Cases*: Rogers Smith, *Civic Ideals: Conflicting Visions of Citizenship in U.S. History* (New Haven: Yale University Press, 1997), 325, 375–377.

38. Foner, *Reconstruction*, 530–531; Smith, *Civic Ideals*, 334–337.

39. "Now for the Remedy," *New York Tribune*, February 4, 1875.

40. See Randall M. Miller, "The Freedmen's Bureau and Reconstruction: An Overview," in *The Freedmen's Bureau and Reconstruction*, ed. Paul A. Cimbala and Randall M. Miller (New York: Fordham University Press, 1999), xiii–xxxii.

41. Gould, *Grand Old Party*, 31–32.

42. Richard Franklin Bensel, *Yankee Leviathan: The Origins of Central State Authority in America, 1859–1877* (Cambridge: Cambridge University Press, 1990), 332–333.

43. Ulysses S. Grant, "Inaugural Address," March 4, 1869, ed. Gerhard Peters and John T. Woolley, *American Presidency Project*, www.presidency.ucsb.edu /ws/?pid=25820.

44. Ibid.; Gretchen Ritter, *Goldbugs and Greenbacks: The Antimonopoly*

*Tradition and the Politics of Finance in America, 1865–1896* (Cambridge: Cambridge University Press, 1997), 36.

45. Bunting, *Ulysses S. Grant*, 94–98; "Wall Street," *New York Tribune*, October 2, 1869.

46. As Bensel notes, the 3% certificate was "negotiable as legal tender and thus held primarily as bank reserves": Bensel, *Yankee Leviathan*, 319.

47. Ibid., 319–322; Irwin Unger, *The Greenback Era: A Social and Political History of American Finance, 1865–1879* (Princeton: Princeton University Press, 1964), 66–67.

48. Samuel DeCanio, "Populism, Paranoia and the Politics of Free Silver," *Studies in American Political Development* 25, no. 1 (2011): 1–26. DeCanio also notes the role played by William Ralston, a powerful California banker, in bringing the legislation to passage.

49. Gerring, *Party Ideologies in America*, 71–73.

50. Perret, *Ulysses S. Grant*, 419–420.

51. Ulysses S. Grant, "Veto Message," April 22, 1874, ed. Gerhard Peters and John T. Woolley, *American Presidency Project*, www.presidency.ucsb.edu /ws/?pid=70417; McFeely, *Grant*, 393–397; Ritter, *Goldbugs and Greenbacks*, 29, 34, 37.

52. Ulysses S. Grant, "Sixth Annual Message," December 7, 1874, ed. Gerhard Peters and John T. Woolley, *American Presidency Project*, www.presidency.ucsb.edu/ws/?pid=29515.

53. Ritter, *Goldbugs and Greenbacks*, 37–38.

54. Boller, *Presidential Campaigns*, 127–132; Gould, *Grand Old Party*, 61–67.

55. Gould, *Grand Old Party*, 61–67. The size of the House after the 1872 election was larger due to reapportionment. Republicans held 56% of House seats at the start of the 1871 session, and 68.2% of seats at the start of the 1873 session. See Party Divisions of the House of Representatives; Party Division in the Senate.

56. See Party Divisions of the House of Representatives; Party Division in the Senate.

57. Foner, *Reconstruction*, 575–582. See also Michael F. Holt, *By One Vote: The Disputed Presidential Election of 1876* (Lawrence: University Press of Kansas, 2008).

## CHAPTER 6. HARRY TRUMAN

1. On FDR's economic vision, see the Commonwealth Club speech during the campaign in 1932: Franklin D. Roosevelt, "Campaign Address on Progressive Government at the Commonwealth Club in San Francisco, California," September 23, 1932, ed. Gerhard Peters and John T. Woolley, *American Presidency Project*, www.presidency.ucsb.edu/ws/?pid=88391. See also Franklin D. Roosevelt, "Inaugural Address," March 4, 1933, ed. Gerhard Peters and John T. Woolley, *American Presidency Project*, www.presidency.ucsb.edu /ws/?pid=14473.

2. Donald A. Ritchie, *Electing FDR: The New Deal Campaign of 1932* (Lawrence: University Press of Kansas, 2007), 176–192.

3. Susan Dunn, *Roosevelt's Purge: How FDR Fought to Change the Democratic Party* (Cambridge, MA: Harvard University Press, 2010), 42.

4. On the passage and impact of the National Labor Relations Act (the Wagner Act), see David Plotke, *Building a Democratic Political Order: Reshaping American Liberalism in the 1930s and 1940s* (Cambridge: Cambridge University Press, 1996), 92–127.

5. Ritchie, *Electing FDR*, 180.

6. Nancy J. Weiss, *Farewell to the Party of Lincoln: Black Politics in the Age of FDR* (Princeton: Princeton University Press, 1983), 53–55; William E. Leuchtenburg, *Franklin D. Roosevelt and the New Deal, 1932–1940* (New York: Harper & Row, 1963), 185; Gary A. Donaldson, *Truman Defeats Dewey* (Lexington: University Press of Kentucky, 1999), 92; Ritchie, *Electing FDR*, 189.

7. Suzanne Mettler, *Soldiers to Citizens: The G.I. Bill and the Making of the Greatest Generation* (New York: Oxford University Press, 2005), 72–76.

8. Franklin D. Roosevelt, "Executive Order 8802—Reaffirming Policy of Full Participation in the Defense Program by All Persons, Regardless of Race, Creed, Color, or National Origin, and Directing Certain Action in Furtherance of Said Policy," June 25, 1941, ed. Gerhard Peters and John T. Woolley, *American Presidency Project*, www.presidency.ucsb.edu/ws/?pid=16134.

9. Jules Witcover, *Party of the People: A History of the Democrats* (New York: Random House, 2003), 373–374.

10. Truman was personally disturbed by the case of Sgt. Isaac Woodard. Just discharged from the army, Woodard was viciously attacked by police in Batesburg, South Carolina, resulting in blindness: David McCullough, *Truman* (New York: Simon & Schuster, 1992), 588–589.

11. McCullough, *Truman*, 469–470; Donaldson, *Truman Defeats Dewey*, 12–13.

12. Henry N. Dorris, "House Votes Lease-Lend Bill, 260–165; Defeats Moves to Limit Future Aid; Landon Attacks Roosevelt's Policy," *New York Times*, February 9, 1941.

13. Franklin D. Roosevelt, "Annual Message to Congress on the State of the Union," January 6, 1941, ed. Gerhard Peters and John T. Woolley, *American Presidency Project*, www.presidency.ucsb.edu/ws/?pid=16092.

14. McCullough, *Truman*, 292–320. The phone conversation between Roosevelt and Truman, held in the hotel room of Democratic National Committee Chairman Robert Hannegan, was more like a presidential guilt trip. Roosevelt asserted that Truman would "break up the Democratic Party in the middle of the war" if he did not accept the nomination. Then the president hung up the phone. Ibid., 314.

15. Ibid., 247, 256–280, 287–289; Donaldson, *Truman Defeats Dewey*, 61–63, 199–203.

16. McCullough, *Truman*, 327–328.

17. Paul F. Boller, Jr., *Essays on the Presidents: Principles and Politics* (Fort Worth: Texas Christian University Press, 2012), 162.

18. Truman's job approval rating averaged 41% in the Gallup Poll. After precipitously declining in the months following the Japanese surrender, Truman's approval ratings surged and declined between 1946 and 1949. In his second term, Truman steadily declined, bottoming out at 23% in November 1951: "Presidential Popularity: A 43 Year Review," Princeton, NJ, Gallup Opinion Index, Report No. 182, October–November 1980, 34–36.

19. Franklin D. Roosevelt, "Annual Message to the Congress on the State of the Union," January 11, 1944, ed. Gerhard Peters and John T. Woolley, *American Presidency Project*, www.presidency.ucsb.edu/ws/?pid=16518.

20. A Gallup Poll taken October 5–10, 1945, revealed an 82% job approval rating for Truman. http://www.gallup.com/poll/124922/Presidential-Approval -Center.aspx; Harry S. Truman, "Special Message to the Congress Presenting a 21-Point Program for the Reconversion Period," September 6, 1945, ed. Gerhard Peters and John T. Woolley, *American Presidency Project*, www.presi dency.ucsb.edu/ws/?pid=12359.

21. Truman, "Message to Congress," September 6, 1945.

22. Ibid.

23. In both chambers of Congress, this coalition was a formidable force by Roosevelt's third term. By the time of Truman's tenure, the Conservative Coalition prevailed 80%–100% of the time when this alliance appeared in Congress. John F. Manley, "The Conservative Coalition in Congress," *American Behavioral Scientist* 17 (1973): 235–239.

24. McCullough, *Truman*, 468–469; Donald R. McCoy, *The Presidency of Harry S. Truman* (Lawrence: University Press of Kansas, 1984), 52.

25. "Federal Employees Pay Act of 1946," *Legisworks*, http://legisworks.org /congress/79/publaw-390.pdf.

26. The Hill-Burton Act "gave hospitals, nursing homes and other health facilities grants and loans for construction and modernization. In return, they agreed to provide a reasonable volume of services to persons unable to pay and to make their services available to all persons residing in the facility's area": US Department of Health and Human Services, www.hrsa.gov/gethealthcare/af fordable/hillburton/; the National Mental Health Act "called for the establishment of a National Institute of Mental Health": National Institutes of Health, www.nih.gov/about/almanac/organization/NIMH.htm.

27. Katelin P. Isaacs, *Credit for Military Service under Civilian Federal Employee Retirement Systems* (Washington, DC: Congressional Research Service, 2014), 2.

28. McCoy, *The Presidency of Harry S. Truman*, 61–62.

29. Harry S. Truman, "Annual Message to the Congress on the State of the Union," January 5, 1949, ed. Gerhard Peters and John T. Woolley, *American Presidency Project*, www.presidency.ucsb.edu/ws/?pid=13293.

30. Harry S. Truman, "Veto of the Taft-Hartley Labor Bill," June 20, 1947, ed. Gerhard Peters and John T. Woolley, *American Presidency Project*, www .presidency.ucsb.edu/ws/?pid=12675.

31. Witcover, *Party of the People*, 443–444; Harry S. Truman, "Statement by the President upon Signing the Housing Act of 1949," July 15, 1949, ed.

Gerhard Peters and John T. Woolley, *American Presidency Project*, www.presi
dency.ucsb.edu/ws/?pid=13246.

32. Geoffrey Kollmann, "Social Security: Summary of Major Changes in the
Cash Benefits Program," Social Security Administration, 2000, www.ssa.gov
/history/reports/crsleghist2.html.

33. On the place of the civil rights movement during the Roosevelt and Truman years, see Plotke, *Building a Democratic Political Order*, 279–297.

34. "To Secure These Rights: The Report of the President's Committee on
Civil Rights," Harry S. Truman Presidential Library and Museum, October 29,
1947, www.trumanlibrary.org/civilrights/srights1.htm#top.

35. McCoy, *The Presidency of Harry S. Truman*, 107–108.

36. Donaldson, *Truman Defeats Dewey*, 189–190.

37. Lewis Wood, "Truman Puts Ban on all Housing Aid Where Bias Exists,"
*New York Times*, December 3, 1949.

38. Michael R. Gardner, *Harry Truman and Civil Rights: Moral Courage and
Political Risks*, 3rd ed. (Carbondale: Southern Illinois University Press, 2003),
163–197.

39. Truman, "Annual Message," January 5, 1949, ed. Gerhard Peters and
John T. Woolley, *American Presidency Project*, www.presidency.ucsb.edu/ws
/?pid=13293.

40. Harry S. Truman, "Commencement Address at Howard University," June
13, 1952, ed. Gerhard Peters and John T. Woolley, *American Presidency Project*, www.presidency.ucsb.edu/ws/?pid=14160.

41. McCullough, *Truman*, 372–373, 486.

42. Ibid., 582–583.

43. Robert J. Donovan, *Tumultuous Years: The Presidency of Harry S. Truman, 1949–1953* (New York: W. W. Norton, 1982), 26–27.

44. McCoy, *The Presidency of Harry S. Truman*, 118–123. That same year,
the influential article "The Sources of Soviet Conduct" appeared in *Foreign Affairs*. Using the anonymous pseudonym "X," George F. Kennan argued on behalf
of a containment policy concerning the Soviet Union. George F. Kennan, "The
Sources of Soviet Conduct," *Foreign Affairs*, July 1947, Department of State,
www.foreignaffairs.com/articles/23331/x/the-sources-of-soviet-conduct.

45. Harry S. Truman, "Special Message to the Congress on Greece and Turkey:
The Truman Doctrine," March 12, 1947, ed. Gerhard Peters and John T. Woolley, *American Presidency Project*, www.presidency.ucsb.edu/ws/?pid=12846.

46. McCoy, *The Presidency of Harry S. Truman*, 122.

47. The label "Cold War" was used in a speech in 1947 by Bernard Baruch, a
confidant of Truman. William Safire, "Islamofascism," *New York Times*, October 1, 2006.

48. Harry S. Truman, *Memoirs*, vol. 2, *Years of Trial and Hope* (Garden City,
NY: Doubleday, 1956), 112–113.

49. McCoy, *The Presidency of Harry S. Truman*, 125–129.

50. Ibid., 116–118.

51. Ibid., 214–216; "A Report to the National Security Council—NSC 68,"

April 12, 1950, President's Secretary's File, Truman Papers, Harry S. Truman Presidential Library, Independence, MO.

52. Donaldson, *Truman Defeats Dewey*, 12–13; McCullough, *Truman*, 498–505.

53. Donaldson, *Truman Defeats Dewey*, 97–98.

54. Ibid., 136–144.

55. Truman had favored a more vague and generic civil rights plank. Convention delegates, led by Minneapolis Mayor Hubert Humphrey, approved more liberal and expansive platform language. McCullough, *Truman*, 639–640.

56. Truman's rhetorical jabs had a kernel of truth: American communists did in fact support Wallace's candidacy very publicly: Donaldson, *Truman Defeats Dewey*, 2, 56. See also Zachary Karabell, *The Last Campaign: How Harry Truman Won the 1948 Election* (New York: Random House, 2000), 71.

57. Witcover, *Party of the People*, 433–436.

58. Harry S. Truman, "Address in Philadelphia upon Accepting the Nomination of the Democratic National Convention," July 15, 1948, ed. Gerhard Peters and John T. Woolley, *American Presidency Project*, www.presidency.ucsb.edu/ws/?pid=12962.

59. Boller, *Essays on the Presidents*, 271.

60. Democratic National Convention Acceptance Address, July 15, 1948, ed. Gerhard Peters and John T. Woolley, *American Presidency Project*, www.presidency.ucsb.edu/ws/?pid=12962.

61. Donaldson, *Truman Defeats Dewey*, 188–90, 192–196, 203.

62. "Blacks and the Democratic Party," Annenberg Public Policy Center: Factcheck.org. Data taken from the Joint Center for Political and Economic Studies, www.factcheck.org/2008/04/blacks-and-the-democratic-party/.

63. United States House of Representatives, "Party Divisions of the House of Representatives," http://history.house.gov/Institution/Party-Divisions/Party-Divisions/; United States Senate, "Party Division in the Senate, 1789–Present," www.senate.gov/pagelayout/history/one_item_and_teasers/partydiv.htm.

64. Steve Crabtree, "The Gallup Brain: Americans and the Korean War," *Gallup Poll*, February 4, 2003, www.gallup.com/poll/7741/gallup-brain-americans-korean-war.aspx.

65. McCoy, *The Presidency of Harry S. Truman*, 279–280.

CHAPTER 7. GEORGE H. W. BUSH

1. Carter, "University of Notre Dame—Address at Commencement Exercises at the University," May 22, 1977, ed. Gerhard Peters and John T. Woolley, *American Presidency Project*, www.presidency.ucsb.edu/ws/?pid=7552.

2. Clark Murdock, *Preparing for a Deep Defense Drawdown* (Washington, DC: Center for Strategic and International Studies, 2013), 7, http://csis.org/event/preparing-deep-defense-drawdown.

3. Abuses were extensively investigated by the Senate Select Committee to Study Governmental Operations with Respect to Intelligence Activities, often

referred to as the Church Committee: US Senate Select Committee on Intelligence, Senate Select Committee to Study Governmental Operations with Respect to Intelligence Activities, www.intelligence.senate.gov/resources /intelligence-related-commissions, 1975–1976.

4. Michael Barone, *Our Country: The Shaping of America from Roosevelt to Reagan* (New York: Free Press, 1990), 645. The author suggests that Reagan's significant electoral success in the 1980s was unthinkable in the 1970s.

5. "Gallup Presidential Election Trial-Heat Trends, 1936–2008," *Gallup Poll*, www.gallup.com/poll/110548/gallup-presidential-election-trialheat-trends -19362004.aspx#2.

6. CBS News and *New York Times* exit polls, 1980–1988, www.washington post.com/wp-srv/politics/interactives/independents/data-party-identification .html.

7. "Economic Recovery Tax Act of 1981," Public Law 97–34, 97th Congress, www.legisworks.org/GPO/STATUTE-95-Pg172.pdf.

8. Defense budgets began slowly rising during the Carter Administration, but the Reagan Administration presided over an increase of about 42% when adjusted for inflation. Benjamin Ginsberg and Martin Shefter, *Politics by Other Means: The Declining Importance of Elections in America* (New York: Basic Books, 1990), 122–126.

9. Ibid., 66–68.

10. "Voodoo Economics," *NBC Nightly News*, February 10, 1982, NBC Universal, https://archives.nbclearn.com/portal/site/k-12/browse/?cuecard=33292.

11. The *Gallup Poll* of January 22–25, 1988, revealed a 49% approval rating, while the *Gallup Poll* of December 27–29, 1988, showed a 63% rating: "Presidential Job Approval Center," *Gallup Poll*, www.gallup.com/poll/124922/Pres idential-Approval-Center.aspx?ref=interactive.

12. Gerald M. Boyd, "Iran Deal Haunting The Bush Campaign," *New York Times*, January 24, 1988; Margaret Garrard Warner, "Bush Battles the 'Wimp Factor,'" *Newsweek*, October 19, 1987.

13. Steven V. Roberts, "Is the President in Favor of a Bush Nomination?," *New York Times*, December 1, 1987.

14. John Robert Greene, *The Presidency of George Bush* (Lawrence: University Press of Kansas, 2000), 24–26.

15. "Dukakis Lead Widens, According to New Poll," *New York Times*, July 26, 1988.

16. The CBS News/*New York Times* exit polls revealed that Reagan won 27% of Democratic voters in 1980, and 26% in 1984. Roper Center Public Opinion Archives, www.ropercenter.uconn.edu/elections/how_groups_voted /voted_80.html, www.ropercenter.uconn.edu/elections/how_groups_voted /voted_84.html.

17. Greene, *The Presidency of George Bush*, 34–37.

18. Ronald Reagan, "Remarks at the Republican National Convention in New Orleans, Louisiana," August 15, 1988, ed. Gerhard Peters and John T. Woolley, *American Presidency Project*, www.presidency.ucsb.edu/ws/?pid=36273. The

"Gipper" refers to George Gipp, a Notre Dame football player. Reagan played Gipp in the film *Knute Rockne, All American*, Warner Brothers, 1940.

19. George Bush, "Address Accepting the Presidential Nomination at the Republican National Convention in New Orleans," August 18, 1988, ed. Gerhard Peters and John T. Woolley, *American Presidency Project*, www.presidency.ucsb.edu/ws/?pid=25955.

20. *Howard Gleckman*, "Dick Darman Still Doesn't Get It," *Business Week*, October 14, 1996, www.businessweek.com/1996/42/b349739.htm, web version updated June 14, 1997.

21. The CBS/*New York Times* exit poll revealed that Bush won 17% of the Democratic vote: Roper Center Public Opinion Archives, www.ropercenter.uconn.edu/elections/how_groups_voted/voted_88.html.

22. United States House of Representatives, "Party Divisions of the House of Representatives," http://history.house.gov/Institution/Party-Divisions/Party-Divisions/; United States Senate, "Party Division in the Senate, 1789–Present," www.senate.gov/pagelayout/history/one_item_and_teasers/partydiv.htm.

23. Greene, *The Presidency of George Bush*, 47–48.

24. George Bush, "Inaugural Address," January 20, 1989, ed. Gerhard Peters and John T. Woolley, *American Presidency Project*, www.presidency.ucsb.edu/ws/?pid=16610.

25. Greene, *The Presidency of George Bush*, 81–83; Robert A. Rosenblatt, "GAO Estimates Final Cost of S & L Bailout at $480.9 Billion," *Los Angeles Times*, July 13, 1996.

26. Greene, *The Presidency of George Bush*, 81–83.

27. Ibid., 80–84.

28. Albert B. Crenshaw, "Tax Breaks for Some, Higher Fees for Others," *Washington Post*, January 30, 1990.

29. John E. Yang and Dana Priest, "President Shifts on Capital Gains; Budget Alternative Tied to Inflation," *Washington Post*, September 28, 1990.

30. William McGurn, "Budget Talking Blues," *National Review* 42, no. 17 (September 3, 1990): 20–21.

31. John E. Yang, "House Democrats Join Revolt on Budget Deal; Vote Counts Show Both Parties Falling Short," *Washington Post*, October 4, 1990; John E. Yang and Tom Kenworthy, "House Rejects Deficit-Reduction Agreement; Federal Shutdown Looms after Budget Vote," *Washington Post*, October 5, 1990; Dan Balz and John E. Yang, "Bush Closes Most Government Operations," *Washington Post*, October 6, 1990.

32. Edward N. Wolff, *The Rich Get Increasingly Richer: Latest Data on Household Wealth During the 1980s* (Washington, DC: Economic Policy Institute, 1993).

33. Jeanne Sahadi, "Taxes: What People Forget about Reagan," CNN, September 10, 2010, http://money.cnn.com/2010/09/08/news/economy/reagan_years_taxes/.

34. David E. Rosenbaum, "Bush Says Budget May Bar a Tax Cut for Capital Gains," *New York Times*, December 19, 1990; "Tax Legislation," Tax Policy

Center, Washington, DC, Urban Institute and Brookings Institution, www.tax policycenter.org/legislation/allyears.cfm#Omnibus1990.

35. "Roll Call Votes 101st Congress: 2nd Session," United States Senate, www.senate.gov/legislative/LIS/roll_call_lists/roll_call_vote_cfm.cfm?congre ss=101&session=2&vote=00326; "Final Vote Results For Roll Call 528," House of Representatives, http://clerk.house.gov/evs/1990/r011528.xml.

36. Seymour M. Hersh, "U.S. Secretly Gave Aid to Iraq Early in Its War against Iran," *New York Times*, January 26, 1992.

37. Greene, *The Presidency of George Bush*, 117–122, 125.

38. Years later, as the United States was mired in another war in Iraq, Bush's national security advisor, Brent Scowcroft, reflected on the decision to leave Hussein in power: "We heard no rumbles of discontent at all. They emerged shortly after, and then for a number of years we heard, 'Why didn't you finish the job?' We don't hear that anymore." *American Experience*, "George H. W. Bush," 2008, www.pbs.org/wgbh/americanexperience/features/transcript/bush-tran script//?flavour=mobile. See also Ryan Chilcote, "Kuwait Still Recovering from Gulf War Fires," *CNN*, January 3, 2003, www.cnn.com/2003/WORLD /meast/01/03/sproject.irq.kuwait.oil.fires/index.html?_s=PM:WORLD; "Pres- idential Job Approval Center," *Gallup Poll*, February 28, 1991–March 3, 1991, www.gallup.com/poll/124922/Presidential-Approval-Center.aspx; Greene, *The Presidency of George Bush*, 129–139.

39. Financial aid from Germany, Japan, and various Arab countries covered an estimated $52 billion from the total $61 billion cost of the war. "Gulf War Fast Facts," *CNN*, September 20, 2014, www.cnn.com/2013/09/15/world /meast/gulf-war-fast-facts/.

40. 102nd Congress, H.J. RES. 77 (1991–1992); and 102nd Congress, S.J. RES. 2 (1991–1992).

41. Greene, *The Presidency of George Bush*, 95–99, 159–161; Douglas Jehl, "Bush Baltic Move Seeks to 'Keep Pressure' on Secession," *Los Angeles Times*, September 3, 1991; William Safire, "After the Fall," *New York Times*, August 29, 1991; the *Gallup Poll* of December 12–15, 1991, revealed a 50% job ap- proval rating, dropping to 46% in the January 3–6, 1992, poll, "Presidential Job Approval Center," *Gallup Poll*, www.gallup.com/poll/124922/Presidential -Approval-Center.aspx.

42. Doyle McManus, "Congress Votes Contra Aid, Supporting Bush Strat- egy," *Los Angeles Times*, April 14, 1989.

43. Doyle McManus, "Noriega Aid to Contras at Behest of U.S. Reported," *Los Angeles Times*, February 14, 1988; Andrew Rosenthal, "Panama Crisis: Disarray Hindered White House," *New York Times*, October 8, 1989; Greene, *The Presidency of George Bush*, 100–106.

44. A fine example of the liberal Democratic critique of the Reagan Revolu- tion (and celebration of New Deal/Great Society liberalism) can be found in the keynote address of New York Governor Mario Cuomo at the 1984 Democratic National Convention: Mario Matthew Cuomo, Democratic National Conven- tion Keynote Address, July 16, 1984, San Francisco, California, www.american rhetoric.com/speeches/mariocuom01984dnc.htm.

45. George Bush, "Address Accepting the Presidential Nomination at the Republican National Convention in New Orleans," August 18, 1988, ed. Gerhard Peters and John T. Woolley, *American Presidency Project*, www.presidency .ucsb.edu/ws/?pid=25955.

46. Greene, *The Presidency of George Bush*, 162–163.

47. Steven A. Holmes, "Rights Bill for Disabled Is Sent to Bush," *New York Times*, July 14, 1990.

48. Janet L. Fix, "Accommodating the Disabled; Firms Face Deadlines to Make Themselves Accessible to the Disabled," *Philadelphia Inquirer*, October 6, 1991.

49. Jessica Lee, "Rights Law Signed amid Furor," *USA Today*, November 22, 1991.

50. George Bush, "Message to the Senate Returning without Approval the Civil Rights Act of 1990," October 22, 1990, ed. Gerhard Peters and John T. Woolley, *American Presidency Project*, www.presidency.ucsb.edu/ws/?pid=18948.

51. Judith A. Johnson, *AIDS Funding for Federal Government Programs: FY1981–FY2006* (Washington, DC: Congressional Research Service, 2005), 1–16.

52. Ryan White was an Indiana boy who was expelled from his public school because he had AIDS. US Department of Health and Human Services, "About the Ryan White HIV/AIDS Program," http://hab.hrsa.gov/abouthab/aboutpro gram.html.

53. Robert Pear, "As Bush Defends AIDS Policy, Its Critics See Flaws," *New York Times*, October 18, 1992.

54. Associated Press, "Bush Signs Major Revision of Anti-Pollution Law," *New York Times*, November 16, 1990.

55. Greene, *The Presidency of George Bush*, 68–71.

56. US Department of Health and Human Services, "Head Start Program Fact Sheet Fiscal Year 2010," http://eclkc.ohs.acf.hhs.gov/hslc/data/factsheets /fheadstartprogr.htm; George Bush, "Statement on Signing the Higher Education Amendments of 1992," July 23, 1992, ed. Gerhard Peters and John T. Woolley, *American Presidency Project*, www.presidency.ucsb.edu/ws/?pid=21259.

57. George Ramos, "Broad New Law Changes Policies on Immigration," *Los Angeles Times*, December 6, 1990; Lyn G. Shoop, "Health Based Exclusion Grounds in United States Immigration Policy: Homosexuals, HIV Infection and the Medical Examination of Aliens," *Journal of Contemporary Health Law & Policy* 9, no. 1 (1993): 521–544.

58. Michael deCourcy Hinds, "A Stunning Upset: Defeat of Republican in Pennsylvania Is Seen as Warning for '92," *New York Times*, November 6, 1991.

59. Robert Ajemian, "Where Is the Real George Bush?," *Time*, January 26, 1987.

60. Bush's busy foreign travel itinerary was a frequent target for criticism. Democrats sold T-shirts commemorating Bush's "Anywhere but America" tour: Paul West, "Bush 'World Tour' T-Shirts Pad Democrats' Pockets," *Baltimore Sun*, November 27, 1991.

61. Peter Goldman, Thomas M. DeFrank, Mark Miller, Andrew Murr, Tom

Matthews, et al., *Quest for the Presidency 1992* (College Station: Texas A & M University Press, 1994), 318–327, 334–353.

62. Ibid., 230, 526–528.

63. In one bizarre interview with CBS's *60 Minutes*, Perot claimed that Republicans plotted to ruin his daughter's wedding. Ibid., 594–596.

64. Ibid., 368–372; Patrick J. Buchanan, "1992 Republican National Convention Speech," August 17, 1992, http://buchanan.org/blog/1992-republican-national-convention-speech-148. Bush also got in on the television analogies. At one campaign stop he said, "We are going to keep on trying to strengthen the American family, to make American families a lot more like *The Waltons* and a lot less like *The Simpsons*." An ill-timed comparison, given that the Waltons were a family struggling through the Great Depression: Steven Herbert, "Clinton Edges Out Bush in Race for TV Ratings," *Los Angeles Times*, August 22, 1992.

65. Goldman et al., 572–573; 733–734; Ann Devroy, "Bush Offers Agenda to Revive Economy," *Washington Post*, September 11, 1992; Greene, *The Presidency of George Bush*, 163–164.

66. Steven A. Holmes, "An Eccentric but No Joke," *New York Times*, November 5, 1992.

67. Roper Center Public Opinion Archives, www.ropercenter.uconn.edu/elections/how_groups_voted/voted_92.html. A scandal involving overdrafts at the bank used by members of the House may have damaged some Democratic incumbents: Timothy Egan, "Of Checks and Balances and the Angry Voters," *New York Times*, March 14, 1992; United States House of Representatives, "Party Divisions of the House of Representatives," http://history.house.gov/Institution/Party-Divisions/Party-Divisions/; United States Senate, "Party Division in the Senate, 1789–Present," www.senate.gov/pagelayout/history/one_item_and_teasers/partydiv.htm.

68. R. W. Apple, Jr., "How Lasting a Majority?," *New York Times*, November 10, 1994; Katharine Q. Seelye, "Gingrich First Mastered the Media and Then Rose to Be King of the Hill," *New York Times*, December 14, 1994.

69. David Johnston, "Bush Diary at Issue: 6-Year Inquiry into Deal of Arms for Hostages All but Swept Away," *New York Times*, December 25, 1992.

70. David A. Crockett, *The Opposition Presidency: Leadership and the Constraints of History* (College Station: Texas A & M University Press, 2002), 175–200.


CHAPTER 8. CONCLUSION

1. Gerhard Peters, "Presidential News Conferences," *American Presidency Project*, ed. John T. Woolley and Gerhard Peters, www.presidency.ucsb.edu/data/newsconferences.php.

2. Andrew Rosenthal, "Now Read His Lips: Bush Says He Erred," *New York Times*, March 4, 1992.

# BIBLIOGRAPHY

BOOKS

Ackerman, Bruce. *We the People.* Volume 1, *Foundations.* Cambridge, MA: Harvard University Press, 1991.

———. *We the People.* Volume 2, *Transformations.* Cambridge, MA: Harvard University Press, 1998.

———. *We the People.* Volume 3, *The Civil Rights Revolution.* Cambridge, MA: Harvard University Press, 2014.

Barone, Michael. *Our Country: The Shaping of America from Roosevelt to Reagan.* New York: Free Press, 1990.

Bensel, Richard Franklin. *Yankee Leviathan: The Origins of Central State Authority in America, 1859–1877.* Cambridge: Cambridge University Press, 1990.

Boller, Paul F., Jr. *Essays on the Presidents: Principles and Politics.* Fort Worth: Texas Christian University Press, 2012.

———. *Presidential Campaigns.* New York: Oxford University Press, 1984.

Bunting, Josiah, III. *Ulysses S. Grant.* New York: Times Books, 2004.

Burnham, Walter Dean. *Voting in American Elections: The Shaping of the American Political Universe since 1788.* Palo Alto, CA: Academica Press, 2010.

Burstein, Andrew, and Nancy Isenberg. *Madison and Jefferson.* New York: Random House, 2010.

Calhoun, Charles W. *Conceiving a New Republic: The Republican Party and the Southern Question, 1869–1900.* Lawrence: University Press of Kansas, 2006.

Califano, Joseph, Jr. *The Triumph and Tragedy of Lyndon Johnson.* New York: Simon & Schuster, 1991.

Castel, Albert. *The Presidency of Andrew Johnson.* Lawrence: University Press of Kansas, 1979.

Cimbala, Paul A., and Randall M. Miller, eds. *The Freedmen's Bureau and Reconstruction.* New York: Fordham University Press, 1999.

Coletta, Paolo E. *The Presidency of William Howard Taft.* Lawrence: University Press of Kansas, 1973.

Cooper, William J., Jr. *The South and the Politics of Slavery, 1828–1856.* Baton Rouge: Louisiana State University Press, 1978.

Crockett, David A. *The Opposition Presidency: Leadership and the Constraints of History*. College Station: Texas A & M University Press, 2002.

———. *Running against the Grain: How Opposition Presidents Win the White House*. College Station: Texas A & M University Press, 2008.

Cunningham, Noble E., Jr. *The Jeffersonian Republicans in Power: Party Operations, 1801–1809*. Chapel Hill: University of North Carolina Press, 1963.

Curtis, James C. *The Fox at Bay: Martin Van Buren and the Presidency, 1837–1841*. Lexington: University Press of Kentucky, 1970.

Dangerfield, George. *The Awakening of American Nationalism, 1815–1828*. New York: Harper & Row, 1965.

Donaldson, Gary A. *Truman Defeats Dewey*. Lexington: University Press of Kentucky, 1999.

Donovan, Robert J. *Tumultuous Years: The Presidency of Harry S. Truman, 1949–1953*. New York: W. W. Norton, 1982.

Duckett, Alvin Laroy. *John Forsyth: Political Tactician*. Athens: University of Georgia Press, 1962.

Dunn, Susan. *Roosevelt's Purge: How FDR Fought to Change the Democratic Party*. Cambridge, MA: Harvard University Press, 2010.

Fischer, David Hackett. *The Revolution of American Conservatism: The Federalist Party in the Era of Jeffersonian Democracy*. New York: Harper & Row, 1965.

Foner, Eric. *Reconstruction: America's Unfinished Revolution, 1863–1877*. New York: Harper & Row, 1988.

Gardner, Michael R. *Harry Truman and Civil Rights: Moral Courage and Political Risks*. 3rd ed. Carbondale: Southern Illinois University Press, 2003.

Gerring, John. *Party Ideologies in America, 1828–1996*. Cambridge: Cambridge University Press, 1998.

Gillette, William. *The Right to Vote: Politics and the Passage of the Fifteenth Amendment*. Baltimore: Johns Hopkins University Press, 1965.

Ginsberg, Benjamin, and Martin Shefter. *Politics by Other Means: The Declining Importance of Elections in America*. New York: Basic Books, 1990.

Goldman, Peter, Thomas M. DeFrank, Mark Miller, Andrew Murr, Tom Matthews, et al., *Quest for the Presidency 1992*. College Station: Texas A & M University Press, 1994.

Gould, Lewis L. *Grand Old Party: A History of the Republicans*. New York: Random House, 2003.

———. *The William Howard Taft Presidency*. Lawrence: University Press of Kansas, 2009.

Greene, John Robert. *The Presidency of George Bush*. Lawrence: University Press of Kansas, 2000.

Hatfield, Mark O., ed., with the Senate Historical Office. *Vice Presidents of the United States, 1789–1993*. Washington, DC: US Government Printing Office, 1997.

Hofstadter, Richard. *The Idea of a Party System: The Rise of Legitimate Opposition in the United States, 1780–1840*. Berkeley: University of California Press, 1969.

Holt, Michael F. *By One Vote: The Disputed Presidential Election of 1876*. Lawrence: University Press of Kansas, 2008.

———. *The Rise and Fall of the American Whig Party: Jacksonian Politics and the Onset of the Civil War*. Oxford: Oxford University Press, 1999.

Isaacs, Katelin P. *Credit for Military Service under Civilian Federal Employee Retirement Systems*. Washington, DC: Congressional Research Service, 2014.

Johnson, Haynes, and David S. Broder. *The System: The American Way of Politics at the Breaking Point*. Boston: Little, Brown, 1996.

Johnson, Judith A. *AIDS Funding for Federal Government Programs: FY1981–FY2006*. Washington, DC: Congressional Research Service, 2005.

Karabell, Zachary. *The Last Campaign: How Harry Truman Won the 1948 Election*. New York: Random House, 2000.

Ketcham, Ralph. *James Madison*. Charlottesville: University of Virginia Press, 1971.

Kleppner, Paul, ed. *The Evolution of American Electoral Systems*. Westport, CT: Greenwood Press, 1981.

Leuchtenburg, William E. *Franklin D. Roosevelt and the New Deal, 1932–1940*. New York: Harper & Row, 1963.

McCoy, Donald R. *The Presidency of Harry S. Truman*. Lawrence: University Press of Kansas, 1984.

McCullough, David. *Truman*. New York: Simon & Schuster, 1992.

McDonald, Forrest. *The Presidency of Thomas Jefferson*. Lawrence: University Press of Kansas, 1976.

McFeely, William S. *Grant: A Biography*. New York: W. W. Norton, 1981.

McJimsey, George. *The Presidency of Franklin Delano Roosevelt*. Lawrence: University Press of Kansas, 2000.

Meacham, Jon. *American Lion: Andrew Jackson in the White House*. New York: Random House, 2008.

Merry, Robert W. *A Country of Vast Designs: James K. Polk, the Mexican War, and the Conquest of the American Continent*. New York: Simon & Schuster, 2009.

Mettler, Suzanne. *Soldiers to Citizens: The G.I. Bill and the Making of the Greatest Generation*. New York: Oxford University Press, 2005.

Milkis, Sidney M. *The President and the Parties: The Transformation of the American Party System since the New Deal*. New York: Oxford University Press, 1993.

Milkis, Sidney M., and Michael Nelson. *The American Presidency: Origins and Development, 1776–2011*. 6th ed. Washington, DC: Congressional Quarterly Press, 2012.

Morris, Edmund. *Theodore Rex*. New York: Random House, 2001.

Neustadt, Richard E. *Presidential Power and the Modern Presidents: The Politics of Leadership from Roosevelt to Reagan*. New York: Free Press, 1990.

Oates, Stephen B. *With Malice toward None: The Life of Abraham Lincoln*. New York: Row, 1977.

Pasley, Jeffrey L. *First Presidential Contest: 1796 and the Founding of American Democracy*. Lawrence: University Press of Kansas, 2013.

Perret, Geoffrey. *Ulysses S. Grant: Soldier & President*. New York: Random House, 1997.

Plotke, David. *Building a Democratic Political Order: Reshaping American Liberalism in the 1930s and 1940s*. Cambridge: Cambridge University Press, 1996.

Pomper, Gerald M., ed. *The Election of 1992*. Chatham, NJ: Chatham House, 1993.

Raphael, Ray. *Mr. President: How and Why the Founders Created a Chief Executive*. New York: Alfred A. Knopf, 2012.

Risjord, Norman K. *The Old Republicans: Southern Conservatism in the Age of Jefferson*. New York: Columbia University Press, 1965.

Ritchie, Donald A. *Electing FDR: The New Deal Campaign of 1932*. Lawrence: University Press of Kansas, 2007.

Ritter, Gretchen. *Goldbugs and Greenbacks: The Antimonopoly Tradition and the Politics of Finance in America, 1865–1896*. Cambridge: Cambridge University Press, 1997.

Rudalevige, Andrew. *The New Imperial Presidency: Renewing Presidential Power after Watergate*. Ann Arbor: University of Michigan Press, 2006.

Rutland, Robert Allen, ed. *James Madison and the American Nation, 1751–1836: An Encyclopedia*. New York: Simon & Schuster, 1994.

———. *The Presidency of James Madison*. Lawrence: University Press of Kansas, 1990.

Schlesinger, Arthur M., Jr. *The Imperial Presidency*. New York: First Mariner, 2004.

Sellers, Charles. *The Market Revolution: Jacksonian America, 1815–1846*. New York: Oxford University Press, 1991.

Silbey, Joel H. *Martin Van Buren and the Emergence of American Popular Politics*. Lanham, MD: Rowman & Littlefield, 2002.

Simpson, Brooks D. *The Reconstruction Presidents*. Lawrence: University Press of Kansas, 1998.

Skocpol, Theda. *Protecting Soldiers and Mothers: The Political Origins of Social Policy in the United States*. Cambridge, MA: Harvard University Press, 1992.

Skowronek, Stephen. *The Politics Presidents Make: Leadership from John Adams to Bill Clinton*. Cambridge, MA: Belknap Press of Harvard University Press, 1997.

Smith, Jean Edward. *Grant*. New York: Simon & Schuster, 2001.

Smith, Rogers. *Civic Ideals: Conflicting Visions of Citizenship in U.S. History*. New Haven: Yale University Press, 1997.

Stagg, J. C. A. *Mr. Madison's War: Politics, Diplomacy and Warfare in the Early American Republic, 1783–1830*. Princeton: Princeton University Press, 1983.

Truman, Harry S. *Memoirs*. Volume 2, *Years of Trial and Hope*. Garden City, NY: Doubleday, 1956.

Tulis, Jeffrey K. *The Rhetorical Presidency*. Princeton: Princeton University Press, 1987.

Unger, Irwin. *The Greenback Era: A Social and Political History of American Finance, 1865–1879*. Princeton: Princeton University Press, 1964.

Weigley, Russell F. *History of the United States Army*. New York: Macmillan, 1967.

Weiss, Nancy J. *Farewell to the Party of Lincoln: Black Politics in the Age of FDR*. Princeton: Princeton University Press, 1983.

Widmer, Ted. *Martin Van Buren*. New York: Times Books, 2005.

Wills, Garry. *James Madison*. New York: Times Books, 2002.

Wilson, Major L. *The Presidency of Martin Van Buren*. Lawrence: University Press of Kansas, 1984.

Witcover, Jules. *Party of the People: A History of the Democrats*. New York: Random House, 2003.

Wolff, Edward N. *The Rich Get Increasingly Richer: Latest Data on Household Wealth during the 1980s*. Washington, DC: Economic Policy Institute, 1993.


NEWSPAPERS

*Baltimore Sun*
*Business Week*
*Los Angeles Times*
*National Review*
*Newsweek*
*New York Times*
*New York Tribune*
*Philadelphia Inquirer*
*Time*
*USA Today*
*Washington Post*


JOURNAL ARTICLES

Adler, William D., and Jonathan Keller. "A Federal Army, Not a Federalist One: Regime Building in the Jeffersonian Era." *Journal of Policy History* 26, no. 2 (2014): 167–187.

DeCanio, Samuel. "Populism, Paranoia and the Politics of Free Silver." *Studies in American Political Development* 25, no. 1 (2011): 1–26.

Johnson, Leland R. "The Suspense Was Hell: The Senate Vote for War in 1812." *Indiana Magazine of History* 65, no. 4 (1969): 247–267.

Kennan, George F. "The Sources of Soviet Conduct." *Foreign Affairs* 25, no. 4 (1947): 566–582.

Manley, John F. "The Conservative Coalition in Congress." *American Behavioral Scientist* 17 (November 1973): 223–247.

Nichols, Curt, and Adam S. Myers. "Exploring the Opportunity for

Reconstructive Leadership: Presidential Responses to Enervated Political Regimes." *American Politics Research* 38, no. 5 (2010): 806–841.

Pancake, John S. "The 'Invisibles': A Chapter in the Opposition to President Madison." *Journal of Southern History* 21, no. 1 (February 1955): 17–37.

Polsky, Andrew J. "Mr. Lincoln's Army Revisited: Partisanship, Institutional Position and Union Army Command, 1861–1865." *Studies in American Political Development* 16 (Fall 2002): 176–207.

———. "Partisan Regimes in American Politics." *Polity* 44, no. 1 (January 2012): 51–80.

Preyer, Norris W. "Southern Support of the Tariff of 1816: A Reappraisal." *Journal of Southern History* 25, no. 3 (August 1959): 306–322.

Shoop, Lyn G. "Health Based Exclusion Grounds in United States Immigration Policy: Homosexuals, HIV Infection and the Medical Examination of Aliens." *Journal of Contemporary Health Law & Policy* 9, no. 1 (1993): 521–544.

Zinman, Donald A. "The Heir Apparent Presidency of James Madison." *Presidential Studies Quarterly* 41, no. 4 (December 2011): 712–726.

———. "Passing the Torch through Political Time: Heir Apparent Presidents and the Governing Party." *White House Studies* 9, no. 1 (2009): 51–65.

## ARTICLES IN EDITED VOLUMES

Bradford, James C. "United States Navy." In Rutland, *James Madison and the American Nation.*

Burnham, Walter Dean. "The Legacy of George Bush: Travails of an Understudy." In Pomper, *The Election of 1992*, 1–38.

Formisano, Ronald P. "Federalists and Republicans: Parties, Yes—System, No." In Kleppner, *The Evolution of American Electoral Systems*, 33–76.

Miller, Randall M. "The Freedmen's Bureau and Reconstruction: An Overview." In Cimbala and Miller, *The Freedmen's Bureau and Reconstruction.*

Pitcavage, Mark. "United States Army." In Rutland, *James Madison and the American Nation.*

## INTERNET

American Rhetoric. Top 100 Speeches. www.americanrhetoric.com.

Buchanan, Patrick J. "1992 Republican National Convention Speech." August 17, 1992. http://buchanan.org/blog/1992-republican-national-convention -speech-148.

Cable News Network. www.cnn.com.

CongressLink. Dirksen Congressional Center. Pekin, IL. www.congresslink .org/.

Crabtree, Steve. "The Gallup Brain: Americans and the Korean War." *Gallup Poll*, February 4, 2003, www.gallup.com/poll/7741/gallup-brain-americans -korean-war.aspx.

Cumberland Road Project. Cumberland, MD. www.cumberlandroadproject
.com/.

Factcheck.org. Annenberg Public Policy Center. Washington, DC. www.fact
check.org.

Gallup Poll. Washington, DC. www.gallup.com.

Govtrack.us. www.govtrack.us/.

Hamilton, Alexander, John Jay, and James Madison. *Federalist Papers*, 1787–
1788. Library of Congress, http://thomas.loc.gov/home/histdox/fedpapers
.html.

Investopedia. www.investopedia.com/.

Kollmann, Geoffrey. "Social Security: Summary of Major Changes in the Cash
Benefits Program." Social Security Administration, 2000. www.ssa.gov/his
tory/reports/crsleghist2.html.

Legal Information Institute. Cornell University. www.law.cornell.edu/.

Legisworks. http://legisworks.org/.

Leip, Dave. *Atlas of US Presidential Elections*. www.uselectionatlas.org/.

Library of Congress. Washington, DC. www.loc.gov/.

Lincoln, Abraham. *Collected Works of Abraham Lincoln*. Ann Arbor, MI.
http://quod.lib.umich.edu/l/lincoln/lincoln1.

Longfellow, Rickie. "Back in Time: The National Road." US Department of
Transportation. www.fhwa.dot.gov/infrastructure/back0103.cfm.

Massachusetts Historical Society. Boston. www.masshist.org.

Miller Center of Public Affairs. Charlottesville, VA. *American President: A
Reference.* http://millercenter.org/president.

Murdock, Clark. *Preparing for a Deep Defense Drawdown*. Washington, DC:
Center for Strategic and International Studies, 2013. http://csis.org/event
/preparing-deep-defense-drawdown.

National Institutes of Health. www.nih.gov/.

Peters, Gerhard, and John T. Woolley. *The American Presidency Project*. www
.presidency.ucsb.edu.

Roper Center Public Opinion Archives. www.ropercenter.uconn.edu/.

Tax Policy Center. Washington, DC. Urban Institute and Brookings Institution. www.taxpolicycenter.org/.

Truman, Harry S. Presidential Library. www.trumanlibrary.org/.

United States Department of Health and Human Services. Washington, DC.
www.hrsa.gov/.

United States House of Representatives. Washington, DC. www.clerk.house
.gov/.

United States Senate. Washington, DC. www.senate.gov.

FILM AND TELEVISION

*60 Minutes*. CBS Productions, 1968– .

American Experience. *George H. W. Bush*. PBS, 2008. www.pbs.org/wgbh
/americanexperience/features/transcript/bush-transcript//?flavour=mobile.

*Knute Rockne, All American.* Warner Brothers, 1940.
*NBC Nightly News.* NBC Universal, 1970.
*The Simpsons.* 20th Century Fox Television, 1989.
*The Waltons.* Lorimar Productions, 1972–1981.

# INDEX